**Local Government in
the German Federal System**

Local Government in the German Federal System

Arthur B. Gunlicks

Duke Press Policy Studies
Duke University Press   Durham 1986

© 1986 Duke University Press
All rights reserved
Printed in the United States of America
on acid-free paper ∞

Library of Congress Cataloging-in-Publication Data
Gunlicks, Arthur B., 1936–
  Local government in the German federal system.
  (Duke Press policy studies)
  Bibliography: p.
  Includes index.
  1. Local government—Germany (West)   I. Title.
II. Series.
JS5395.G86   1986   352.043   86-6350
ISBN 0-8223-0674-3

Frido Wagener

25 May 1926

6 January 1985

Contents

Preface xi
1 Introduction 1
2 The Development of Local Government in Germany, 1808–1949 5
3 The German Administrative Tradition, the Federal Framework, and Local Government Institutional Structure 32
4 Territorial and Administrative Reforms at the Local Level 48
5 The Legal Framework of German Local Government 67
6 Local Government and the Distribution of Administrative Responsibilities 84
7 Local Government Finance 119
8 The Public Service and the Organization of Local Bureaucracies 143
9 Local Councillors, Parties, and Elections 155
10 Local Government and Intergovernmental Relations 181
11 Intergovernmental Relations and the Undermining of Traditional Administrative Systems 200
12 German and American Local Government: Some Comparisons and Conclusions 208
Notes 215
Index 239

Tables and Figures

Tables

3.1 *Länder* of the Federal Republic of Germany and their representation in the *Bundesrat*   36
4.1 Independent (county-free) cities, counties, and municipalities in the Federal Republic before and after the territorial reforms   58
4.2 Counties in the Federal Republic after the reforms, 1978   60
6.1 Administrative tasks at the federal level   87
6.2 Administrative tasks at the *Land* level   90
6.3 Administrative tasks at the government administrative district (*Regierungsbezirk*) and regional level   91
6.4 Distribution of local government affairs (*Selbstverwaltungsaufgaben*) between municipalities and counties (based on the example of North-Rhine Westphalia)   106
6.5 Distribution of delegated functions (*Auftragsangelegenheiten* or *Pflichtaufgaben nach Weisung*) between municipalities and counties (based on the example of North-Rhine Westphalia)   110
7.1 Local government income (all municipalities and counties), 1950–1985   136
7.2 Cost coverage of user fees for selected services and fee increases, 1982–1983   138
7.3 Local government expenditures (all municipalities and counties), 1950–1985   140
8.1 Proportion of public servants to total working population, 1965–1980   144
8.2 *Beamten* categories, pay scales, and educational requirements   145
8.3 Administrative organizational plan of the KGSt for municipalities   152

9.1 Proportion of council seats to population in the municipalities and counties of Hesse   157
9.2 Application of the d'Hondt and Hare-Niemeyer methods of calculation   176

Figures

3.1 Structure of administration in the Federal Republic of Germany   45
5.1 Forms of local government in the Federal Republic of Germany   74
7.1 Distribution of federal and *Land* grants   129
7.2 Make-up of local government tax revenues by source, 1961–1984   133
11.1 Two basic models of administrative organization and the division of state powers   205

Preface

While writing a dissertation on political parties at the local level in the German state of Lower Saxony in the mid-1960s and working on several studies of local government boundary reforms in the 1970s, it became necessary for me to learn something about German local government. Two things quickly became apparent to me. One, that local government in Germany is more complex than in the United States, and, two, that there is very little material written in English that would help Americans or other English-speaking foreigners understand German local government. Perhaps it is the complexity of German local government that explains why the subject is generally disregarded in all but a few English-language books on German government and politics, and why, when it is mentioned, it is usually given little attention.

German local government deserves better. It is an important subject, not only for inherent reasons, but also because the system of public administration in Germany traditionally has relied on local governments to a much greater extent than is the case in the United States. The German states, or *Länder*, are responsible for executing as matters of their own concern most national laws, a large majority of which in turn are given to the local governments which serve also as field agencies. Local governments also execute most state (*Land*) laws, in addition to the ordinances and regulations passed by the local councils in their roles as instruments of local self-government. Thus the local level is the primary focus for the administration of the laws and regulations of all levels in Germany. Some understanding of local government in Germany is therefore required of anyone who wishes to gain a better understanding of the manner in which that country is governed. The purpose of this book is to provide the foundation for such an understanding.

All references to post-World War II Germany are to be understood as the Federal Republic of Germany, or West Germany. The German Democratic

Republic, or East Germany, has imposed party rule within an institutional framework adopted from the Soviet Union, and older German administrative traditions are of limited relevance today in that part of Germany. All translations from the German are my own, and any errors or misinterpretations are mine as well.

Thanks are due to a number of persons and institutions that have assisted me with this project. Some parts of the manuscript were read by Professor Joachim-Jens Hesse of the Post-Graduate School of Public Administration in Speyer, and chapter 2 was carefully scrutinized by my colleague at the University of Richmond, Hugh West. I have benefitted from informal discussions with several scholars and practitioners in Germany who will remain anonymous. I thank both the named and the anonymous for their comments, suggestions and insights; they are not responsible for any shortcomings that the reader may find. I thank the faculty and staff at the Post-Graduate School of Public Administration in Speyer for their generous support during a sabbatical leave in 1982–83 and brief returns in 1984 and 1985. Special thanks go to the library staff and to the staff at the school's Research Institute for Public Administration, in particular to Frau Hannelore Fehr and Frau Sigrid Hübers for their competent and cheerfully rendered secretarial services. I also wish to thank the Max Planck Institute for Foreign and International Law in Heidelberg for the use of their excellent library facilities and for their friendly assistance. Without the sabbatical leave granted by the University of Richmond, I would not have been able to do the research necessary for this book, and my efforts would have been made more difficult without the financial assistance given by the Faculty Research Committee. My wife and sons deserve some credit for putting up with me during the time I have been working on this book, as does Dr. Christoph Sattler, who shared his house in Heidelberg with us.

Above all I wish to thank Professor Frido Wagener, the long-time director of the Research Institute for Public Administration in Speyer, who invited me to spend my sabbatical year in Speyer as a visiting professor and research fellow, made arrangements for numerous support services, and encouraged me during my work on this project through his comments and suggestions. In spite of a busy schedule, he always found time to join me in conversations about his favorite subject, German public administration. Any substantive weaknesses in this book are the result of the fact that Professor Wagener was able to read only about half of the manuscript. His untimely death in January 1985 represents a severe loss not only to his own family, but also to the discipline of public administration in Germany, to his faculty colleagues and friends in Speyer, to his students in Speyer and Heidelberg, and to me personally. This book is dedicated to his memory.

1
Introduction

Few modern nations have had as traumatic a history with as many wrenching political changes as Germany since 1871, when Germany finally achieved unity under Bismarck's direction as a semi-constitutional monarchy with a federal territorial organization. From this monarchical Kaiserreich to the Weimar Republic, from that first German experiment with parliamentary democracy to the Third Reich, from the disastrous Nazi reign to Allied occupation and the loss of one-fourth of the territory of the German state in its boundaries of 1937, and from separation into four separate administrative zones, each under the control of a former enemy with a different political and administrative tradition, to the creation in 1949 of the Federal Republic of Germany (West) and German Democratic Republic (East), Germans have had more opportunities than perhaps any other people to learn about and also to be confronted by foreign political and administrative principles and techniques that were not a part of their original political-administrative culture.

While the nature, time frame and scope of this confrontation may be unique in Western history, neither foreign occupation nor the strong influence of foreign political-administrative practices is new in German history. Indeed, during the final years of the eighteenth and the first years of the nineteenth century, most of what is today the Federal Republic was occupied by or fell under the strong influence of Napoleonic French forces. French political and in particular French administrative principles and practices had a deep and lasting impact in some of these areas, especially along the Rhine, and French influence was not without some importance in central and southern Germany as well. Even the far-reaching municipal government reforms introduced by the anti-French Baron vom Stein of Prussia in 1808 were probably based in part on a French model of reform that never took root in France itself.

Given the division of Germany into hundreds of territorial units before Napoleon and about forty units during most of the nineteenth century, and considering the dramatic discontinuities in German political institutions, it would not be unreasonable to assume that German administrative arrangements and practices have gone through significant changes as well; however, this is not the case. Of course, there have been changes over the decades, and changes continue to be made today. Nevertheless, what is striking about German history over the past one hundred years and more are the *continuities* in German administration. This is not, of course, peculiar to Germany. F. F. Ridley has noted that "the fact that governments change but administrations remain may be a cliché, but it is true for all that."[1]

Administrative continuities are especially apparent at the local level, where most administration in the German tradition has taken place. Like nineteenth-century France, central state laws in Prussia were delegated to regional administrative districts and local governments for implementation; however, unlike the highly centralized French state, Prussia was organized into eight provinces, each of which had certain unique administrative features, including somewhat different systems of local government. After 1808, with the introduction of the City Charter Law of Baron vom Stein, the trend was toward relatively strong and autonomous municipal governments that enjoyed a degree of discretionary authority never achieved by local governments in France. With the creation of the Bismarck Reich of 1871 as a federal state, the constituent states were given the responsibility of administering most central state laws,[2] so that a kind of dualism between policy-making and administration developed which stood in contrast to the American system of dual federalism in which each level of government retained responsibility for both policy-making and administration in separate general areas of concern. The German states enjoyed considerable autonomy in their administration of national laws, as did the local governments, especially the cities, in their implementation of the national and state laws that were delegated to them. In spite of the dramatic developments of the past one hundred years, this system of dual administration has remained a feature of German administration.

Because the administration of most national legislation is delegated to the states, which in turn delegate most national and state laws to the local governments for implementation under the technical supervision of regional administrative district officers, parallels are sometimes drawn between the German, and especially Prussian, system of administration and French prefectorial administration.[3] While numerous similarities exist between the Prussian-German and French administrative traditions (for example, the efforts to ensure administrative coordination by a chief administrator within a specific territory), a key distinction can be found in the relative autonomy from the central government enjoyed by the *Länder* and their local governments. German "prefectorialism," to the extent that it can be called such, does not represent the kind of "centralization" that Daniel

Elazar sees emerging in the United States;[4] rather, it is a form of "decentralized,"[5] or, in Elazar's terms, "noncentralized"[6] administration that is different from the American model and not well understood outside of Germany. One of the purposes of this book, and especially chapter 2, is to trace the development of the German administrative tradition at the local level from the beginning of the nineteenth century to the present and to clarify some of the similarities and differences between the "classical" German and French administrative models on the one hand and to help explain the distinction between these and the American model on the other hand.

Germany shares with the United States a noncentralized administrative framework, yet both countries have been affected by centralizing trends that tend to undermine or at least weaken their respective noncentralized administrative traditions. During the past decades, through a process called "cooperative federalism," and then "intergovernmental relations," the United States and the Federal Republic have become more similar in some important respects. In both political systems the national and/or state governments set policy and provide grant money for an increasing number of activities, while the state or local governments deliver the services or regulate the behavior required by the "higher" levels. Given their different administrative traditions, however, differences between American and German intergovernmental relations can be found in the greater administrative autonomy which German states and local governments appear to enjoy in the implementation of national or state laws and in the relatively greater focus in the United States on separate, functional administration of programs as opposed to the continuing German efforts to ensure a coordinated spatial, or territorial, administration. A second purpose of this book is to describe and analyze the trend in Germany toward growing complexity of administration, pressures toward national uniformity, and efforts to resist centralizing tendencies, and at the same time to provide some comparisons with the United States. This is done throughout the book, but most explicitly in chapters 10, 11, and 12.

While distinctions between German and American federalism and the growth of intergovernmental relations in both systems represent the grander themes of this book, chapter 3 provides a description of the institutional framework within which German administration operates, chapter 4 covers the rationale for and the implementation of recent significant local administrative and territorial reforms, and chapters 5, 6 and 7 focus on a description, and to some extent an analysis, of the legal setting, the functions, and the financing of local governments in Germany. Chapter 8 discusses the personnel and organization of local government bureaucracies, and chapter 9 focuses on political parties and elections.

Much of the material that follows will not be the customary fare for the nonspecialist reader, whose interests are usually directed more toward general studies of current affairs, such as foreign and defense policies, national election analyses, and, of course, national political personalities. On the other hand, some knowledge of the German administrative system, including the system of local government, is crucial to those who wish to gain a broader and deeper understanding of German government. In this sense, it is surprising that so little is written in English about German administrative practices and developments. Again, to quote F. F. Ridley: "If administrative systems cannot be understood except by reference to their political environment, the point here for the political scientist . . . is that political systems cannot be understood without study of the administration."[7] Ridley also echoes Max Weber ("*Herrschaft ist im Alltag primär Verwaltung*"[8]) when he reminds his readers that, when "measured by the work of its personnel, . . . government is overwhelmingly about administration."[9]

2

The Development of

Local Government in Germany,

1808–1949

During the sixteenth, seventeenth and eighteenth centuries, when England, France and Spain were establishing nation-states under the strong central authority of an absolute monarchy, many German cities were still able to enjoy an autonomous status as constituent parts of the highly decentralized feudal German Empire. For some students of Germany, these imperial free or "Reich" cities serve as early models of local self-government in Central Europe. One can, indeed, point to a series of historical developments which lend support to this view: the transition of medieval cities from associations to legal corporations, to judicial persons, the increasing role played by the city council and the change from the principle of unanimity to majority rule, the formation of factions and groups, the differentiation which was finally made between private and public spheres, the connection between certain freedoms which were to be associated later with democratic rights, and the development of administrative principles and administrative law.[1] Following the Reformation, however, the struggle of German states to replace the fragmented feudal order with a more centralized, absolutist authority occurred not only at the expense of the nobility and the loosely organized empire; the Reich cities also were weakened and reduced in number. The small proportion of the city dwellers who enjoyed the rights of citizenship shrank even further, city councillors became identified increasingly with a small group of notables, and city rule came close to approximating the absolutist rule of the German princes.[2] While princely incursions into city autonomy came to be welcomed by many city dwellers who sought relief from local oligarchical rule, there was a heavy price to pay in terms of state bureaucratic control and supervision.[3]

Since one cannot point to a progressive and continuing development of older German cities toward self-government, the focus of this chapter is on the legal origins of German local self-government in the nineteenth century. The end of the first decade of the century brought a promising new beginning for German cities;

however, for more than a hundred years thereafter, most efforts to build upon the earlier foundation met with frustration and disappointment.

From Napoleon to the Revolution of 1848

The French Revolution and the Napoleonic Wars which followed had a dramatic impact on the territorial organization of Germany. In 1789 the German Empire, including Austria, consisted of 314 secular and church territories and Reich cities and 1,475 special knightly estates which enjoyed a measure of autonomy from higher authority.[4] The Peace of Lunéville in 1801 represented a kind of "legal revolution" in that it sanctioned large territorial losses west of the Rhine and brought about a dramatic reshuffling of territories east of the Rhine. The church lost all of its lands in the empire, most church property was absorbed by the various annexing states, and the bishops lost their once-substantial political power. In addition forty-one Reich cities were disbanded and annexed by surrounding states east of the Rhine. Only Hamburg, Bremen, Lübeck, Augsburg, Frankfurt and Nuremberg remained autonomous, and the latter three cities lost their autonomy during the course of the nineteenth century.[5]

The dissolution of these church territories and cities, which was designed to compensate the larger states east of the Rhine for their losses in the West, was given official recognition in 1803 by an assembly of deputies from constituent parts of the empire. It was one of the last decisions that would be made by the empire before its dissolution in 1806 under the pressure of Napoleon.

The dissolution of the empire, the attack on the old feudal order—which included the elimination of church territories and autonomous cities—and the creation in the West and South of several medium-sized German states dependent on France were major political accomplishments for Napoleon. Later, these states would serve as the foundation for modern German federalism.[6] More ironically, French policies also helped pave the way for the rise of Prussia after the final defeat of Napoleon's armies in 1815.

In the first years of the century Prussian losses to France west of the Rhine were compensated by gains in the East. However, these territories and others west of the Elbe River were lost after Prussian military defeats suffered in 1806. With the loss of more than one-half of its pre-1806 territory and with French occupation forces stationed in the remaining lands until heavy reparations payments were made, the power and authority of the Prussian king and state were severely weakened. Various groups reacted to the crisis in Prussia by advocating solutions ranging from French-style revolution to absolutist reaction, but the two major tendencies were the parties of reform and restoration. The reform party prevailed until 1819; thereafter, the restoration party gained the upper hand.[7]

City government reform in Prussia. At the time of its humiliation by France in 1806, Prussian absolutism had brought about a distance between state and people which, according to the reform party, had to be overcome in order to promote stronger feelings of loyalty and commitment to the state by its subjects. Prussian cities were governed by state-appointed bureaucrats who acted under central authority and were responsible for every detail of local administration. In the cities where Prussian troops were permanently stationed, there was frequent interference in local administration by the aristocratic officer corps. Aristocratic authoritarianism and contempt for the new middle class in the cities led to growing bitterness and estrangement.[8]

Baron vom Stein, who served briefly as the Chief Minister of Prussia in 1807 and 1808, was convinced of the need for far-reaching reforms at all levels of the state. While his ideas included the creation of representative institutions (with restricted suffrage) at the local, regional and national levels, he was successful in the short time available to him only in his proposals for city government reform. This reform, contained in the City Charter Law of 1808, was to serve as the foundation of German local self-government throughout the nineteenth century, and its influence can be felt up to the present time in a number of German *Länder* (states).

Given the background of the French Revolution and Prussian defeat by Napoleon, Stein's major concern was to "awaken the sleeping energy of the passive subjects,"[9] to encourage a spirit of community and citizen duty, to revive feelings of patriotism and national honor, and to counter the idea that the state was the concern of the monarch alone.[10] His reform proposals were to serve as an instrument of national education, a device for promoting first a love for the locality, then for the province, and finally for the country.[11] A secondary consideration was the replacement of an expensive and offensive state bureaucracy at the local level by unpaid part-time citizen administrators.[12] Former subjects were to be promoted to citizens, whose energy would rejuvenate the state. The participation of merchants especially would simplify and improve local administration and make it more effective.[13]

Stein's City Charter Law[14] divided Prussian cities into three classes: large (10,000 or more inhabitants), medium (3,500 to 10,000), and small (less than 3,500). In accordance with Montesquieu's thinking about separation of powers, it provided for two organs of city administration: a legislative council of elected representatives and an executive *Magistrat* whose members were elected by the council. The size of each organ depended on the population of the city. Given the traditional, that is, feudal, selection of councillors by guilds and corporate bodies, the election of councillors by secret ballot in city districts for overlapping three-year terms by eligible citizens (Bürger), educated professionals, artists and in general those with some property and income, was a revolutionary change.[15] As a precaution against too much "adventurism," two-thirds of the councillors had to own houses in the cities. The councillors were responsible only to the entire city; they were not to be bound by instructions from guilds, their district, or from other sources. The council could raise revenue, determine the budget, decide all questions within its own sphere of activities (later to be called *eigener Wirkungskreis*), and control the administration. The administrative organ of the city was the collegial *Magistrat*, which consisted both of paid professionals and lay citizen members. The paid professionals were elected by the council for a term of twelve years with pension rights if removed, that is, not re-elected, before normal retirement age. The lay members were unpaid local citizens elected by the council for six years. These citizens served in functional committees of the *Magistrat* which were chaired by a paid professional member. The mayor, who was a professional administrator and head of the *Magistrat*, was elected for six years.[16]

While state tutelage and control were sharply reduced, Stein's reform was hardly intended or designed to turn the Prussian cities into small republics with a kind of medieval autonomy.[17] Prussian ruling elites, like their counterparts in other states in Germany and Europe, were still very much attached to the idea of indivisible state sovereignty and were certainly wary of turning over too much authority to potentially centrifugal and fragmenting forces in local areas. Thus the state retained the right to exercise a general supervision over the cities, including the right to check city accounting procedures and documents, to review decisions regarding citizen complaints, to approve new city ordinances, and to confirm the election of members to the *Magistrat*,[18] which was to administer not only local regulations but also state laws. In the larger cities state supervision went beyond the right of confirmation in that the council could only present three candidates from whom state authorities would select the lord mayor. Supervision and confirmation rights regarding the administration of state laws were based apparently on the assumption that the cities otherwise would not carry out correctly state activities delegated to them. The state also retained the right to supervise the cities in matters of their own concern, so that city actions could not contradict general state laws. On the other hand, cities were allowed a generous discretionary power (in contrast to the British and American traditions of ultra vires) to deal on their own responsibility with matters of local concern (*eigener Wirkungskreis*).[19]

In addition to retaining a general right of supervision, the state assumed the police and judicial functions formerly performed by the cities.[20] State assumption of these functions can be interpreted, however, as a progressive act in the context of the times. Equal justice could not be achieved if each city operated its own system of courts. And police powers were so broadly conceived that they included the regulation of trade and industry, schools, churches, health, food distribution and poor laws. State responsibility for these activities was also required in order to provide equality of treatment in the various cities. Stein's City Charter Law delegated the state's authority for police to the city *Magistrat*, but a clear division of responsibility between the higher police bureaucracy and the city *Magistrat* for specific police activities was not made. Stein's best-known biographer, Gerhard Ritter, argues that the failure to place limits on the potential power of a state police authority to interfere in local government administration was the most serious weakness of the Stein reform law. Prussian cities had to acquire numerous powers necessary for self-government in a struggle with the state that lasted for decades.[21]

Stein's fame rests in large part on the fact that his reform created for most of Prussia until the 1848 revolution relatively autonomous, self-governing units in an otherwise hierarchically governed, absolutist monarchy, in spite of the traditional right of police interference[22] and the victory which the Prussian reaction achieved after 1819 over the reform party. The Stein Charter Law is seen as having had a direct connection with the flourishing German cities of the nineteenth century. Their freedom lay in Stein's conception of the city as an "autonomous corporation distinct from the state, the citizens of which were to take responsibility for administering themselves their own sphere of activities."[23] While his reforms applied initially only to those territories of Prussia east of the Elbe where there were relatively few cities, they influenced South German states after 1815 and Hanover in 1848. They had also a considerable impact on the western provinces of Prussia after 1850.[24]

The 1831 revision of the Prussian City Charter Law. The defeat of Napoleon led to a redistribution of territories in Europe at the Congress of Vienna in 1815, and Prussia regained and added significant lands on both banks of the Rhine. The restoration party had been agitating for changes in the Stein City Charter Law even before 1815, and the acquisition of new territories provided the opportunity to revise the Charter Law and apply it to all of the cities in the greatly enlarged state. With the victory in 1819 of the restoration forces over the reform party headed then by Chief Minister Hardenberg, Stein's reform-minded successor from 1808 to 1822, the way seemed clear for policies that would revise, if not replace, the Stein and Hardenberg reforms. Still, it was not until 1831 that the City Charter Law revisions went into effect.

In accordance with the restoration sentiment which prevailed at the time, the revisions provided in general for a strengthening of the role of the state bureaucracy over the city administration and city council. Opportunities for state intervention were increased, and the state could even propose new local laws in addition to its right under the law of 1808 to reject or revise a law passed by council. This was close to a return to pre-1808 conditions. The king, rather than the state bureaucracy, was given the right to select the lord mayor from among the three candidates proposed by council, and the state was given more control over the *Magistrat*. As in any system of divided powers, there had been struggles at times between the city council and the *Magistrat* under the 1808 law, and the revisions resolved such potential tensions by giving the *Magistrat* the power to challenge every decision of council; in cases of unresolved disputes, the state would decide the issue. The state also could dissolve the council if it "continuously neglected its duties." Thus the state, rather than the citizens, could determine whether the council was competent. Responsibility for the police was delegated to the mayor rather than the *Magistrat* as a collegial body, and the term of office for the mayor and other *Magistrat* professionals was changed from six to twelve years.[25] A minor liberalization in the code was a reduction from two-thirds to one-half in the proportion of house owners required in the council membership.

Because most of the cities in the core areas of Prussia east of the Elbe were satisfied with the 1808 law and resisted the changes in the 1831 version, they were given the option of selecting between the two. Only three cities chose the revised version.[26] The newly acquired lands on the left bank of the Rhine also were exempted from the revised charter law. These territories had been under French administration for twenty years, and French law and administrative practice had taken root. Middle-class (*bürgerliche*) elements were stronger and more numerous in the West than in the more feudal eastern territories, and the French bureaucratic system was seen as an improvement over the older Prussian system. This applied also to the French system of local government, which was rational, simple and effective even though its emphasis on centralized control practically destroyed any real semblance of "self" government. The French *mairie* system thus became the Rhenish strong mayor system (*Bürgermeisterverfassung*). Equality between city, small town and village in the application of local government law adapted from France also fit the economic and social conditions of the Rhineland better than the separate treatment of urban and rural areas which remained a characteristic of the more backward East. French influence in the Rhineland was manifested also in the creation of associations of smaller villages (*Samtgemeinden*) for administrative purposes.[27]

French influence between the Rhine and Elbe rivers was far less deeply rooted, though not without some impact. In 1831 the Prussian province of Westphalia adopted the revised City Charter Law. In 1841 it implemented a separate rural local government law which contained certain features of the Rhenish *Bürgermeister* system; for example, it called for an appointed mayor and the association of small villages into an *Amt* rather than a *Samtgemeinde*.[28]

City government in other German states. In Prussia the reform of city government followed in the wake of military defeat and the loss of one-half of its territory. For the newly enlarged South German states, in contrast, local reform was made necessary by the annexation of numerous small territories and Reich cities. The goal was the establishment of central control over the centrifugal remnants of an earlier feudal era. The (comparatively) absolute monarchies created during the Napoleonic era believed that only a strict submission of local government to state authority would conform to the new principle of undivided state sovereignty and secure the unity of the realm.[29] Officials in Bavaria, for example, accepted the view that an "autonomous political activity by the citizens —even if only in the small arena of the city—would endanger or slow the process of state-building."[30] Thus state bureaucracies strengthened their control over cities in the South just as a new and quite modern form of self-government was being introduced in Prussia.

With the defeat of Napoleon and the reduction of French influence in the West and South of Germany, a new series of local reforms was carried out. Bavaria introduced a local government law that was based on Stein's Charter but called for a greater role for the bureaucracy and for a more limited suffrage. Württemberg's local government law was similar to Bavaria's, but its suffrage provisions were more democratic. Baden's reform efforts failed at first, but in 1831 the relatively progressive monarchy introduced the most liberal city charter law in South Germany. Indeed, this reform so disturbed the reactionary great powers—Austria, Prussia and Russia—that Baden was forced to revise its law in 1837 in a more conservative direction. For example, the direct election of the mayor, city council and the more powerful "small committee" by a relatively broad-based electorate was changed to indirect selection by a "large citizen committee" elected in turn in accordance with a plutocratic three-class electoral system.[31]

Rural government. In the decades following the promulgation of Stein's City Charter Law of 1808, local self-government in Prussian cities became an anomoly in the otherwise absolutist, bureaucratic order of the Prussian state. The contrast between local government in the cities and the administration of rural areas was especially striking, as were the social and economic differences that separated city and country in the Prussian East.

Stein had hoped to weaken if not eliminate the traditional role of the landed nobility (*Rittergutsbesitzer*) in the administration of the rural areas of Prussia east of the Elbe River. The freeing of the serfs in 1807 was the first modest step in this direction, but his proposals for county (*Kreis*) government were not ready for submission to the king when he was dismissed in November 1808. Stein's successor, Prince Hardenberg, was also of the reform party, even though he and Stein disagreed on many subjects. Among his many reform bills was the rural police edict (*Gendarmerieedikt*) of 1812 which represented the first codification of law concerning county administration. In this "county edict" the term "county administration" (*Kreisverwaltung*) was used for the first time; it was also in this law that counties were given equal status as corporations with first class, that is, large, cities. It called for a county government made up of a powerful, state-appointed county administrator (*Landrat*), whose appointment by the king was designed to weaken the hold of the feudal landed nobility; a city judge from the county seat; and six deputies—two each from the towns, the landed nobility and the peasants. These were to be nominated by an electoral assembly made up equally of the above groups. County boundaries were to be redrawn according to population size.[32] Feudal opposition to the county edict of 1812 was strong, and in 1814 the landed nobility succeeded in having it suspended. The traditional system of rural government was essentially reinstated in 1815, and all further reform efforts ended in 1821 with the final victory of the restoration party and Hardenberg's death in 1822.[33]

The restoration party's victory consisted of a decision by the king to allow each province of Prussia to have its own system of rural government. In the Rhineland this meant retention of the French *Bürgermeister* system in the rural towns and villages, equal legal status for urban and rural areas, and in that province and in Westphalia it meant also the formation of associations of villages into *Samtgemeinden* or *Ämter*. In the East, however, victory by the forces of reaction meant return to the patrimonial rule by the mostly noble estate owners, the *Junker*. Most villages in the East were too small to provide services such as schools and road maintenance, yet the ruling nobility resisted the introduction of the Western *Samtgemeinde*.[34] The estate owners retained responsibility for local justice, police and church administration. They also named the village spokesmen. While this system of rural government was hardly self-government from the perspective of the majority peasant population, it was nevertheless a highly decentralized, basically feudal, order. It would have been undermined to a considerable extent by a strong system of county government as envisaged by Hardenberg's edict of 1812. The effectiveness of the resistance to reform by the estate owners of the Eastern provinces is reflected in the fact that no new comprehensive law concerning the government of villages and towns in their territories was passed until 1891.[35]

In the 1820s the various Prussian provinces adopted their own separate county charter laws. These were similar in some respects, for example, in their provisions granting one vote in the county council to each estate owner, whose number was far greater in the East, one vote to each city, and three votes to the majority peasants. In the West each *Samtgemeinde* also had a vote. The result of this system of representation could be seen in a county council which might be composed of more than one hundred estate owners, one or two town representatives with several thousand inhabitants each, and three peasant representatives for tens of thousands of rural inhabitants. In addition the estate owners, the *Junker*, had the right to nominate for state approval the *Landrat*, the chief county administrative official who came from their ranks. While on the average the number of estate owners was about ten, they were still able to dominate the county council.[36]

Intermediate levels of government. The county *Landrat* and the city mayor, together with the city *Magistrat*, were to become key elements in the Prussian administrative system after 1815. Though Hardenberg's county reform failed in 1814, it became necessary to reorganize the administration of Prussia above the county and city level with the accession of large amounts of territory in 1815. In that year the reconstituted Prussian state was divided into ten—in 1824 into eight—provinces, each headed by a provincial governor (*Oberpräsident*). The provinces were divided further into twenty-eight—after 1824, twenty-five —administrative districts (*Regierungsbezirke*) headed by a district officer (*Regierungspräsident*). Both of these institutions had been created by Stein in 1807 for a much smaller Prussia.[37]

While the provinces west of the Elbe were formed by combining a number of older territories, the Eastern provinces remained essentially the same as before 1815. Even in the West, however, older traditions and boundaries were not ignored, and the provinces gained considerable political autonomy over the years in spite of the fact that Prussia was a unitary state. The members of provincial assemblies were elected by the county councils, which resulted in a dramatic overrepresentation of *Junker* elements.

Though the provincial governor was given some administrative duties, his functions were primarily ceremonial. Later, in 1817 and 1825, his position was strengthened. He was given the right to supervise the administrative districts, though not to interfere in the details of their work. He was to resolve conflicts between administrative districts, and he enjoyed certain emergency powers. With these and other duties, the provincial governors gained the status of an intermediate administrative level (*Mittelinstanz*) between the central ministries and the local governments.[38]

In contrast to the provinces, whose boundaries corresponded frequently with cultural distinctiveness and historical tradition, the administrative districts were artificial creations established for bureaucratic purposes only. They were directly responsible for the supervision or administration of virtually all domestic functions, their most important duties consisting of the supervision of the actual operating agencies. These were the county administrations under the direction of the *Landrat* and the larger city administrations (*Magistrate*) headed by the mayor. Given their responsibility for detailed administrative supervision of state activities, the administrative districts were more genuine *Mittelinstanzen* than were the provinces.

Even though Prussia was a unitary state with a bureaucratized, absolute monarchy, Prussian administration was decentralized to a striking degree when compared with France or even England. Local administrators were the operating agents for the central ministries, which delegated the responsibility for supervision to the district officers who, in turn, were "observed" by the provincial governors. In contrast to their role in the administration of state laws, Prussian cities were permitted by law to regulate their own sphere of activities with little supervision.

However, the decentralized administrative structure of Prussia, in spite of the heavy hand of bureaucracy everywhere in Germany, did not mean that there was a well-developed system of *self-government* in the sense of popular participation. Government in the rural areas was primarily the responsibility of the *Junker* in the East of Prussia and of bureaucrats everywhere else. Bureaucratic government was also the major characteristic of cities outside of Prussia and in the western provinces of Prussia. In the Prussian East the Stein City Charter Law of 1808 provided for a considerable degree of local administration but only a limited amount of popular self-government. Male suffrage, while broadly based given the historical context, was not universal; members of the *Magistrat* and the mayor had to be confirmed by the district officers (in the large cities the lord mayor was selected by the king from three candidates); the role of the local bureaucracy was growing, for example, in reviewing city council decisions; and supervision by the administrative districts over *Magistrat* administration was increasing. The Prussian provincial assemblies created in 1823 were corporate, rather than representative, bodies, the membership of which was weighted heavily in favor of the nobility and land owners. The promise by the king to create a Prussian-wide assembly was not carried out at all. For the growing Liberal movement in the German states and Prussian provinces, especially in the West and South, the lack of middle-class (*bürgerliche*) participation in government at all levels had become intolerable.

Local Government in Germany, 1848–1914

During the 1840s Liberals agitated not only for the creation of a Prussian parliament, which had been promised in 1810, but also for more effective middle-class participation in provincial and local governments. In all German states Liberals demanded a united Germany under a constitutional monarchy and parliamentary government. During the first months of the 1848 revolution, it appeared that these goals might be achieved. The revolutionaries enjoyed dramatic initial successes, and the forces of the old order were everywhere in retreat. In 1849 the Frankfurt National Assembly passed a Liberal constitution which provided for a united, "small" German Reich (Austria and certain other territories were not included). This national constitution contained provisions which would have required a number of reforms of German local governments, especially in eastern Prussia.[39] That the revolution failed, and the Frankfurter Constitution was never put into effect, was a tragedy not only for local self-government in Germany but for democratic principles in general.

Local government from 1848 to 1871. In the various German states certain provisions of the 1849 National Constitution did find expression in new local government laws. More progressive features were introduced in South Germany in 1848 and 1849, although Baden's especially modern law of 1849 was never put into effect. Hanover implemented a new kingdom-wide city charter law in 1851 which replaced the older separate city charters. While based on Stein's City Charter Law of 1808, the new Hanover law gave cities control over local police; on the other hand, suffrage provisions were less generous. A rural government law was passed in 1852 which favored large farmers but not the landed nobility as in eastern Prussia. Both of these local government laws were revised in a more conservative direction in 1858 and 1859.[40]

In Prussia local government reform proposals were directed above all against the patrimonial rule of the landed nobility over the villages in the eastern provinces. Liberals called also for ending the differences in regulations for urban and rural administrations. The equality of the French system as adopted by the Rhineland became the model for Prussian villages and towns, while Belgium was the model for the county, district and provincial levels.[41]

In spite of his reassertion of authority and power by the end of 1848, the Prussian monarch acquiesced to the passage of a constitution in December 1848 and to the establishment of a Prussian parliament in 1849. Election to this parliament was according to a three-class electoral system which made representation in the parliament dependent on the amount of taxes paid (for example, a group that paid one-third of the taxes received one-third of the representation). It was copied from the 1837 local government law of Baden and the 1845 village and town charter of the Rhineland. It became the electoral system for all levels of government in Prussia until 1918.[42]

In the revised Prussian constitution of 1850, the essential features of the 1849 Frankfurt Constitution's provisions concerning local government were retained: each municipality was guaranteed the right to elect its own mayor and council and the right to autonomous self-government in the areas of its own sphere of activities.[43] A combined city, town, and village charter law of 1850 provided the equal treatment among municipalities that Liberals had long demanded, and it applied to all of Prussia, replacing the individual and often quite different provincial charters. At the same time new regulations for all Prussian counties, administrative districts and provinces were passed.[44] These laws, in addition to the new police regulations, represented a frontal attack on the privileges of the *Junker* in the East, although the overall thrust was the creation of a unified system of local government for the entire realm. State supervision was reduced somewhat and placed in part in the hands of county and provincial deputies. The three-class electoral system was introduced in the cities and towns, and large farmers replaced in part the nobility in the county councils. The effect of the plutocratic electoral system, to which most middle class Liberals did not object, was accentuated by indirect election to bodies above the municipalities, i.e., to the county, district and provincial councils. While these and other provisions favored wealth and property, on the grounds that such elements were more deserving of representation, they also served to undermine government by the nobility and the bureaucrats in favor of the middle classes. It is not surprising that the forces of reaction objected to these changes, and when they regained control in 1851 they repealed the self-government provisions (article 105) of the 1850 constitution and the 1850 laws which had liberalized, unified, and extended self-government in the municipalities, counties, and provinces.[45]

In 1853 the now-dominant reactionary forces pushed through the two houses of the Prussian parliament their own city charter law for the six eastern provinces.[46] Separate city charter laws were passed in 1856 for the two western provinces, Rhineland and Westphalia. In accordance with its own tradition, the Rhineland was granted at the same time a charter law for small towns and villages; its city charter also provided for an elected strong mayor rather than a *Magistrat* as the executive authority.[47]

While the 1853 City Charter Law for the Prussian East represented in a number of ways a liberalization of the 1808 and 1831 charter laws and incorporated many of the features of the 1850 Municipal Charter Law, it was distinctly a step backward from the 1850 law. Indeed, the differences between the Municipal Charter Law of 1850 and the City Charter Law of 1853 reflect in many ways the tension between the urban Liberals and the rural nobility. Bismarck even expressed doubts that "true Prussians" lived in the larger cities.[48] While the nobility had little influence in the cities, the state bureaucracy did, and in the new City Charter Law of 1853 it was able to strengthen its influence through supervision both at the administrative district and *Magistrat* levels. In contrast to the 1850 law, for example, the members of the *Magistrat* were again subject to approval by state authorities—thus discouraging Liberal candidates—and the *Magistrat* was strengthened in its relations with the council. Councillors were no longer to be elected by secret ballot, and their terms were extended to six years. Elections for one-third of the council were held every two years.

For the rural areas, counties and provinces of eastern Prussia, the repeal of the 1850 law meant a return to the situation before 1848, except that some county and provincial powers had now been assumed by the new Prussian parliament. State bureaucratic control over these levels also was strengthened. However, the landed nobility retained their patrimonial administration of the rural countryside except for their judicial powers which became a responsibility of the state.[49]

The city charter laws of 1853 and 1856 allowed cities to choose between the *Magistrat* and the Rhenish *Bürgermeister* form of government, the latter of which now called for election rather than appointment of the mayor and other administrative professionals. However, few cities in one part of Prussia adopted the system typical of the other. In fact, the similarities between the local government system for Prussian cities were greater than the differences in spite of the two separate laws of 1853 and 1856. These laws were to remain the basis for the government of Prussian cities until well into the twentieth century.[50]

In the other German states, too, the Liberal reforms of 1848–50 were overturned as a result of Prussian and Austrian pressures, especially if the local conservative forces were too weak to do the job alone. The role of the bureaucracy was strengthened again, while in some parts of northern Germany, particularly in Mecklenburg, feudal elements were given new impetus. Only in the free Hanseatic cities of Bremen, Hamburg and Lübeck was it possible to retain some of the progressive reforms of the 1848 revolutionary period.[51]

During the "new era" which replaced the post-1850 time of reaction in Prussia and elsewhere, Liberal influence in legislative assemblies grew, and reforms were passed in numerous states of Europe. In Prussia this era began in 1858 with the accession to the throne of William I. A number of Liberals became Prussian ministers, and Liberals gained a majority in the Prussian parliament. Still, Liberal efforts in 1860 and 1862 to reform rural government in the East remained stillborn. The new era ended in Prussia with the dissolution of the parliament in 1862 and the replacement of the Liberal ministers by conservatives. The appointment of the conservative Bismarck as Chancellor later in the year put an end to all progressive institutional reform efforts.[52]

In Baden and Bavaria, in contrast, the new era set the stage for a number of changes. The friendly relations between the monarch of Baden and Liberals led to a progressive county reform in 1863 which provided for an elected county council and a county executive committee. The chief county administrator (*Landrat*) was the only official requiring state confirmation. The state continued its supervision of local governments, but citizens were given some administrative influence at this level. In Bavaria local reforms were introduced in 1869. State supervision was reduced, and suffrage remained broader than in Prussia.[53]

With the annexation by Prussia of Hanover, Hessen-Nassau and Schleswig-Holstein in 1866, three provinces were added which strengthened the influence of the West in the Prussian parliament. The new provinces also were given parliaments in which the influence of the landed nobility was less strong than in the East. City and large peasant interests were also better represented in the county councils than in eastern Prussia. Of the new provinces, only Schleswig-Holstein introduced major changes in its local government laws after annexation.[54]

By the end of the decade and before the establishment of the Bismarck Reich in 1871, self-government in the various German states and even in the unitary state of Prussia could be found in an almost confusing variety of forms. French influence in the west and southwest of Germany was reflected in the laws providing for equal treatment of urban and rural areas and in the *Bürgermeister* form of local government. In central and eastern Prussia the relatively progressive Stein City Charter Law of 1808, revised in 1831 and 1853, applied in the cities, while an almost feudal system of rural local government persisted in the eastern provinces. Promising reforms in the various states which would have increased local responsibility and eliminated the most obnoxious provisions of rural government in Prussia were repealed or weakened by the conservative reaction which followed the unsuccessful revolution of 1848. Though varying in its degree of control among the different states, the heavy hand of bureaucracy was felt everywhere in the cities and counties. That the spirit and practice of local self-government did develop in German cities during the nineteenth century occurred as much in spite of as because of some of the local government laws.[55]

From the Bismarck Reich to World War I. With the victory over France and the emergence of the Second Reich in 1871, proposals were made which would have created a unitary German state on the model of France, Britain or Spain. Even though Prussia made up three-fifths of the population and two-thirds of the territory of the new Germany, Bismarck rejected these ideas and created a federal state instead; indeed, one could even argue that the special rights given to Bavaria went beyond federalism to a kind of confederal particularism, well within the traditions of the old empire. In spite of its weaknesses, the federal solution did make it easier not just for Bavaria but also for other middle states such as Baden, Württemberg, and Saxony to join the new empire which contained twenty-five states in all.

Federalism in the new German Empire guaranteed the continued diversity of local government systems in various parts of the country, and it meant that changes in the structures or functions at the local level would still come from the constituent states which were once sovereign unitary states in their own right. Only Prussia, however, which was the sole state to have gained territory, had reason to change its local government laws.

The first and most important revision in Prussia following the establishment of the Bismarck Reich was the County Charter Law of 1872.[56] At first the law applied only to the eastern provinces, but in the 1880s it was extended to central and western Prussia, thus creating for the first time a common Prussian county government system.[57]

By the 1880s a clear distinction was being drawn between a *Landkreis* (rural county) and *Stadtkreis* (city-county or county-free city). Before, only the term *Kreis* had been used. The concept for both kinds of *Kreis* was clear: the *Kreis*, whether *Landkreis* or *Stadtkreis*, was an incorporated territory (*Gebietskörperschaft*), and all persons living within its boundaries were "subjects" (*Kreisangehörige*). In the case of *Landkreise*, this included the towns and villages within the territory, since they were also corporations and thus legal persons. Only cities of 25,000 or more inhabitants could become county-free, or *Stadtkreise*.[58]

In accordance with the prevailing European spirit of the times, which did not favor suffrage for the working classes or peasants, the County Charter Law of 1872 provided for a plutocratic election procedure for the county council. Its members were elected indirectly in the towns by the town council, by "first class" taxpayers (that is, those with some wealth) in the villages, and by large landowners. The number of councillors and the proportion of town and country representatives in the county council depended on the population size and distribution; however, the city representatives were not permitted to exceed one-half of the county council.

The county council had the right to decide all important matters which fell within the sphere of county activities. It enjoyed legislative autonomy, and it could revise the decisions of the six-member county executive committee (*Kreisausschuss*) which was elected by the membership of the council and had the responsibility for handling routine questions as well as serving as an executive organ for the council. The chief administrative officer, the *Landrat*, was a member and chairman both of this committee and of the council.

Since the county was an administrative district for the state as well as an incorporated, self-governing territory, the county organs—and especially the *Landrat*—were responsible for the administration of certain functions delegated by higher state authorities as well as for matters within the sphere of local responsibility. Some state-imposed functions were the administrative responsibility of the *Landrat* alone, which demonstrates clearly his dual role of state bureaucrat and local official. The county administrative offices consisted of two sections: one for the administration by state bureaucrats of state functions, and one for the county government activities, administered by local bureaucrats. The *Landrat*, as the key county official, was nominated by the county council; however, because of his role in the administration of state functions, his appointment was by the king. This method of selection virtually guaranteed the conservative character of the Prussian *Landrat* until well into the twentieth century. The percentage of *Landräte* who were from the landed nobility declined as the professional legal qualifications for the position grew, but the nobility still represented half of the 231 Prussian *Landräte* in 1888.[59]

In spite of its conservative features, the County Charter Law of 1872 broke the feudal tradition of rural government in the eastern provinces. The county executive committee was not necessarily dominated by the nobility; the executive committee, rather than the noble estate owners, supervised the villages and served also the first instance of the administrative court system. For the first time since the freeing of the serfs in 1807, the villages in eastern Prussia could elect their own local spokesmen; however, the estates of the nobility retained their autonomy, and the influence of the aristocracy in the rural counties remained strong in spite of the assumption of greater power by non-aristocratic wealth and by the state bureaucracy.[60]

The County Law of 1872 was followed in Prussia by the Provincial Charter Law of 1875.[61] The role of the province was enlarged as a field agency for central ministries; as an institution of self-government, it was concerned primarily with roads, but also with welfare, agricultural schools, and cultural matters. The provincial councils were elected by the county and city councils. Election by the latter was a guarantee that at least a minority of the provincial council would consist of Liberal city mayors; but election by the county councils meant that rural conservative forces would be dominant and that they would be represented especially by *Landräte*.[62] Election of civil servants, in this case mayors and *Landräte*, to parliamentary office was by this time a well-established tradition which not even Bismarck could break. It was defended on the grounds that civil servants possessed expertise which would benefit both the parliament and the government bodies from which they came.[63]

Following the passage of the new charters for counties and provinces, a city charter bill was introduced in the Prussian parliament in 1876. This bill was more in conformity than the existing law with Liberal wishes, since it withdrew the right of the state to confirm members of the city *Magistrat* with the exception of the mayor and his deputy. The plutocratic three-class electoral system was to be retained, but elections were to be made secret. State supervision was also to be reduced. This bill was passed and even liberalized by the lower house, but it was defeated in the conservative upper house. Both houses refused to compromise before the end of the legislative session, and the bill was defeated.[64]

In spite of the changes brought about by the county and provincial charter laws of 1872 and 1875, the cities of Prussia and elsewhere in Germany remained the focus of attention with respect to the concept of self-government. Economic developments, and especially the industrial revolution, accompanied by rapid population growth in the urban areas, required city governments to adapt to rapid and far-reaching changes. While the state assumed responsibility for activities such as mail and telegraph services and railroads, cities provided for gas, water, street car transportation, slaughterhouses and other modern activities which changed the character of the traditional city. Indeed, most modern German city services date from this period.[65] In the process of this development some of the ideas which Stein and others had pushed, such as the administration of city affairs by unpaid middle-class citizens, were becoming increasingly difficult to sustain against an advancing professional local bureaucracy.[66]

In 1883 two laws were passed in Prussia which reordered the administrative court system down to the local level and filled certain gaps concerning the state supervision of city governments. Afterwards, between 1884 and 1888, new county and provincial charter laws were passed in the Prussian parliament for the central and western provinces, and, in the Prussian tradition, these allowed for various regional differences derived from past practices and experience. The laws of 1872, 1875, 1883 and 1884–88 formed the basis of the Prussian administrative system during the period up to World War I, and many of their features persisted thereafter. Only modest changes were made in rural government in the Rural Village Law (*Landgemeindeordnung*) of 1891 which applied to eastern Prussia only. Village mayors and their deputies were generally unpaid; however, if the village had more than 3,000 inhabitants, local officials could be employed. For the smallest villages, of which there were many in the East, a general assembly of all qualified voters was authorized, while an elected council was to serve in the larger villages. Agricultural workers were given the right to vote along with the peasants; however, the three-class electoral system applied here as elsewhere. Contrary to Liberal demands, the feudal autonomy of the landed estates was hardly affected by this law, although in theory the estates could be consolidated with nearby villages. The rights and privileges of the landed nobility remained sufficient, however, to prevent the undermining of their autonomous position in the government of rural eastern Prussia until after World War I.[67]

The German Empire of 1871 to 1918 was characterized by a wide variety of local government systems in the twenty-five constituent states. Prussia alone had by 1900 six different village charters, seven city charter laws, one municipal charter law which covered both cities and counties, six different county and provincial codes, and other laws concerning administrative courts, state supervision of local governments, etc.[68] While there were important differences among these local government systems, the degree of self-government which existed in the sense of broad public participation and self-determination remained in the final analysis quite limited. In the rural areas local government in the villages and counties was dominated by conservative land owners, and in eastern Prussia the landed nobility and their friends dominated local governments until World War I. The free Hanseatic cities, in contrast, especially Hamburg, were strongholds of Liberalism, as were the Southwest German states of Baden and Württemberg. And, in spite of the conservative and often even reactionary pressures in Prussia, the larger cities of the state were often able to remain relative bastions of Liberal politics.[69] Indeed, state supervision was frequently greater in theory than in practice. But the growth of the bureaucracy, brought about not only by the absolutist tradition but also by the industrial revolution and the accompanying population explosion, created new and formidable barriers for those who demanded more local self-government by the citizenry.

Self-government was also limited by the three-class electoral system. The system of equal, universal male suffrage adopted for the national Reichstag was never applied to most of the state, provincial, or local levels of Prussia, nor was it found in most other German states. Only in the Kingdom of Saxony, in Württemberg, in Frankfurt, and in the Prussian provinces of Hanover and Schleswig-Holstein was there an electoral system which provided for a broad electorate to participate equally. In the cities, towns, counties, and provinces in the rest of Germany, the plutocratic principle prevailed. The three-class electoral system led to such anomalies as the election by Friedrich Krupp alone of one-third of the city council of Essen. In Berlin in 1880 about 2 percent of the voters were in the first class, about 10 percent in the second class, and all the rest were in the third class.[70] On the other hand, it should be remembered that French local government councils were not made elective until 1881, and not until 1884 did the British introduce broad male suffrage.

The three-class system of election was generally supported by middle-class Liberals, even though it benefitted also their conservative opponents who were close to the landed nobility and state bureaucracy. The Liberals failed to push for a broader electorate at the local level for a number of reasons, but their fear of the Social Democratic Party (SPD) and its hostile working-class supporters was a primary concern. Even though Bismarck had the Reichstag ban the SPD from 1878 to 1890, the Liberal parties declined in strength. After 1890 the SPD became the largest party in the Reichstag, but it was still denied entrance to most local, county and provincial parliaments by the electoral system.[71] To an even lesser extent than their counterparts in France and Britain, German Liberals were not successful in replacing the conservatives as the main political force in society before they had to meet the overwhelming political challenge from the working class.

Even more important than plutocratic electoral arrangements, however, were the nondemocratic and frequently antidemocratic political environment and institutional framework at the regional and national levels within which German local governments operated. In Great Britain and the United States, local self-government was one aspect of self-government at all levels, a logical consequence of the success of Liberalism and of a general political development toward increasing democracy. In Germany the advocates of self-government at the local level had to struggle against both an absolutist tradition of bureaucratic control and supervision and the remnants of a reactionary, particularistic feudal order. These elements had been weakened during the 1848 revolution, but they soon regained their strength. From 1850 until World War I, they dominated government and politics everywhere except in the cities and in certain regions such as southwest Germany. They were especially strong in the eastern half of Prussia,[72] and they succeeded in defeating every meaningful general reform bill for local and provincial government since the efforts of Baron vom Stein. That German Liberalism enjoyed as much success as it did in obtaining and retaining some degree of self-government for the cities is a tribute to the tenacity of its supporters. That they were less successful in achieving a greater degree of democracy at the state and national levels carried consequences for Germany and Europe that went beyond local government.

In spite of the cultural and institutional obstacles facing the advocates of self-government, democratic pressures increased during the first decade of the twentieth century. Electoral laws were liberalized in a number of state parliaments, and the parties of the left, especially the SPD, continued to grow under conditions of rapid industrialization and economic change. Some reforms which liberalized certain local government practices were introduced in southwest Germany, and the SPD demanded a democratization of local government at its party convention in 1904. Prussia, however, remained immune to these developments.[73] Until the final months of World War I, when it was too late, the Kaiser and his governments were unwilling or unable to find a compromise between the traditional view that the monarch has been called to serve his people by means of a bureaucratic hierarchy and the modern view of the state as an organized people who govern themselves.

The Weimar Era, 1919–1933

The constitutional scholar Hugo Preuss, who played a major role in drawing up the Weimar Constitution, had observed in discussing the Stein reforms that genuine local self-government in Germany could be achieved only under a democratic political order (at the head of which a less powerful constitutional monarch along British lines could have served) that would eliminate the inherent conflict and contradiction between elected organs of local governments and the state bureaucratic authorities at higher levels.[74] Under the circumstances of the times, this would have required a revolution which was most unlikely; however, a revolutionary change did come with World War I and the collapse of the Kaiserreich in 1918. The ushering in of the republic in 1918 and the promulgation of a new constitution in Weimar in 1919 introduced for the first time democratic institutions and procedures at all levels throughout the land. Suffrage was extended to women, and the electoral system provided for an equal and secret ballot with proportional representation for all levels of government. Article 127 of the constitution guaranteed local government the right to self-government "within the limits of the laws." In 1929 a national court interpreted this provision to mean that the constitution guaranteed local self-government as an institution which could not be threatened by state authorities either directly or indirectly, for example, through administrative or financial pressures.[75]

But the new democratic local autonomy was more easily proclaimed than practiced. In spite of the dramatic changes brought about under the new republic, local government could not prosper in the conditions of hunger, inflation, political polarization, and general distress in the period 1918–23.[76] These challenges taxed severely the ability of German local governments to provide even the most basic services. Political polarization and extremism were probably encouraged by proportional representation which helped to fragment and divide local politics when united action was called for.[77] It may be that the politicization of local governments in the cities and industrial towns had begun even before 1918,[78] and that party politics before the war had merely been covered up by the homogeneity of the dominant middle class.[79] It seems clear, however, that the degree to which party politics had become a major factor in local government created a new and difficult situation in many German towns and cities. Alone the dramatic rise of proletarian party influence and the decline of the traditionally dominant middle class represented a significant change, as did the sheer number (forty-two in one city) of competing parties.[80]

Though the Weimar Republic was a federation like its predecessor, now with eighteen rather than twenty-five states, the pressures toward centralization were strong even when one ignores the conditions that obtained in the first years following the war. Some, including Hugo Preuss, had proposed that the new republic be constituted as a unitary state, or that Prussia be broken up into several states[81] and that the smaller states be annexed by larger neighbors. Resistance to such ideas proved to be too strong, but the new national representative organ of the states—now degraded to the designation *Länder*—was a weakened *Reichsrat*. The *Länder* were required to give to the central government a number of their former powers, and the finance reform law of 1919 shifted most of the taxing power from the regional to the central authorities.[82]

Confronted by the combined centralizing pressures of the central government and its bureaucracy, the national parliament (*Reichstag*) and the nationwide impact of its legislation, and the centralized political party organizations,[83] there was little opportunity for the further development of self-government at the local level. Indeed, some six hundred Prussian cities and towns were placed under the control of state commissars during the turbulent years of the republic.[84]

A proposed reform which would have unified and moved in a more democratic direction the Prussian laws for provinces, cities, counties, and rural municipalities was not passed, and these units of government continued to operate on the basis of their charters derived from the nineteenth century. Some changes, of course, did occur. Greater Berlin was created in 1920, and the city was divided into twenty separate districts, each with its own mayor and organs of government. The central government of the city was headed by a lord mayor. The autonomy of the rural estates of eastern Prussia was finally eliminated in 1927.[85] Prussian counties also were given more authority vis-à-vis their towns and villages in a 1929 law.[86]

Other German *Länder* were more successful than Prussia in initiating changes in their local government charters, especially under the influence of the Social Democrats. In Württemberg and Bavaria the dualistic principle of the Stein *Magistrat* system, which provided for a separation of powers between the council and *Magistrat*, was replaced in 1919 by a monocratic city council in which the elected councillors and professional officials served together. Baden introduced also a new city charter law in 1921, but it retained the older Stein system while strengthening the position of the council and mayor vis-à-vis the bureaucracy.

The Bavarian and Württemberg city council system (*Gemeinderatsverfassung*) was similar to the Rhenish *Bürgermeister* system in its monocratic structure; however, the South German system differed in a number of ways from the basically French pattern of the Rhineland. The mayor, while chairman of the council as in the Rhineland, was not the only one responsible for the administration; rather, the council had both legislative and administrative control. In addition the mayor was not the administrative superior of the other paid officials, and he was elected directly by the people rather than by the council. In practice the mayor became far more important in the administration of the city than the charter law suggested.[87]

In contrast to South Germany, Mecklenburg-Schwerin, which had had an almost feudal system of local government until the war, adopted in 1919 the Stein *Magistrat* charter. In Thuringia Social Democratic influence was demonstrated in 1922 by the passage of a city and county charter law which introduced a strict form of parliamentarism in local governments; however, this charter law was repealed in 1926 by a middle-class state government which replaced it with a system similar to the Rhenish *Bürgermeister* system. This system had been adopted also by Saxony, although most larger cities in that *Land* took the option of retaining the older *Magistrat* system.[88]

World War I and the developments following the war encouraged the further assumption of responsibility by local governments for numerous activities and services which in some countries, especially in the United States, have remained largely in the private sphere. While German cities had pursued a politics of "municipal socialism" even under the Liberals in the latter nineteenth century,[89] the counties also began to take on broad responsibilities in the early twentieth century.[90] These were in addition to the responsibility for state activities delegated to them by higher authorities, so that local governments became major distributors of a wide variety of services. Municipal socialism, because of competition with the private sector, was subjected to strong criticism by industry, commerce, and banking interests, but it remains a characteristic of German local government to this day.

During the brief period of "normalcy" from 1924 to 1929, German local governments were barely able to recover from the turmoil and strain of the previous years. With the depression of 1929–33, they faced virtual collapse. Demands for public services far exceeded the capacity to deliver them at near adequate levels, and the desperate economic and social conditions weakened the cities' ability to confront political extremism and to resist Nazi incursions.[91]

Local Government and the Third Reich, 1933–1945

Given the economic and social conditions in the cities and towns of Germany, it is perhaps understandable that the Nazi call for a "central coordination" or "synchronization" (*Gleichschaltung*) of German institutions was not met with strong resistance. According to the new *Führer* principle—"authority downwards, responsibility upwards"—leading officials in most larger local government units were replaced by Nazi supporters.[92] In 1933, for example, three-fifths of the mayors were replaced in cities with more than 20,000 inhabitants.[93] First the Communists, then the Social Democrats, and finally all party councillors other than Nazis were replaced.

In 1935 the Nazis promulgated a new German Municipal Charter Law (*Deutsche Gemeindeordnung*—DGO) which, in its political provisions, reflected the Nazi *Führer* principle. The mayor was given the over-all responsibility for his municipality, and council members were restricted to an advisory role. All officials, including councillors, were appointed, not elected. Party interference now exceeded the traditional supervision by state authorities.

On the other hand, the DGO overcame previous barriers and created for the first time in Germany a unified system of local government administration for the entire country. Some features regarding matters of finance, budget and economic regulations had been advocated by non-Nazis before 1933 and did not represent a break with older traditions. Indeed, many provisions of the 1935 DGO contained sound administrative ideas and were carried over by the West German *Länder* after 1945.[94]

The Nazi regime did not pass a new county charter law. The villages and towns in the counties were covered by the DGO, but the administration of the counties themselves was left relatively untouched. The changes which were made, for example, the appointment of six county councillors to advise the *Landrat* as the person responsible for the administration of the county, were largely political rather than functional.[95]

Allied Occupation and Local Government, 1945–1949

With the conquest of western territories (from now on the discussion will concern West Germany only) and the capitulation of the Third Reich in May 1945, the

Allies entered cities and towns that had suffered immense destruction.[96] They also found administrative structures in a state of collapse. Leading Nazi officials had "melted away," and "the first task facing the Allies was to decide who should be put in their place."[97]

> Buergermeister and Landraete were selected from previously furnished lists. Generally the Military Government officer called in the town or country priest or minister, the local school teacher, a few local citizens and asked them to suggest a Buergermeister or Landrat. After several conferences and as much investigation as possible, and clearance of political questionnaires, a provisional administrative chief was selected, and he in turn appointed other professional leaders, such as police and fire chiefs, food office head, local clerk, motor vehicle supervisor, and other needed officials. Through these appointed officials, the local Military Government officers began to bring order out of complete chaos, restore circulation, remove hazards to life, such as partially destroyed buildings, start cleaning out rubble, and feed the starving population.[98]

At first these newly established local governments under the supervision of Military Government teams were the only units of administration in which Germans were actively involved. "Reconstruction therefore started with the Gemeinde and Kreis and only after several months with the Regierungsbezirk and the Land."[99] The municipalities and counties would become, along with the churches, unions, and political parties, one of the most important foundations for the reconstruction of post-war Germany.[100]

Practical necessity was a major factor in the attention which the Allies paid to local governments; however, there were also important political reasons. In July and August at the Potsdam Conference, the Four Powers called for a "decentralization of the political structure and the development of local responsibility." This was to be accomplished through the restoration of local self-government "throughout Germany on democratic principles and in particular through elective councils." Democratic parties were to be allowed and encouraged, and representative institutions at regional levels were to be introduced "as rapidly as may be justified by the successful application of these principles in local self-government."[101]

From the beginning, each of the Western Allies differed somewhat in timing and approach toward the reestablishment of local government in its zone of occupation. The Americans and French promoted a policy of "restoration." Americans were accustomed to the diversity of local government institutions which characterized pre-1933 Germany, and they believed apparently that Germany had enjoyed basically healthy local political institutions before Hitler. As a result they moved quickly to reestablish local government in their zone with only limited changes from older patterns. The French were satisfied generally with local government traditions in their zone, since local charter laws in the Rhineland and in Baden had been influenced strongly by France during the Napoleonic era.[102]

The British probably had planned also to restore local governments according to past structural patterns, until Professor William Robson at the London School of Economics suggested that democratic self-government in the British sense had never really existed in Germany and that major reforms were called for. The new Labour Government apparently listened to this criticism, and British occupation authorities proceeded to introduce in their zone certain provisions for local government for which the British system served as a model.[103]

The Americans also moved more quickly than the British and French in reestablishing *Land* (state) governments. Governments for the old state of Bavaria, Württemberg-Baden (joined in 1953 with the French-occupied Baden and Württemberg-Hohenzollern to form the new *Land* of Baden-Württemberg) and the newly created *Land* of Hesse were formed under new constitutions in December 1946, and a new government for Bremen began operating in October 1947. In the same year the French permitted the establishment of new governments in Baden, Württemberg-Hohenzollern (both to become parts of Baden-Württemberg in 1953), in the newly created Rhineland-Palatinate and in the Saarland. The British created three new *Länder* in 1946 and 1947 from the former Prussian provinces and small states which made up its zone; these *Länder*, North-Rhine Westphalia, Lower Saxony and Schleswig-Holstein, operated under temporary charters until the early 1950s. Whether promulgated in 1946 (Bavaria) or not until the early 1950s (the three *Länder* in the British zone), each of the constitutions in the new German *Länder* would contain provisions guaranteeing counties, cities and towns the right of self-government.

Political parties were allowed to form in the American zone in August 1945, in the English and French zones in September and December. The first local elections were held in the American zone in January 1946 for small- and medium-sized municipalities, in the spring for counties and larger cities. The French allowed municipal elections in the summer of 1946 and county elections in the fall of 1946. The British wanted to give their appointed councillors some time to gain practical experience and did not hold local elections until the fall of 1946.

The reestablishment in 1946 of local governments with elected officials required new local government charter laws to replace the DGO of 1935. In the American zone Bavaria and Württemberg-Baden returned to the *Ratsverfassung*, with the council as the major organ of local government and the directly elected mayor as the head of the administration. In the new state of Hesse the *Bürgermeister* system was introduced with an option permitted for the old Prussian *Magistrat* system. The French decreed local government laws during the summer of 1946 which returned local governments in their zone to the traditional *Bürgermeister* system.

Only the British, who were in less of a hurry, insisted on changing the traditional institutions of local government in their zone, which before 1933 had operated either under Stein's "ungenuine" (*unechtes*) *Magistrat* Charter Law of 1808 or the revised "genuine" (*echtes*) *Magistrat* system of 1831. The British saw especially in the latter system a *Magistrat* so powerful as to create a dualism between citizens and local bureaucrats. In their regulations for the municipalities in the three newly created states in the zone, the British separated the legislative from the administrative functions of the mayor, giving the latter to the town clerk (British) or city manager (U.S.) and his staff of nonpolitical local civil servants. The mayor, as head of the council, was to be a layman rather than a professional administrator. In the larger cities an executive committee was formed from the membership of the council to furnish administrative leadership. The same principles applied in the counties.[104]

Germans who visited Britain in order to observe British self-government in operation were generally impressed by the role of the local council. On the other hand, some were skeptical that such a system could operate effectively without local "notables" (*Honoratioren*).[105] The dominance of such middle and upper middle-class elements in German cities had ended to a considerable extent with the politicization following World War I. German local government councils were somewhat more socially diverse and more partisan than the English model. There were also problems in the changes which the British introduced for assessing responsibility for administrative inaction. In several cases after 1945, county governments refused to carry out *Land* directives, and, with the county council serving as the head of the administration, no one person was legally responsible. This was changed later, when the leading civil servant at the local level was made generally responsible for implementing delegated functions.[106]

Another important change introduced by the British was the decentralization of the police. The British argued that local control would make it more difficult for a future would-be dictator to gain control of the central government, and they pointed to the Nazi assumption of power in Prussia in July 1932 and to the Communist takeover in Czechoslovakia in 1948 as examples of their concern. While some Germans agreed, others argued that the threat to democracy came from the local level and took as examples the situation in Germany before 1932. They also believed that centralization would facilitate personnel reviews to weed out undesirable elements and promote the democratic education of police forces. Communist support for local control also was seen as supporting their case.[107]

In the years after the Federal Republic became sovereign in 1949, the responsibility for police was returned to the *Land* government in each of the *Länder* in the former British zone as it had been already in the other zones. Whether the changes introduced by the British in the relationships between the mayor, council and professional administration should remain in effect was also a subject of debate. To oversimplify, the question appeared to be how much democracy (role of the elected council) there should be as opposed to efficiency of administration (role of the local bureaucracy). Schleswig-Holstein returned to the older Prussian "ungenuine" *Magistrat* system in 1950; however, lobbying efforts by council members, mayors and *Landräte*, who had become accustomed to the British regulations—and generational change—led to the retention of the essential features of the British reforms in the local charter laws of North-Rhine Westphalia (1952) and Lower Saxony (1955).[108]

There was no effort made by the Allies to coordinate local government laws in their three zones, and some attempts in the post-war years by Germans to promote a uniform charter law for municipalities and counties which each *Land* would adopt had only a limited impact. German local government laws, especially with respect to political-institutional organization, have retained their traditional diversity. The major difference between pre-1933 and post-1945 laws is that a number of British reforms have been added to the influence of older French and indigenous models.

Conclusion

The tradition of local self-government in Germany, insofar as it has had a discernible influence on present-day patterns, dates back to the reforms of Baron vom Stein in 1808. These reforms and the *Magistrat* system which they created applied to cities in eastern Prussia only, but their impact in western Prussia and in the other German states was felt throughout the nineteenth century, either in the "ungenuine" Stein form or in the "genuine" revised form of 1831. The *Bürgermeister* system of the German Rhineland was adopted from the French Napoleonic model, and it came to represent a second traditional form of local government in Germany. A third form, the *Ratsverfassung*, a significant revision of the *Magistrat* form, was adopted in Bavaria and Württemberg in the early twentieth century. All of these forms of local government were or became strongly bureaucratized, even though elements of self-government remained. While the mayor was a local elected official, he was also a state official responsible for the administration of state functions as well as local activities. Self-government in the smaller towns and villages and in the counties was even more restricted than in the cities, because of the powerful administrative position of the *Landrat* and the limited opportunities for participation by the town and rural population. In eastern Prussia the landed nobility retained control over the small villages until 1872, and they remained influential in rural government until the end of the Weimar Republic.

Even though the plutocratic electoral system of the old order was replaced by a radically democratic proportional representation after World War I, and even though a democratic parliamentary system was introduced at national and state levels, local self-government in Germany could not prosper under the post-war conditions of famine, inflation, depression and political turmoil. In part because of these conditions, centralizing pressures from the central government's administrative authorities, from *Reichstag* legislation, and from centralized party organization undermined further the efforts of those who wanted to sustain some local self-determination. Thus Ernst Reuter, who would become lord mayor of West Berlin after World War II, complained in 1924 that there was local self-government only for the local bureaucrats and the ruling mayors, not for the local citizenry.[109]

Following the disaster of the Third Reich, traditional local government patterns returned in the American and French zones, but certain reform provisions introduced by the British in their zone were adopted permanently in the 1950s by German *Land* governments in two of the largest states. Local self-government was strengthened everywhere in West Germany, however, because of the positive reputation and esteem local officials gained as a result of their success and effectiveness after 1945 in dealing with rubble, destruction, and almost twelve million refugees from the eastern provinces of the now-extinct Prussia and from other parts of Eastern Europe. The brief period between 1945 and 1949, when local governments were free of any state supervision and responsible only to the occupying powers for their services and activities, strengthened dramatically the self-confidence of local officials.

The guarantee of local autonomy never became an issue anywhere in the post-war *Länder*, all of which have constitutions containing provisions which protect the institution of local self-government. The constitution of the Federal Republic, which was created in 1949, also contains a provision guaranteeing local self-government. With the democratic parliamentary system reestablished at the national and state levels, the development of a new, far less fragmented and more moderate party system, the dramatic growth of the economy and the rise in the standard of living to previously unknown heights, and the strong position which it enjoyed when the new era of sovereignty for West Germany began, local self-government was to gain a place in German society which few other systems of local government could match.

3

The German Administrative Tradition, the Federal Framework, and Local Government Institutional Structure

At the beginning of the nineteenth century, the French and Prussian states introduced administrative reforms that made both systems famous for their rational and effective administration of state affairs. While there is considerable controversy over the question of whether Baron vom Stein and Prince von Hardenberg copied important ideas from the Napoleonic reforms, the fact remains that in many respects French and Prussian administrative principles were remarkably similar.

The Spatial Model of Administration

Both countries adopted a system of administration based on territory or area. According to this *spatial* model of organization, the central government or "state" is responsible for general policy making for the entire territory. Unless the policy deals with certain specified areas, however, such as defense, railways or postal services, it is not administered directly by a central ministry, but rather it is delegated by that ministry to regional subnational general purpose units. These units carry out a wide range of tasks delegated to them by the constitution and laws of the central state. In case the regional subnational units are too large for the implementation of certain services or activities, these are delegated to local governments which are both basic units of state administration and levels of administration that are responsible for local concerns. The local governments are under the control or supervision of the regional subnational units, especially with respect to their administration of delegated central state functions.

A guiding principle of this system of administration is unity of command or unity of administration (*Einheit der Verwaltung*). This means that at each level of administration each general purpose unit is responsible for all public functions within its territory. A single chief administrative officer is responsible for the coordination within his unit of all administrative activities and services. He is also responsible to the next higher supervisory administrative unit for the administrative performance of his unit or at least for the legality of the actions of his administration.

In France the chain of command has run traditionally from the central ministry, in particular the Ministry of the Interior in Paris, to the ninety or so departments headed by prefects who were directly responsible to the ministry for most activities within their departments' territories. The departments, in turn, were subdivided into more than 450 *arrondissements* headed by subprefects responsible to the prefect for almost all activities within their territory. The *arrondissements* were then subdivided into about 38,000 communes, for most of whose administration the mayor was responsible to the subprefect.[1] This "classical" model of administration, though altered in a variety of ways since 1800, still applies in general outline to France today. The most significant formal institutional changes probably have been the further division of the country into twenty-two regions during the Gaullist era of the Fifth Republic and the prefectoral reforms of President Mitterrand. The effects of Mitterrand's decentralization efforts are not clear at this time (1984), though there is reason to believe that they have been more limited than many thought would be the case when they were introduced.

While Prussia adopted a form of administration based also on territory and stressing unity of administration, the Prussian unitary state was more decentralized than France. Most of the time between 1815 and 1871, Prussia was divided into eight provinces, twenty-five subnational administrative districts (*Regierungsbezirke*)—which were comparable to but larger than the French departments—and the counties (both city and rural). The rural counties in turn were composed of the thousands of small towns and villages in Prussia. The chief administrative officer for each level—the provincial governor, the district officer, the lord mayor or country *Landrat*, and the town or village mayor—was legally responsible for supervising or performing all public services and activities within his jurisdiction and ensuring their conformity to the law of the central state. But the concept of *Allzuständigkeit*, noted in chapter 2, according to which local governments could perform any task within their own sphere of activity within the law, gave them a limited but important degree of autonomy which French communes did not enjoy until 1884 at the earliest. Stein's City Charter Law of 1808 also provided for an elected city council and an elected lord mayor, whereas these were appointed under Napoleon. Even after 1831, when French municipal councils were made elective, they had only limited decision-making authority. And only after 1884 did they enjoy in law if not in practice full discretion in matters of purely local concern. French mayors were not elected by local councils until 1881.[2] Prussian decentralization is demonstrated also by the different forms of city government that existed among the provinces and by the different organizational forms between rural municipal government and city government in the eastern provinces. In France, by contrast, a single form of local government applied then and today to all communes regardless of size.

In 1871 the German Empire united twenty-five states in a federation which retained the spatial administrative principles of the unitary Prussian state. Thus the national capital, Berlin, became the center of policy making, but most of the policies were turned over to the states for administration. Of these, only Prussia had provinces as the highest level of sub-state administration; however, most of these states—excluding the smallest "territorial" states and the city states—were also divided into administrative districts, city and rural counties, and municipalities, each with a chief administrative officer responsible for all administrative activities in his territory. While it was more centralized than its predecessor, the Weimar Republic of 1919–33 also followed to a considerable extent the pattern set by the Bismarck Reich of 1871–1918.

In the Federal Republic of Germany, the central federal state is responsible for establishing basic policies, rules and regulations for a wide variety of activities; however, the administration of most of these activities has been turned over to the eleven *Länder*. The larger of these have divided their territory into administrative districts (*Regierungsbezirke*), the purpose of which is to coordinate and implement the many functions delegated by the *Land* to them and to supervise the administration of the even more numerous state activities that have been delegated to the cities and counties. The cities and counties have the dual function of serving both as basic central state administrative units and as autonomous institutions of local self-government. With numerous exceptions, such as the central state's local bureaucracies for postal and rail services, *Land* courts and insurance offices, and certain cooperative arrangements between or among local governments in the form of special purpose authorities, the city and county general purpose governments are responsible for all administrative activities within their territory according to the principle of unity of administration. Thus in spite of wrenching political changes between 1918 and 1949, administrative principles in the Federal Republic follow the traditional scheme of German administrative organization.

The German Spatial-Federal Model Today

While the roots of spatial administration in Germany today can be traced back to Prussian reforms in the first decade of the nineteenth century, the origins of the West German federal system emerged in 1867 with the formation of the North German Confederation and then in 1871 with the creation of the Bismarck Reich. There have been more changes in the organization and practice of German federalism, however, than in the older principles of spatial administration.

In the Bismarck Reich the nonelected upper house of parliament, the *Bundesrat*, represented the mostly conservative, traditional twenty-five states with the most conservative state of all, Prussia, playing the dominant role. The *Bundesrat* served as a powerful check on the popularly elected lower house, the *Reichstag*. The chancellor and his cabinet were responsible to the Kaiser, not to the *Reichstag*, as would have been the case in a genuine parliamentary democracy. The Kaiser considered himself to be responsible only to God.

In the Weimar Republic the upper house, the *Reichsrat*, continued to be the nonelected representative of the now democratically governed states (*Länder*), which were reduced in number to eighteen. Its powers were severely weakened, however, and it ceased to play an important role in the political process. In other words, the Weimar Republic was more a spatial-unitary than a spatial-federal state. The chancellor and the cabinet were made responsible to the popularly elected *Reichstag*, but the fragmentation and polarization of the political parties prevented the parliamentary system from functioning as planned. Increasing reliance was placed on the popularly elected President of the republic, who served as an ersatz monarch. The important powers granted him by the Weimar Constitution when the *Reichstag* was unable to form a majority government proved fatal in the hands of President Hindenburg, who turned over the chancellorship to Adolf Hitler in January 1933.

A number of parallels can be drawn between the national political structures and administrative organization of the Bonn Federal Republic and its predecessors, even though there are, of course, important differences as well. Like the Weimar Republic, the Federal Republic is a parliamentary democracy with a popularly elected lower house, the *Bundestag*. The chancellor and his cabinet are responsible to this body; however, under the unique constructive vote of nonconfidence, the chancellor can be removed only if the *Bundestag* can find a majority for his successor. In contrast to Weimar, the President is elected by an assembly consisting of parliamentary deputies from the *Bundestag* and the *Land* parliaments, and his functions are almost entirely ceremonial. The German three-party system (CDU/CSU, SPD and FDP), which has functioned basically as a two-bloc system in recent years, has been far more responsible for political stability than have institutional devices. The parties have been able to form majority governments, and extremist parties of the left and right have had little success at the polls. Whether the new Green party will become a permanent feature of the political landscape remains to be seen. That it received 5.6 percent of the vote in the 1983 *Bundestag* elections and entered parliament with 27 seats means at least that the party will be a factor in German national politics during the rest of the 1980s; it has been a factor at the *Land* and local level in parts of Germany since the late 1970s.

Like the Bismarck Reich, the Federal Republic is a spatial federation with a

Table 3.1. *Länder* of the Federal Republic of Germany and their representation in the *Bundesrat*

Land	Population (1981)	Votes in Bundesrat
Territorial states (*Flächenstaaten*)		
North-Rhine Westphalia	17,049,000	5
Bavaria	10,942,000	5
Baden-Württemberg	9,275,000	5
Lower Saxony	7,262,000	5
Hesse	5,605,000	4
Rhineland Palatinate	3,642,000	4
Schleswig-Holstein	2,616,000	4
Saarland	1,065,000	3
City states (*Stadtstaaten*)		
Hamburg	1,641,000	3
Bremen	693,000	3
West Berlin	1,892,000	4 (advisory only)
Total	61,682,000	45

Source for population data: Statistisches Bundesamt, *Statistisches Jahrbuch 1982 für die Bundesrepublik Deutschland* (Stuttgart: W. Kohlhammer Verlag, 1982), 50.

nonelected upper house, the *Bundesrat*, representing the constituent states (*Länder*); see table 3.1. In contrast to the Bismarck Reich, however, the *Land* delegations represent democratic parliamentary governments, and none of the eleven *Länder* (including West Berlin) is in a position to dominate the *Bundesrat*.

The larger group of four *Länder* have five votes each, the three middle-size *Länder* have four votes each, and the two city states (Hamburg, Bremen) and the Saarland have three votes each. West Berlin's four votes are advisory only; its delegations in the *Bundesrat* and *Bundestag* participate in committee deliberations and plenary debates, but they do not vote officially on legislation.

The Five Levels of Administration

The spatial-federal system of the Federal Republic is made up of political-administrative institutions at five levels of administration: (1) the federal government, (2) the *Länder* governments, (3) the administrative districts (*Regierungsbezirke*), (4) the counties and county-free cities, and (5) the municipalities belonging to a county and associations of small municipalities. In addition there are certain institutions of intergovernmental cooperation which exist at the third, fourth and fifth levels of administration.[3]

The national level. The federal government in Bonn, the first level of administration, consists of the chancellory and sixteen ministries. In general these ministries are concerned more with general policy and political planning than with the implementation of their programs and activities, which is largely the responsibility of the *Länder*. Only a few federal authorities have field agencies, examples of which would include those for the foreign service, federal finance administration (to the regional level only), postal service, railways, armed forces, waterways and shipping, air traffic control, frontier police, and the federal labor authority.

Authorities which perform specific functions for the federation, normally without field agencies, include the federal offices for crime control, statistics, protection of the constitution, cartels, patents, health, insurance, and aviation. Certain technical functions are performed, for example, by semi-autonomous bodies, such as the Federal Office for Aviation Security and the German Weather Service. Finally, there are certain semi-autonomous institutions subject to federal supervision, such as the Federal Labor Authority and the German Federal Bank; both of these have field agencies at the regional and local levels.[4]

The Land *level.* Excluding West Berlin, which has a special legal status, there are ten *Länder* in the Federal Republic, ranging in population from 700,000 to 17,000,000 (see table 3.1). Eight *Länder* are so-called territorial or area states (*Flächenstaaten*), and three are city states. All *Länder* are organized as parliamentary systems, although the city states differ somewhat in political structure from the territorial states. The head of government in the territorial states is the minister-president, in the city states the lord mayor (who is known by a different title in each of the city states). Each head of government is responsible to a one-house popularly elected legislature, called the *Landtag* in the territorial states; other terms are used for the parliaments in the city states.

The focus of activities in the *Länder* is on the administration of national and *Land* laws and on the system of justice. National laws are administered as matters of the *Länders'* own responsibility (*eigene Angelegenheiten*). The administrative district staff in the six larger *Länder* serve as regional field agents with the primary function of coordinating and supervising the actual implementation of national and *Land* laws by the municipal and rural counties. Relationships between the federal government and the *Länder* are not of a hierarchical, superior-inferior order. They are characterized rather by a cooperating, though unequal, partnership. A similar relationship exists between the *Land* government and the local governments.[5]

As the second level of administration in the Federal Republic, the *Land* government, consisting of the minister-president (in the three city states, the lord mayor) and the ministries (in the city states, the *Senat*) are the highest *Land* authorities. There are usually eight to ten ministries in the *Länder* which employ

2,000 to 6,500 public servants. The general accounting agencies for the *Länder* also are highest *Land* authorities, but their directors are not cabinet ministers. A number of other agencies with *Land*-wide responsibilities for several functions can be found directly below the highest authorities in the administrative chain of command. These include, in some *Länder*, the *Land* Statistical Office, the *Land* Computer Office, the *Land* Survey Office, and, in Lower Saxony only, the *Land* Administration Office. Finally, there are a few special-purpose organizations, such as the office responsible for weights and measures, which perform specific functions for the *Länder* and have field offices at the local level.

There are also a number of self-governing corporations, institutions, and foundations that belong to the *Land* level of organization and that fall under the legal supervision of the *Land* governments. These include social insurance funds, universities, chambers of trade (crafts, agriculture, lawyers, physicians, etc.), *Land* banks, fire insurance funds, home construction credit institutions, and radio and television. One should also include here certain institutions operating under private law, such as *Land* theaters.

Regierungsbezirk level. The *Regierungsbezirk*, or administrative district, is a general-purpose regional *Land* institution of administration. It is found only in the six larger territorial states. Schleswig-Holstein, the Saarland and the three city states do not have such a regional middle-level administration (*Mittelinstanz*). The district officer (*Regierungspräsident*) and his staff are appointed civil servants responsible to the *Land* ministries, in particular to the Ministry of Interior. The district officer and his staff together are called the *Bezirksregierung* or, in Baden-Württemberg, *Regierungspräsidium*, and they are the only nonelected body among the five levels of the German administrative system.

While there are a number of functional *Land* agencies with field offices at the regional level of the *Regierungsbezirk*, such as school, police, forest and finance authorities, the general purpose of this district is to serve as the key instrument of coordination in the German system of spatial administration. We noted above that most national legislation is administered by the *Länder*; however, most of this administration does not take place at the second level of the highest *Land* authorities but rather is delegated to the third level *Bezirksregierung* and the fourth level county and independent city governments. The *Bezirksregierung* collects and coordinates the numerous tasks assigned to it, and the district officer supervises according to *Land* law the counties and large cities in their execution of the large number of remaining delegated tasks. It is at the level of the *Regierungsbezirk* that the concept of unity of administration is applied most consistently, since the goal is to subsume for coordination under the authority of the district officer as many national and *Land* administrative tasks as possible. In many respects, then, the *Regierungspräsident* is analogous to the French prefect and the *Regierungs-*

bezirk to the French department, traditionally the key instruments in the French system of spatial administration.

In the two smaller territorial states, Schleswig-Holstein and the Saarland, the Ministries of Interior assume the functions of the *Regierungsbezirke* and delegate administrative tasks to local governments. Even though there are no middle levels in the city states, the *Senat* in each city state does delegate a number of functions to city districts for administration (see below, p. 41).

Counties and county-free independent cities. In sharp contrast to the United States, virtually all territory in the Federal Republic — as in France — is incorporated, and the German county (*Landkreis*) is, among other things, an association of small- to medium-sized municipal corporations. If large and important enough (defined usually as a city with at least 100,000 inhabitants), a city may become county-free (*kreisfrei*) or, in other words, a city-county (*Stadtkreis*). A roughly similar kind of city-county separation existed in England before 1974. In the United States only Virginia provides for city-county separation; in all other states separation from surrounding counties is an exception to the general rule.

Like the *Regierungsbezirke*, the counties and county-free cities are general purpose institutions with a high degree of unity of administration. They have both coordinating and implementing functions, and they serve as the lowest level of state (that is, *Land* and, more indirectly, national) administration. They carry out state administrative functions delegated to them by the *Land*, and they are supervised and may be given instructions (*Fachaufsicht*) by the district officer in their implementation of these functions.

In some *Länder* state functions are delegated not to the county-level administrations but to the chief administrative officer, the county *Landrat* (the *Oberkreisdirektor* in North-Rhine Westphalia) who is "loaned" to the *Land* as an organ (*Organleihe*) for performing certain tasks at this lowest level of state administration. In the county-free cities the functions of lowest-level state administration are carried out by the city administration headed by the lord mayor (*Oberbürgermeister*) or city manager (*Oberstadtdirektor* in North-Rhine Westphalia and Lower Saxony).

As at other levels of administration, there are exceptions at the county and county-free city level to the spatial principle of unity of administration. Thus the national government, for example, has post offices and railway stations at this level, while the *Land* government's functional bureaucracies responsible directly to higher authorities include, depending on the *Land*, offices for police, agriculture and veterinary medicine and special agencies for weights and measures, forestry, finance, etc. There are sixteen different areas of responsibility organized functionally in one or more of the *Länder* at the lower level of a spatial authority.[6]

While numerous state tasks are administered at the level of the counties and county-free cities, the fourth level of administration, these units are essentially institutions of local self-government. Each has a popularly elected council and a chief executive officer who is responsible politically to the council for the execution of local government functions; however, the chief officer is responsible to the *Regierungspräsident*, that is, the district officer, for the legal quality of his administration. Thus the chief administrative officers of the counties and the cities have the dual responsibility of executing both delegated and self-government functions according to the principle of unity of administration.

The city-counties, like all municipalities (*Gemeinden*), have the legal right to perform any functions of local government (*Allzuständigkeit*) as long as these are not contrary to *Land* and national law and have not been assumed already by a *Land* or national authority. The potential scope of action is limited, of course, by the scale of activities already regulated by national and *Land* law, the requirements of various other laws, financial resources and political pressures. The counties, which also are institutions of self-government, enjoy a general discretionary power only for activities beyond the capacities of the individual municipalities.

As we saw above, the district officers supervise the counties and county-free cities in their administration of state-delegated tasks (*Auftragsangelegenheiten*); these delegated functions are performed, then, on behalf of the state (*übertragener Wirkungskreis*). The county-free cities, the municipal corporations which constitute the areas of the counties, and the counties also carry out local government functions (*Selbstverwaltungsangelegenheiten*) which are administered as matters within their own sphere of activity (*eigener Wirkungskreis*). The municipalities are supervised in administering these local government functions, too; however, in contrast to the more detailed functional supervision (*Fachaufsicht*) over state-delegated tasks, supervision over the local government tasks is only for the purpose of ensuring their legality (*Rechtsaufsicht*). The city-counties are under the legal supervision of the district officers, while most other municipalities fall under the legal supervision of the chief county administrative officers. In some *Länder* larger cities that are not county-free may be supervised directly by the district officer rather than by the chief county administrative officer. In Schleswig-Holstein and the Saarland, which do not have *Regierungsbezirke*, supervision of the larger cities and counties is performed by the *Land* Ministry of the Interior. It should be noted that, as a general rule, the larger the city and the more likely it is to have highly qualified specialized employees, the less actual supervision there is.

Rural municipalities and associations of municipalities. Because of the population density of the Federal Republic, the contrast between rural and urban areas frequently is less sharp than in North America or even France. The difference is sometimes more one of degree than of kind. With few exceptions, all of the territory of rural areas is incorporated, and the combined land area of the municipal corporations forms the county. While most of these municipalities are small villages, many are medium-sized towns and some are quite large, in a few cases even cities with more than 100,000 inhabitants. Though large enough to be county-free, such large cities have not been given this status because of the problems this would create for the surrounding "rural area."[7]

At the fifth and lowest level of administration, that is, below the county level, there is in principle no state bureaucracy except national postal and *Land* police services.[8] State administrative tasks (*Land* and national) are the responsibility of the counties and county-free cities. The municipalities administer all of their activities according to the principle of unity of administration, and they have the general discretionary power to act within the law. Since their small size prevents most municipalities from performing many required or desirable public services, the county serves as an institutional device enabling municipalities to combine their resources for the execution of numerous functions. The county serves also as a means of equalizing service levels among its member municipalities.

In five of the eight territorial states (Baden-Württemberg, Bavaria, Lower Saxony, Rhineland-Palatinate and Schleswig-Holstein), small municipalities are permitted to form an association of villages, a kind of municipal federation (called in various *Länder Verbandsgemeinde, Verwaltungsgemeinschaft, Samtgemeinde* or *Amt*) which assumes responsibility for tasks that require greater resources in personnel and revenue than the member villages possess on their own. The association council is elected directly in Lower Saxony and Rhineland-Palatinate, whereas it is composed of delegates from the associated municipalities in the other three *Länder*.

If the county and association of municipalities are units of local government designed to combine resources and promote coordination and cooperation, it might be asked whether units of local government also exist which provide for a degree of decentralization in the larger cities and towns. For the large cities there is an institution of decentralization dating back to nineteenth-century Prussia, namely the city district (*Bezirk*). The most prominent examples of city districts are found in the three city states. Other examples, though not numerous, can be found in several large city-counties, that is, county-free independent cities. The district constitutions and powers differ somewhat from *Land* to *Land*, but they all have elected councils, some limited powers and in most cases a small administrative staff.[9]

In recent reforms in some of the *Länder*, especially in North-Rhine Westphalia, large villages or towns have annexed surrounding small villages to form enlarged unitary municipalities (*Einheitsgemeinden*). This is the consolidationist alternative to the association of municipalities described above. In order to preserve some degree of community and political attachment to the preconsolidated village, some of these have been given a status analogous to the big city districts. Thus the council for the unitary municipality which is responsible for the entire area of its jurisdiction may form districts (*Ortschaften*) based on the old boundaries of the annexed villages. These have elected councils, whose powers are limited to those granted by the parent council.

Intergovernmental cooperation at the regional and local levels. While it is useful to describe the German spatial-federal system in terms of five levels of administration, there are functional administrative institutions that do not fit neatly in this scheme. These institutions range from large, complex, multi-purpose regional associations with elected councils and thousands of employees located at the second or third levels of administration to small, simple, single-purpose associations formed between two or more local corporations at the fourth or fifth level.

The largest and most complex of the regional associations are the *Landschaftsverband Rheinland* and the *Landschaftsverband Westfalen-Lippe* in North-Rhine Westphalia. Created in 1953, their origins go back to the Prussian provinces. These are self-governing public law corporations with assemblies elected by county and county-free city councils. Members of the local councils and local government officials are eligible for election to the assembly, which meets about three times a year. The other organs of these two associations are an executive committee and a director, who is elected by a two-thirds vote of the assembly for an eight-year term of office. Each association is responsible for a wide variety of tasks, the most important of which are psychiatric hospitals and highway construction.[10]

The *Landschaftsverband Hessen* is a *Land*-wide association created also in 1953 for the purpose of providing social welfare and public health services. In Lower Saxony there are two regional associations: the *Ostfriesische Landschaft*, a unique kind of public corporation in Germany concerned essentially with historical preservation, cultural activities and regional traditions; and the *Oldenburgischer Bezirksverband*, a self-governing public corporation, members of which include the six counties and three county-free cities of the old *Land* of Oldenburg. The *Bezirksverband Pfalz* in the Rhineland-Palatinate has its origins in the French occupation under Napoleon. It consists of seven county-free cities and eight counties, and its activities include health, schools, historical preservation, culture, tourism, and economic development. There are two regional *Landeswohlfahrtsverbände* in Baden-Württemberg, one for Baden and one for Württemberg-Hohenzollern. As the name suggests, these associations are concerned with various social welfare activities.[11]

The final example of third-level regional associations are the Bavarian *Bezirke*, which date from 1822. These are local government institutions that have the right to administer those affairs that are beyond the capacities of the county-free cities and counties (these are normally smaller in Bavaria than in other *Länder*). Each *Bezirk* has an elected assembly, an executive committee and other functional committees. The chief executive officer is the *Bezirkspräsident*, elected by the assembly. Responsibilities include a variety of social services, health care for the mentally and physically disabled, youth services, special schools, etc.

At the fourth level of administration, examples of intergovernmental cooperation can be found in numerous metropolitan associations (*Stadt-Umland-Verbände*).[12] Neighborhood associations (*Nachbarschaftsverbände*), which promote cooperation in land-use planning between cities and their surrounding territories and more often between two cities in close proximity to each other, can be found in Baden-Württemberg and, in a somewhat looser form with a broader focus, in the Rhineland-Palatinate and in Schleswig-Holstein.

A much larger multi-purpose metropolitan association is the *Umlandverband Frankfurt*, created in 1975. Members include the cities of Frankfurt and Offenbach, three counties and parts of three other counties. While land-use planning is the major function of this association, it is responsible also for water services, waste disposal, and regional sport centers, recreation areas and slaughterhouses. The *Stadtverband Saarbrücken* was created in 1974 as a means of dealing with problems of coordination between the city and its surrounding area. The association performs all of the functions of a county but with additional responsibilities for land use and economic development planning. The *Verband Grossraum Hannover* was created in 1974 and became the best known and in its activities the most comprehensive regional association in Germany. It had a popularly elected assembly, 134 employees and a budget of DM 180 million. It was responsible especially for regional transportation and, at least in theory, for regional planning for hospitals, adult education, water and energy supply, waste and sewerage disposal, streets and schools. Continuing conflict between the virtually autonomous association and the city of Hanover and the surrounding county of Hanover led to the association's dissolution in 1980. The metropolitan association for Braunschweig (Brunswick), formed in 1973, was dissolved in 1978 for similar reasons. Since 1980 the city and county of Hanover have formed on the basis of a *Land* law a special-purpose association for regional transportation and other limited regional tasks. A final example of regional intergovernmental cooperation can be found in the *Kommunalverband Ruhrgebiet*, an association covering not only one metropolitan area but an entire region of dense population and several large cities. Formed in 1979, it consists of fifteen county-free cities and counties and is concerned primarily with environmental matters, including parks, recreation areas, surveys, scenic planning and protection, and waste disposal.

At level five intergovernmental cooperation between and among municipalities takes on a number of legal forms.[13] It is a general rule that municipalities with a minimum of 5,000–8,000 inhabitants should be able to administer local government functions on their own. Since only about 20 percent of the municipalities in Germany in 1977 met the size requirement, even after comprehensive territorial reforms during the 1960s and 1970s, associations of small municipalities (see above, p. 41), were formed so that the association could assume local government tasks. While the territorial reforms reduced the need for intergovernmental cooperation, it continues to serve a useful purpose.

The loosest form of cooperation is the "working group" (*Arbeitsgemeinschaft*). The working group is based on the agreement of the participants, and it has no legal standing. It is designed to serve as a forum for the discussion of common concerns and to plan, coordinate and make non-binding decisions. A legal basis may result from the signing of a contract, according to which the working group is to coordinate certain functions. The founding participants must be municipalities, associations of municipalities, or counties. Thereafter, other legal and natural persons may join.

A somewhat more institutionalized form of intergovernmental cooperation is the "public law agreement" (*öffentlich-rechtliche Vereinbarung*) between a working group and a special-purpose association. While the agreements of the working group are binding only internally, the public law agreement is binding externally. The characteristic feature of the public law agreement is that one participant assumes the administrative responsibility for one or more common functions or permits use by other units of its facilities. The public law agreement is a popular and flexible instrument of cooperation; as a general rule, only municipalities, associations of municipalities, and counties may participate in such agreements. Even associations of municipalities may be formed on the basis of voluntary or non-voluntary public law agreements.

The most common device for promoting intergovernmental cooperation at the local level is the special-purpose association (*Zweckverband*). The *Zweckverband* differs from the two forms discussed above in that it is a public corporation created for the purpose of executing one or more public tasks. There are different kinds of *Zweckverbände*, most of which are voluntary; however, nonvoluntary associations may be formed for the purpose of completing certain required tasks. They fall under the supervision of the district officer, which is also the case for working groups and public law agreements. Before the local government reforms of the 1960s and 1970s, *Zweckverbände* were formed most commonly for elementary schools, fire protection, cultural promotion, the construction of roads and paths, waste disposal and certain welfare and youth programs. These have been sharply reduced in number since the reforms, but new *Zweckverbände* for special education, adult education, local savings banks and recreation areas appear to be emerging in their place though in smaller numbers.[14] Though

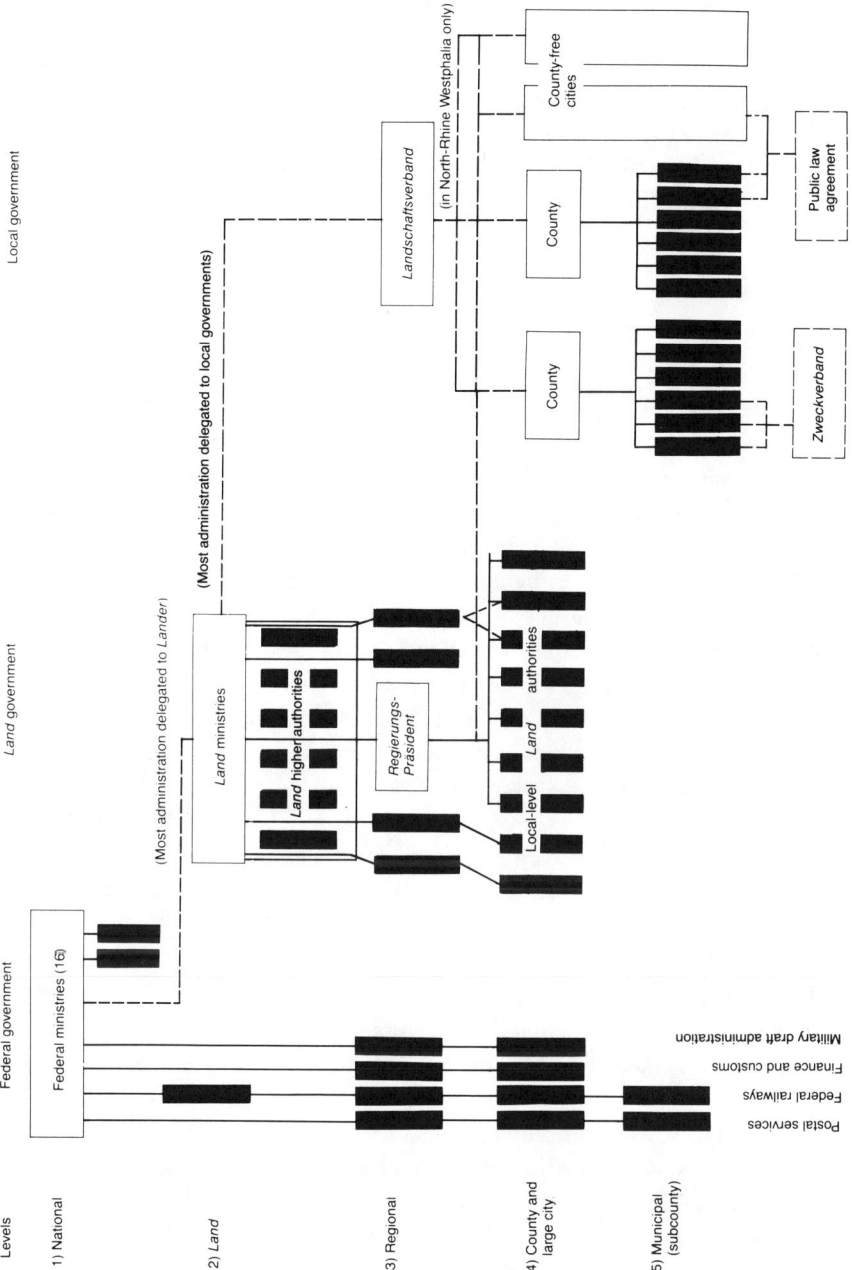

Figure 3.1. Structure of administration in the Federal Republic of Germany

Source: Adapted from Frido Wagener, "Äusserer Aufbau von Staat und Verwaltung," in Öffentliche Verwaltung in der Bundesrepublik Deutschland, ed. Klaus König, H. J. von Oertzen, and Frido Wagener (Baden-Baden: Nomos Verlagsgesellschaft, 1981), 80.

roughly analogous to the American special district, the *Zweckverband* must always be formed by two or more municipalities or counties which, respectively, fall under the supervision of the chief executive officer of the county or district officer. American-type special districts, which may focus on a narrow function within a single county or municipality, would violate the German principle of spatial administration.[15]

Conclusion

While France and Germany are both classic examples of states with spatial administration, they differ significantly in the focus on a highly centralized administration within a unitary organization of state power in France and a decentralized administration within a federal division of powers in Germany. Both countries have served as models of a rational, highly developed, efficient, systematic bureaucratic order. The German spatial model is made more complex than the French model, however, by the addition of the federal feature. In contrast to France, Germany's first level of administration, the federal government, does not supervise directly the execution of national laws by lower levels of administration. Rather, the second-level eleven German *Land* governments assume major responsibility for the administration of "state" laws, both national and *Land*.

In the eight territorial states, the *Land* governments delegate the actual implementation of most laws to still lower levels of administration. In the six largest states the third level is the *Regierungsbezirk*, the regional administrative district. This is the only level in Germany without an elected assembly or executive officer, since it is conceived as exercising purely administrative functions on behalf of the elected, publicly responsible *Land* government (in particular the *Land* Ministry of Interior). While some *Land* functions are executed at this level by functional specialists, the district officer and his staff are concerned mostly with coordination and *functional* supervision of tasks delegated by *Land* law to the county and county-free city governments for execution; they are concerned also with the *legal* supervision of those tasks which these local governments exercise on their own authority as units of self-government. In the two smaller territorial states, Schleswig-Holstein and the Saarland, the functions of the third-level district officers are assumed by the ministries of interior.

At the fourth level of administration, the counties and county-free cities implement under the supervision of the district officer (except in the two small states noted above) both the delegated state functions and their own activities for which they are responsible as units of self-government. The chief administrative officer of the county, in turn, supervises the activities of the fifth-level administrative units, the self-governing municipalities, which are also the constituent parts of the counties.

While the model of spatial administration calls for unity of administration at each level, German practice has, in fact, been quite flexible in allowing for the functional administration of some tasks and for intergovernmental cooperation in other areas. There are a number of examples of functions that are administered by national or *Land* government agencies with field offices that reach down to the local level, and there are even more numerous examples of intergovernmental cooperation at the third, fourth and fifth level of administration. In contrast to the special districts in the United States, however, special-purpose associations in Germany must consist of general-purpose local governments; individual functions may not be performed by a special authority within a county or municipality.

Figure 3.1 is a simplified reflection of the spatial-federal model in Germany. It suggests a higher degree of complexity, however, than actually exists. This is not to imply that German administration is a model of simplicity, as is sometimes claimed for the French model. The administrative decentralization of German federalism introduces into the German model a degree of complexity which the French presumably would not tolerate. On the other hand, the principles of the German spatial-federal model are clear and explicit. Once these principles are grasped, the numerous exceptions to the rules become less difficult to master.

4

Territorial and Administrative Reforms at the Local Level

The logic of the spatial administrative system, the classical model of administration, requires that subnational levels operate according to the principles of unity of administration. Numerous exceptions to this principle may exist in the form of functionally organized activities, but the general rule will still apply that as much administrative activity as possible should be brought together in one general-purpose government with a single administrative chief responsible for proper implementation under the legal and/or functional supervision of higher authorities. If the spatial administrative system is to provide for democratic self-government as well, then the subnational levels must be more than mere agents of the state, executing the laws of the central government. In the West German spatial-federal system, the *Länder* as self-governing units have a sphere of activity which they can regulate on their own authority; of even greater relevance to this study, the local governments are able to govern themselves in those areas not regulated by the state or in those matters assumed voluntarily and on their own responsibility. The principle of unity of administration, then, is combined with democratic principles of direct election of legislative bodies and indirect or direct popular control of the chief administrative officer.

The logical consequences of the democratic spatial-federal system are underlined by the requirements of article 28 of the Basic Law, according to which there must be democratic government at the local level. Furthermore, the municipalities must be guaranteed the right to regulate on their own responsibility all matters affecting the local community within the framework of the laws.

To some extent developments after World War II seemed to be challenging both the logical consequences of spatial administrative theory and the principles of local self-government. A rapid increase in the number and extent of state activities delegated to the local levels for administration led to an overburdening especially of smaller local units. Increasing demands for public services within the sphere of local self-government also became difficult to meet. The smaller the unit of local government, the less likely it was to be in a position financially and administratively to handle its responsibilities under the principle of unity of administration. The smaller the unit the less likely it was also to be able financially or administratively to meet its obligations of self-government. The result was a growing gap between the theory of democratic spatial administration at the local level and the practice of inadequate fiscal and administrative capacity and increasing use of functional structures, such as special-purpose joint authorities (*Zweckverbände*), which contradicted the principle of unity of administration.

During the 1960s and 1970s, the response to the shortcomings of local self-government and the local administration of state laws was a redrawing of municipal, county and administrative district boundaries, a dramatic reduction in the number of local units, and a considerable effort toward redistributing, that is, decentralizing, administrative functions. Proposals to redraw the boundaries of the *Länder* and to eliminate several of them in the process were discussed but not acted upon.

The Rationale and Standards for Reform

The situation before the reforms. In 1968 there were 24,278 municipalities in the Federal Republic, two-thirds of which had fewer than one thousand inhabitants, 95 percent fewer than 5,000 inhabitants. All but 135 of the larger municipalities —which were independent or county-free (*kreisfrei*)—were constituent parts of the 425 counties. There were wide variations among the counties in terms of population and area both among and within the *Länder*.

By the early 1960s a number of serious problems were perceived to exist in the spatial administrative system at the local and regional levels.[1] The traditional emphasis on law and order and basic security had changed to a focus on the provision of services. The majority of municipalities were simply too small to offer the range of services demanded. The lack of an adequate tax base, administrative personnel and sufficient population to make the services cost effective led to the provision of such services, if at all, by larger neighboring municipalities or special-purpose joint authorities. This undermined local self-government in the first instance and the principle of unity of administration in the second. Local self-government also was undermined by the increasing reliance on categorical grants from higher levels to finance numerous local projects.

A second major problem was the lack of coordination among local government units in built-up areas, roughly analogous to metropolitan areas in the United States. In these areas the central city or cities usually had sufficient administrative capacity to provide the necessary range of services, but there was insufficient space for recreation areas, new housing and economic development. Competition among area municipalities for business enterprises, use of leisure and cultural facilities by residents of other municipalities, and lack of coordination and cooperation in areas such as housing and transportation were the multiple causes of growing dissatisfaction. Intermunicipal cooperation existed, but increasing reliance on its various forms raised questions concerning the principle of local self-government in the sense of *Allzuständigkeit* (the general power to act in all matters of local concern) and effective democratic control over executive-dominated joint authorities. Local government boundaries were the result of history and tradition, and frequently they were perceived as having become serious barriers to the solution of current problems.

A third important factor was the growing importance of planning in the 1960s. Federal and *Land* planning laws required rational planning units at the local level, and this meant the elimination or reduction of so many small, ineffective local units and overlapping jurisdictions. The advocates of planning had little patience especially with the lack of cooperation and coordination which characterized the municipal relationships in many built up areas.

Finally, it was thought by some scholars and practitioners as well that there were too many administrative levels. The elimination of small, ineffective municipalities and an increase in the size and capacity of the remaining municipalities should make it possible for these to perform functions carried out previously by the larger municipalities. This would relieve the county administrations, which could then assume the responsibilities of the administrative districts. The administrative districts, for all practical purposes the third level of administration, could then be dissolved. As the reform movement progressed, however, it was decided that the administrative districts could be reduced in number but not eliminated altogether.[2]

By the early 1960s it had become apparent that the spatial administrative system was in need of reform. In May 1963 the minister-president (the German counterpart to the American governor) of the Rhineland-Palatinate announced that his government intended to take up the question of local government reform.[3] The real impetus for local reforms, however, is usually seen to have been the forty-fifth annual meeting of German legal scholars in 1964, when problems of local government structures and planning were the major theme of discussion.[4]

Reform goals. In a broader sense the overall goal of local government reforms was seen by many Germans to be the fulfillment of certain provisions of the Basic Law, or constitution. Article 20, paragraph 1, declares the Federal Republic to be a "democratic and socially just (*sozialer*) federal state." This provision can be and frequently is interpreted to mean that the well-established—and by American standards very generous—network of government subsidies, services and social welfare programs must be available to all Germans in spite of the federal organization of West Germany (the spatial-federal system is much less of a potential hurdle for the implementation of national domestic policies than is the functional-federal system of the United States). Article 72, paragraph 2; article 104a, paragraph 4; and article 106, paragraph 2, speak even more directly of government responsibility for securing the unity of living conditions in the territory of the federation. Article 28, as we have noted, guarantees the municipalities a general power to act, and both municipalities and counties enjoy the right of self-government.

It could be and was argued that there was an unnecessary gap between constitutional theory and practice before the reforms. How could social justice and equality in living conditions become a reality (in a rather perfectionist sense) when some states were considerably poorer than others and, in particular, when there were substantial differences in the administrative and service capacities (*Leistungsfähigkeit*) among the various counties and municipalities?[5] The differences between the weaker rural municipalities and the urban centers in the provision of a wide variety of public services—in spite of fiscal transfers and federal aid—were seen to have become especially intolerable in a modern, democratic welfare state. In addition it was argued that one could hardly speak of "genuine" local self-government as guaranteed by article 28, when most of the municipalities and many counties were not in a financial and administrative position to meet their constitutional responsibilities.

Thus the constitutional goals of local government reform were derived from the principles of equality *and* freedom—or self-government—which were seen to be complementary. If local governments could not provide their citizens with more uniform levels of services, then their citizens would demand more assistance from the federal and *Land* governments, further eroding local self-government. It was assumed that such demands could be avoided only in a system of *reformed* local units which were in a position to provide strong and effective, that is, "genuine" local self-government.

In order to achieve the conditions of this rather abstract grand design, the reformers set three concrete general goals: improvements in the administrative and service capacity (*Leistungsfähigkeit*) of the municipalities, optimization of the municipal political form, and adjustments of boundaries and functions to meet area or regional needs.[6] Improvements in the administrative and service capacity of the municipalities meant that municipalities would have to become large enough to hire professional staff that would not need counsel from supervisory authorities at higher levels. Local governments would have to have more facilities and provide more and better services, both delegated and self-government. They would need to be able to engage in rational land-use planning and zoning, to take advantage of economies of scale, and to provide efficient local transportation, road networks, bicycle paths, etc. In effect, the ability of local councillors and administrators to make meaningful decisions for the local unit was to be improved.

The political functions of the municipality were to be strengthened, and especially the contact between the citizen and the local administration (*Bürgernähe*) were to be improved. This was to be achieved less in terms of geography—the municipalities were, after all, to be increased in size—than in information flow. That is, a professional local administration would increase contacts with citizens through better information, with the result that citizen concerns would be better accommodated. The importance of a large number of councillors in providing communication between government and citizen before the reform was recognized, but it was important also that the citizen have a competent administration to deal with, an administration that he could trust to deal effectively with his concerns. If the municipality were to become too large, the advantages of larger size could be lost, in which case some form of two-tier decentralization might be an appropriate solution. Finally, political standards were to be improved by the greater clarity and transparency of the reformed structures of local government and the strengthened unity of administration.

Adjustments of boundaries were necessary to meet area or regional needs especially in terms of planning and land-use. Not only municipalities but also counties were to fall within one planning region. In order to provide for more equality in the provision of services in rural areas, it was necessary to place strong and weak municipalities together in one county, which could then perform its balancing or equalization functions in a more effective manner. It was also deemed necessary to have the boundaries of state special authorities and other special public institutions correspond to the enlarged boundaries of local government units.

Overall reductions in the costs of local government were not a goal of the reforms. If the reformed local units were to offer more services, have more facilities, and hire more professional staff, they could hardly do so at lower cost than before. On the other hand, certain savings might be realized through economies of scale, more effective administration, reduction in the number of joint authorities, etc. Costs, like history and traditional boundaries, took a back seat to the efficient provision of increased services by local professional staff. The goal of local territorial reform, as one student of the reforms has written, was "the simplification, rationalization and strengthening of self-government, so that in the future every municipality could again assume on its own as many tasks as possible."[7]

Goal application and standards. As concrete plans for comprehensive local reforms began to be drawn up in the scholarly literature[8] and in commission reports sponsored by the various *Land* governments,[9] it became evident that there would be goal conflicts and that one goal might have to take precedence over another. It also became clear that there would be disagreements over which standards should apply.

In the reform of rural municipalities a general consensus was reached that in principle a municipality should have about 8,000 inhabitants, depending somewhat on the *Land* and the density of population. In Lower Saxony, for example, the goal was to create municipalities with 7,000–8,000 inhabitants; however, in neighboring North-Rhine Westphalia, the goal was set at 7,000–10,000. In some cases, especially in more rural areas and in Bavaria, 5,000 became an acceptable number.[10]

A second question was how to form municipalities of adequate size. In contrast to the situation in most of the United States, municipalities in Germany are generally separated by no more than a few kilometers, and in flat, agricultural areas several towns or villages may be visible from one point. In cases where most of these were small villages, the issue became one of consolidation and annexation or association through a form of federation. In some *Länder*, namely North-Rhine Westphalia, Hesse and the Saarland, the decision was made to form only consolidated "unitary municipalities" (*Einheitsgemeinden*). In the other five territorial *Länder*, provisions were made for an association or federation of municipalities (*engerer Gemeindeverband*). These are called *Verbandsgemeinde* (Rhineland-Palatinate), *Verwaltungsgemeinschaft* (Baden-Württemberg and Bavaria), *Samtgemeinde* (Lower Saxony), and *Amt* (Schleswig-Holstein). Minimum population standards, which varied from 200 to 2,000, were applied in these *Länder* for membership in an association of municipalities.

A factor which had also to be taken into account was distance. Outlying villages subject to consolidation by a larger, centrally located village or town or several villages interested in associating were not to be located more than 7–10 kilometers from the core unit. Of course the condition of area roads became an element in such calculations as well.

In the reform of the counties, history and tradition were to be even less important than in the case of municipalities. Size criteria were not quite so important with the counties, since the focus of attention was on economic relationships and the view that there should be a correspondence between administrative and economic areas. On the other hand population size was important, and notable differences existed among the *Länder* in terms of size criteria (for example, a minimum of 80,000 inhabitants in Bavaria, 200,000 in North-Rhine Westphalia). The number of unitary municipalities and associations of municipalities in a county was a factor to be considered, and ten was thought to be about right. No one municipality was to dominate the county, and counties were to contain a combination of strong and weak municipalities, if possible, in order that the county could serve as an instrument of equalization in the provision of services and the distribution of revenues.

Next to the rural municipalities and the counties, there was the question of which county-free larger cities should be reintegrated into a county. It was obvious that this would affect the smaller county-free cities first, but size criteria varied among the *Länder* both before and after the beginning of the reform (during the reform, for example, 50,000 in Bavaria and 200,000 in North-Rhine Westphalia). In densely populated areas, especially in North-Rhine Westphalia, a number of medium-sized cities were annexed by larger cities and some large cities with more than 100,000 inhabitants were returned to a county, though at least as the county seat.

While territorial and administrative reforms frequently were referred to as separate programs, the two were closely intertwined from the beginning. Indeed, it can be argued that boundary changes were the primary means for securing administrative, or functional, reform, although such changes were deemed necessary for purposes of land-use and regional planning as well. Nevertheless, the relationship between the two became an issue, and in some *Länder* there were partisan divisions over which should come first.[11]

The overall goal of the administrative reforms was to provide the local units with the capacity to perform as many tasks as possible. The idea was to increase the size of the municipalities and counties to the point that numerous functions could then be redistributed from higher to lower levels. At the municipal level this meant that some functions previously administered at the county level could now become the responsibility of the enlarged municipal government; however, this unit was to be enlarged at the expense of the smaller units which had been annexed and no longer enjoyed self-government. Whether in the county-free cities, which were to become even larger (unless returned to a county), or in the enlarged unitary municipalities in the counties, it was deemed necessary to provide improved means of citizen participation to compensate for the loss of councillor positions that would occur with the dissolution of so many smaller local governments.

To provide more opportunities for citizen participation in spite of a dramatic reduction in the number of local government units, districts were to be formed in the large county-free cities and *Ortschaften* in the smaller unitary municipalities. The *Ortschaften* were to be coterminous with the newly annexed villages. While both districts and *Ortschaften* would have elected councillors and, in some cases, a decentralized administrative apparatus at their disposal, they were not to become autonomous areas; instead, their powers would be determined generally by the local general purpose government, that is, in particular by the council elected by all of the inhabitants of the enlarged local unit.

Other means of improving citizen participation included the revision of election laws to readjust the proportion of local councillors to citizens, improvements in citizen information, provisions for local citizen initiatives, and opportunities for citizen hearings in local organs.[12] The latter included expanded opportunities for participation in the local planning process.

Though a major goal of the local reform movement was the strengthening of unity of administration, it was clear—or became clear—that not all state functions should be turned over to the enlarged county-free cities and counties. Functional organizations, such as *Land* tax offices, veterinary offices, weights and measures, and school supervisory authorities, were retained by the *Länder* as activities to be administered directly by the state. On the other hand, it was considered desirable that the boundaries of these organizations correspond to the boundaries of the reformed local governments (*Einräumigkeit*).

Implementation and Results

Implementation. Far-reaching, comprehensive reforms are usually carried out by governments only in times of crisis or immediately following a revolution. There was neither a crisis—comparable, for example, to the situation confronting Baron vom Stein in 1807–8—nor a revolution in the Federal Republic. Yet there are few examples in history that would match the dramatic reorganization of local governments which altered the German administrative-political map in the decade between 1968 and 1978. These changes were made voluntarily by eight territorial *Länder* without the pressure of a central government which might have been expected to have had some role in the planning, coordination and direction of such a massive undertaking. They were made by eight *Länder* with different political party majorities and constellations of interests in the individual *Land* parliaments. They were made by eight *Länder* with different historical traditions, ranging from an artificially created post-war Lower Saxony to a proud, thousand-year-old Bavaria. And they were made with relatively little public and partisan political opposition. Indeed, there seemed to be a consensus among legal scholars, high-level bureaucrats, politicians—especially in the larger cities, the mass media, and the attentive public that local government reforms were necessary. Disagreements existed primarily over the extent, timing and details of the reforms, not over their desirability.

Why was there so much apparent consensus in favor of the reforms? First, and probably most important, was the impact made on the attentive public and leading politicians by legal-administrative scholars, practitioners, and the numerous professional journals which carried their message. Irrespective of their political orientations, opinion makers appeared to be persuaded by the arguments of the advocates of reform.[13] Second, there was a general climate of opinion in Europe in the 1960s and early 1970s favoring reform in education, marriage and divorce, life-styles, employer-employee relations, social services, pensions, foreign policy, and in a number of other areas. Local governments were merely another example of institutions deemed to be in need of change. Third, the reforms were to be carried out by the party-controlled *Land* governments and parliaments based on a general, comprehensive plan for the territory of the *Land*. Voluntary combinations on the part of individual municipal governments were to be encouraged, but American-style "volunteerism" was seen as an unacceptable barrier to meaningful reform efforts. Indeed, volunteerism can be equated with no reform.[14]

The first *Land* government to introduce a local government reform bill was the Rhineland-Palatinate in 1965. In the years that followed, each *Land* began step by step, first by modifying a number of laws which would help expedite the boundary and administrative changes. These included regulating the terms of office of local officials, freezing local government positions, preventing small municipalities subject to annexation from increasing dramatically their indebtedness for new facilities, and altering local election dates so that they would not fall shortly before or after the reforms. The means of implementation varied from *Land* to *Land*, but everywhere affected municipalities were permitted to participate in the process through hearings, interest group or political party channels. In some *Länder* the reform took place region by region, in others the entire territory was reformed in one package. Territorial reform came first in some *Länder*, administrative reform in others. In some *Länder* the counties were reformed first, in others the municipalities, and in still other cases they were reformed together. A voluntary phase was typical, but even with the threat of action by the *Land* government, voluntary action alone was never adequate for a comprehensive reform.[15]

It would not have been possible to engage in such a dramatic reform effort without majority support in each *Land* parliament. In general the CDU or CSU (Bavaria) had a majority in the South, the SPD alone or together with the FDP in the North (except in Schleswig-Holstein). There was no opposition of principle by the respective minority parties; however, in some *Länder* various aspects of the reform became a partisan issue. Indeed, it is possible to conclude that at least in Lower Saxony, in spite of agreement in principle, the SPD was more in favor of achieving the reform goals concerned with equality (more equitable distribution of services achieved through large-scale annexations and consolidations and a bias in favor of unitary municipalities), while the CDU was more sensitive to the goals concerned with freedom (administrative decentralization but opposition to the argument that "bigger is better"; a bias in favor of associations of municipalities and historical boundaries where possible).[16] Assuming that these basic positions were not confined to Lower Saxony, the differences in partisan majorities are one factor in explaining the reasons for the generally larger units that emerged in the North and the exclusive focus on unitary municipalities in the SPD-controlled *Länder* North-Rhine Westphalia and Hesse.

Results. A comparison of the situation before and after the territorial reforms can be seen in table 4.1. To say that the number of municipalities has been reduced from over 24,000 to 8,409 is somewhat misleading in so far as 6,032 of the latter number are members of 1,041 associations of municipalities. In other words, it would be just as accurate to speak of a reduction from 24,000 to 3,418 local general-purpose administrative units.

Based on a slightly different set of figures, Mattenklodt[17] calculated a 64.9 percent reduction in municipalities in the Federal Republic from 1968–78. The range by *Land* was from 17.9 percent in Schleswig-Holstein and 20.1 percent in Rhineland-Palatinate to 82.6 percent in North-Rhine Westphalia and 84.3 percent in Hesse. While about 44 percent of the more than 24,000 municipalities had fewer than 500 inhabitants in 1968, only 20.5 percent of the 8,400 municipalities were of that size in 1978. More than two-thirds of all municipalities had fewer than 1,000 inhabitants in 1968; somewhat more than one-third of the sharply reduced number of municipalities was so small in 1978.[18] The number of cities with more than 100,000 inhabitants increased from 57 in 1968 to 68 in 1978.

Because of increases in size and considerations of administrative capacity and impact on surrounding municipalities, the number of independent cities was reduced from 135 to 87. On the other hand, all of the *Länder* made special provisions for larger cities belonging to a county (for example, cities with more than 20,000–30,000 population) which gave them a somewhat different legal and psychological status from smaller municipalities. These 281 nonindependent cities with special status are designated by different terms in each of the *Länder*.[19]

The reduction in the number of counties from 425 to 237 is also a remarkable accomplishment, considering the fact that the boundaries for most of these were at least 200 years old. Table 4.2 shows that North-Rhine Westphalia applied by far the strictest standards for population size, while Bavaria and the Rhineland-Palatinate were the most lenient. Otherwise it is not so easy to generalize about differences between North and South; both Baden-Württemberg and the Saarland have above average county populations, while Lower Saxony has below-average populations. The average population of counties in Lower Saxony would probably have been higher if the SPD-FDP coalition which was preparing the county reforms had not collapsed in 1976 and been replaced by the CDU, and later, by a CDU-FDP coalition which actually implemented a revised county reform plan.[20]

In addition to the municipalities, counties, and county-free independent cities, the number of administrative districts (*Regierungsbezirke*) also was reduced from 33 to 25: in Hesse, from 3 to 2; in Lower Saxony, from 8 to 4; in North-Rhine Westphalia, from 6 to 5; and in the Rhineland-Palatinate, from 5 to 3. The number of administrative districts in Bavaria and Baden-Württemberg remained unchanged at 7 and 4, respectively. The 25 new and remaining administrative

Table 4.1. Independent (county-free) cities, counties, and municipalities in the Federal Republic before and after the territorial reforms

Land	Independent cities		Counties	
	1968	1980	1968	1980
Baden-Württemberg	9	9	63	35
Bavaria	48	25	143	71
Hesse	9	5	39	21
Lower Saxony	15	9	60	38
North-Rhine Westphalia	37	23	57	31
Rhineland-Palatinate	12	12	39	24
Saarland	1	—	7	6
Schleswig-Holstein	4	4	17	11
Federal Republic (without city-states)	135	87	425	237

Source: Adapted from Heinz Köstering, "Das Verhältnis zwischen Gemeinde- und Kreisaufgaben einschliesslich der Funktionalreform," in *Handbuch der kommunalen Wissenschaft*

districts were increased in number to 26 in 1981 when Hesse returned to 3 districts.[21]

Institutional-administrative impact. The reforms affected not only municipal, county and administrative district boundaries but also many other aspects of public administration. At the local level, for example, many old public buildings became unsuited for the new responsibilities of their occupants. In other cases they were now located in the wrong area. The construction of new facilities added, of course, to the costs of the reform without contributing much to the improvements which the reforms were supposed to bring. At the *Land* level election districts for the *Land* parliaments had to be changed and various administrative adjustments had to be made, including boundary changes for various courts and agencies administered directly by the *Land*. These adjustments usually led to improvements in unity of administration or at least to a better correspon-

Table 4.1. (continued)

Municipalities		Remarks
1968	1980	
3,370	1,102	179 of these 1,102 municipalities are unitary municipalities; the remainder form 272 associations of municipalities (*Verwaltungsgemeinschaften*)
7,029	2,023	940 of these 2,023 municipalities are unitary municipalities; the remainder form 345 associations of municipalities (*Verwaltungsgemeinschaften*)
2,675	422	All 422 municipalities are unitary municipalities
4,216	1,020	274 of these 1,020 municipalities are unitary municipalities; the remainder form 142 associations of municipalities (*Samtgemeinden*)
2,240	373	All 373 municipalities are unitary municipalities
2,893	2,291	38 of these 2,291 municipalities are unitary municipalities; the remainder form 163 associations of municipalities (*Verbandsgemeinden*)
346	50	All 50 municipalities are unitary municipalities; one of the 6 counties is the Saarbrücken metropolitan association
1,374	1,128	101 of these 1,128 municipalities are unitary municipalities; the remainder form 119 associations of municipalities (*Ämter*)
24,136	8,409	2,377 of these 8,409 municipalities are unitary municipalities; the remainder form 1,041 associations of municipalities.

und Praxis, vol. 3: *Kommunale Aufgaben und Instrumente der Aufgabenerfüllung*, 2d ed., ed. Günter Püttner (Berlin and Heidelberg: Springer-Verlag, 1983), 39–40.

dence of boundaries for *Land* and local government functions (*Einräumigkeit*). *Land* planning was also tied closely to the territorial reforms. This was especially the case for Lower Saxony, where the counties were given the responsibility for regional planning in spite of criticisms that they are too small for this purpose.[22]

The *Länder* were affected mostly, of course, by the new distribution of administrative functions among the second, third, fourth and fifth levels of administration. The process of decentralization, the redistribution of numerous tasks from higher levels to the strengthened lower levels, depended to a considerable extent on the federal government, since most laws administered by the *Länder* and their local governments are federal laws that frequently specify the units responsible for administration. This problem was resolved to a considerable extent by a federal law which loosened these requirements. The actual amount of administrative reform, that is, decentralization, that took effect varied among the *Länder*. It seems fair to say that in many instances meaningful decentralization has occurred,

Table 4.2. Counties in the Federal Republic after the reforms, 1978

	Counties	Average population	Range in population (1,000)	Average area (km²)	Range in area (km²)
Baden-Württemberg	35	210,000	83–450	986	(519–1854)
Bavaria	71	104,000	69–231	964	(307–1972)
Hesse	21	201,000	83–354	971	(222–1848)
Lower Saxony	38	149,000	49–541	1213	(540–2860)
North-Rhine Westphalia	31	302,000	122–632	973	(406–1958)
Rhineland-Palatinate	24	110,000	56–190	782	(305–1626)
Saarland	6	181,000	91–366	428	(250– 555)
Schleswig-Holstein	11	178,000	113–253	1386	(662–2071)
Federal Republic	237	166,000		996	

Source: Werner Thieme and Günter Prillwitz, *Durchführung und Ergebnisse der kommunalen Gebietsreform* (Baden-Baden: Nomos Verlagsgesellschaft, 1981), 75, and Günter Seele, "Die Kreisverfassungssysteme," in *Handbuch der kommunalen Wissenschaft und Praxis*, vol ?· *Kommunalverfassung*, 2d ed., ed. Günter Püttner (Berlin and Heidelberg: Springer Verlag, 1982), 344.

or that improvements in information and consultation have been made.[23] In both instances it can be argued that government has been brought closer to the people (*Bürgernähe*). On the other hand, there is much criticism that there was more rationalization than decentralization,[24] that most of the decentralized tasks are relatively unimportant or that expectations were exaggerated[25] and that in any case these and older local government functions are now performed by enlarged local units in which the physical — and often the psychological — distance between local government administrators and councillors and the citizens they serve has increased. Districts and *Ortschaften* may have helped, but they have hardly solved this problem.[26]

The federal government, as the central government in the German spatial-federal system, was affected in a number of ways by the reforms. It had an interest above all in a strong, effective, and reasonably uniform system of local governments administering most federal laws. Like the *Länder*, the federal government had to redraw electoral district lines for the federal parliament, and it had to adjust the boundaries of a number of federal bureaucracies with local field agencies (for example, the postal and telecommunication services). Through the numerous annexations and consolidations, certain aspects of the system of "cooperative federalism" also were affected.[27] As noted above, however, the federal government's role in the local government reforms was minor.

Finally, the reforms had an impact on numerous autonomous public institutions of self-government, such as the professional and occupational chambers (for example, chambers of lawyers, physicians, and craftsmen). Social insurance agencies were affected, especially the field agencies concerned with health care and old age insurance activities. And, of course, political party organizations were affected, not only in the sense of party structure but also in the new opportunities opened by the larger—and therefore potentially more politicized —local units.[28]

Opposition to the reforms. From an American perspective one of the most remarkable features of the more than ten years of reform activity was the relative lack of public opposition. This is not to say that there were no protests of any significance—there were, indeed, isolated examples of widespread citizen protest, but these were hardly typical reactions. They also occurred mostly in the North, where the annexations and consolidations tended to be more far-reaching. In most cases where opposition did develop, it was expressed in legal terms in the administrative and constitutional courts.[29]

The most dramatic case of a boundary reorganization arousing opposition, and even ridicule and contempt, was in Hesse. The SPD-FDP state government decided to combine the two tradition-laden cities of Giessen and Wetzlar, with fourteen villages that surrounded them, into a new and much larger city, which was to be called Lahn after the river that runs through it. This proposal, which had much merit from the point of view of administrative efficiency, economic development and especially planning rationality, advocated the creation of an entirely artificial city with little consideration for the wishes of the population, the distance to be traveled to the new city hall, the names of century-old institutions, such as the university in Giessen, the impact on maps, train schedules, turnpike exits, and so on. "Lahnstadt" became such an effective rallying cry for the opponents of reform that it threatened to discredit the local government reforms everywhere in West Germany. Without doubt, Chancellor Helmut Schmidt was thinking of the bad example of Lahnstadt when he criticized local government reforms for their "arrogance with respect to long-standing institutions" (*Arroganz gegenüber gewachsenen Gebilden*).

The SPD and FDP paid dearly for the implementation of their reform of Lahnstadt, with the SPD losing control of the new city council to the CDU by a landslide in the local election of March 1977. With the next *Land* elections scheduled for October 1978 and the CDU campaign geared toward achieving an absolute majority, the SPD-FDP government retreated from the Lahnstadt model and presented plans for the re-separation of Wetzlar and Giessen. At first, this plan called for the establishment of a new umbrella institution, a "city region," for serving the two cities and the surrounding villages in such areas as planning, zoning, hospital, water, and waste disposal. After the *Land* election and a narrow victory by the SPD-FDP, this was changed, and in 1979 the two cities were simply placed in a newly formed county. While Giessen did regain separate status, it lost its old standing as an independent county-free (*kreisfrei*) city.[30]

Assessment

The more than decade-long period of local government reforms was concluded, with a few exceptions, such as the controversy over "Lahnstadt" in Hesse, by the end of 1978. What can be said at this time about the success or failure of this massive reform effort?[31] The answer that one receives to this question will depend for some time on the perspective of the respondent and the examples that he cites. Whether one's home municipality or county gained or lost in the reorganization, whether one was engaged positively in the reform process, whether one identified with the party responsible for the reform, and so forth, may have some impact on the response.

A more serious problem in formulating an answer to the question is the difficulty of making an objective assessment. The materials and data that one would have to collect and evaluate would require a massive effort. Even if one cleared this hurdle, there would be the problem of quantifying many of the goals and assessing the extent to which they were achieved. An analysis of the situation before and after the reforms would suffer also from an unknown number of intervening variables for which one could hardly adopt adequate controls.[32]

Thieme and Prillwitz, whose book is the most comprehensive and recent review of the territorial reforms, suggest that "one always may assume that to a considerable extent the reform measures have had a positive effect. One also may assume that the reform has had a negative impact here and there. Furthermore, one may assume in any case that at the end of an evaluation of this reform process no total balance of success and failure is possible but always only partial assessments can be made."[33] Given the unlikelihood that empirical methods of evaluation will be very successful, Thieme and Prillwitz offer a deductive assessment which includes the following theses:[34]

(1) The larger municipalities created in rural areas have led to an improvement in administrative capacity. Full-time specialized staff have increased subject competence at the local level and promoted better citizen service. On the other hand, some municipalities were probably made too large and given more bureaucracy than is desirable.

(2) The capacity of the municipalities to provide better and more facilities has been increased. On the other hand, some municipalities went too far in constructing facilities, for example, indoor swimming pools, which they are now finding difficult to maintain at a reasonable cost.

(3) The reforms have had a positive effect in the planning process. Especially larger cities and their surrounding areas have benefitted from this result. On the

other hand, large city interests are now given more weight than the metropolitan periphery, an interesting contrast to the American scene.

(4) The county reforms have had a relatively small impact on county land-use planning, although county development planning might prove to be of some value in the future. The counties in Lower Saxony are too small for the regional planning functions they have been given.

(5) The relationship between the citizens and the reformed local units remains uncertain. Whether the goal of an administration closer to the people (*bürgernahe Verwaltung*) was achieved depends to a considerable degree on the extent to which administrative reform, that is, decentralization, occurred. Some decentralization occurred automatically as a result of the territorial reorganization, but that there has been less decentralization than was expected is a common complaint.

(6) There is, of course, less close contact between the citizen and his local government (*Bürgernähe*) because of the physical distance separating them and the reduction in the number of councillors. On the other hand, there are other aspects of *Bürgernähe* to be considered; for example, the citizen today is closer to a competent local bureaucracy, and the local councillor, though representing a larger number of constituents than before, is in a position to make more important decisions. He is probably also better qualified than before.

(7) The decision-making capacity of local units has been improved. This has meant probably an improvement in the quality of decisions as well.

(8) The larger units of local government have opened new opportunities for the political parties. Parties have been active participants in the counties and larger municipalities, including larger villages, since 1946; however, nonparty voter groups (*Wählergruppen*) were the dominant factors in the smaller villages until the local reforms went into effect. Whether the increased politicization of local elections in rural municipalities is a positive or negative factor depends to some extent on one's perspective and expectations.

(9) The goal of simplification and increased transparency of local government structures has probably been achieved only partially, if at all. To compensate for the loss of *Bürgernähe* resulting from enlarged municipalities, districts in the cities and *Ortschaften* in the "unitary municipalities" were created. While these have provided some degree of decentralization, they have had the effect also of making the administrative structure of the affected municipalities more complex. And though the achievement of the goal of greater unity of administration was to eliminate all or most of the functional joint authorities (*Zweckverbände*), these are still common.[35] Nevertheless, considerable improvements in the unity of administration were made through the county reforms.

(10) The costs of local government have risen. Lower costs as such were never a goal of the local reforms, since improving the services and administrative capacity of the municipalities meant higher costs for personnel and facilities.

Whether scales of economy and improvements in costs to benefits have been achieved remains uncertain.

Some of these deductive theses have been confirmed in an empirical study of the reforms in Lower Saxony.[36] Members of the *Land* parliament, most of whom are members of municipal or county councils as well, were asked to assess the municipal reforms in 1976 and to evaluate both the municipal and county reforms in 1980. The SPD carried out the municipal reforms with a one-vote majority in the legislative period 1970–74, while a CDU-FDP coalition implemented the county reforms in 1977. As a result, the assessments of the reform vary significantly in some cases according to the party of the respondent deputy.

In spite of the differences by party concerning the results of the territorial and administrative reforms in Lower Saxony, there was widespread agreement in 1980 that the reforms had brought about improvements in administrative capacity at the municipal level and also, but to a lesser extent, at the county level. There also was agreement in 1980 between the parties that efficiency in the municipalities had been improved through increased unity of administration, and that there is now more equality in the provision of various services. A majority of the SPD, but only a plurality or less of the CDU *Land* deputies agreed that municipal efficiency had been increased through a better spatial distribution of population, that local administrative structures had been simplified, that the differences between urban and rural areas had been reduced, and that there had been improvements regarding the core cities and their surrounding areas. A majority of the CDU and a plurality of the SPD deputies agreed that there had been a significant redistribution of functions to lower levels, and that the reform had raised permanently the costs of local government. A plurality of SPD deputies agreed that there was now closer contact between citizens and local governments, while a sizeable majority of CDU deputies disagreed. This is not surprising, given the fact that the SPD was more in favor of larger unitary municipalities, while the CDU advocated smaller reformed units and, where possible, associations of municipalities (*Samtgemeinden*).[37] Somewhat in contrast to theses six and seven above, only a minority of deputies in both parties agreed that local democracy had been strengthened in the sense that the municipal councils now had more authority, thereby encouraging a more intensive citizen participation in local politics.

When asked to assess the attitudes of their voters or local citizens to the municipal reforms, the deputies gave a wide variety of responses. Some deputies insisted that a large majority of citizens had a positive orientation, though admitting that a minority had negative feelings. Some distinguished between inhabitants of cities (mostly unaffected and unconcerned) and rural areas (more negative attitudes). CDU deputies were more likely than their SPD counterparts to respond that their voters had negative feelings, probably because the CDU has more support in the small villages that were the major targets of the reorganization.

Many agreed that the vast majority of citizens were uninterested and basically without an opinion unless they felt that they (for example, former councillors) or their municipality had been "victims" of the reform. This popular disinterest and personal lack of concern in the reform results emerges especially with respect to the county reforms. On the other hand, if a municipality lost its previous status as a county seat, its inhabitants might still be angry and disappointed.

Given the high expectations,[38] focus of attention and tremendous expenditure of time and effort on the local government reforms, the opposition, widespread resignation and, above all, yawning apathy of the affected citizenry have to be a disappointment to many reform advocates and participants. It is possible that the apparent lack of public enthusiasm for the reforms is a reflection of what many in West Germany came to call by the mid-1970s "reform fatigue" (*Reformmüdigkeit*). Local reforms were merely one example of a whole series of reforms and changes in foreign and domestic policies in Germany since the mid- and late-1960s. Disappointment with the gap between promise and performance, especially in educational reforms which affected directly the local level, sometimes bitter controversy over certain reforms, and the passage of time have eroded much of the original goodwill which probably existed in the later 1960s when the local government reforms began to go into effect. By the mid-1970s the more skeptical and sober view of social change had not spared the reforms of local governments.

It is also clear that local government reforms have been dealt a serious blow by the economic recession which began in 1974 and sharpened in the 1980s. Many of the expectations of the reformers were based on the assumption that the German economy would continue to grow and that public revenues would continue to increase above inflation, thus providing the financial base for additional professional staff and improved public services. At the moment at least, it appears that a major weakness of the conceptual framework of the local government reforms was the lack of attention paid to the question of providing adequate long-term financing for the reform goals. Another expectation based on trends of the 1960s was that there would be continued population growth. That "the pill" and changed attitudes about family size would bring about by the end of the 1970s the lowest birthrate in the world was hardly anticipated by those who drew up plans for educational, territorial, and other reforms.

Another explanation for the lack of public enthusiasm for the local reforms might be that the initiative for the reforms came from elites rather than from public pressure for change. The difficulty with this argument is that most reforms, including the efforts of Baron vom Stein, were the work of a relatively small number of elites, and the test of their success comes only after several decades. That the local government reforms of the 1960s and 1970s were the work of elites can hardly be disputed; however, the number and the variety of elites involved was relatively large. They came from all eight territorial states, and they included high-level bureaucrats, numerous *Land* and local politicians, lawyers and judges, and interested and affected citizens. The writings and discussions of hundreds of academicians, especially legal scholars in the discipline of public administration, but also economists, planners, and to a small extent sociologists and political scientists, had some part, however modest it may have been in most cases, in influencing the course of events. In spite of the admittedly strong influence of elites, there was probably more widespread participation in the German local government reforms of the 1960s and 1970s than in most comparable reform efforts.

5

The Legal Framework
of German Local Government

The role of law in German government and society can hardly be exaggerated,[1] and any discussion of German local government must of necessity include a strong legal component. From Baron vom Stein's City Charter Law of 1808 to the present time, the definitions, description, regulations and procedures contained in the general charter laws for municipalities and counties have been detailed and comprehensive. There were thirty-five German states in the middle of the nineteenth century, and German federalism preserved in large part the separate local government traditions of the twenty-five states of the 1871 Bismarck Reich and of the eighteen member states of the Weimar Republic. The short-lived German Municipal Charter Law of 1935 which was introduced by the Nazi regime was the only nationwide local government law in German history. It has had some lasting influence in certain of its nonpolitical administrative provisions, but after 1945 each newly constituted *Land* in the Federal Republic (Bavaria is the only "territorial state" with a pre-1945 tradition) passed its own general charter laws for the municipalities and counties within its boundaries.

Since the abortive Frankfurt Constitution of 1849, German constitutions have contained provisions concerning local governments and guaranteeing their right of self-government. Until 1918, however, more emphasis was placed on decentralized self-administration by bureaucrats than on self-government by local citizens, although self-government was not lacking entirely. While self-government was stronger in theory in the Weimar Republic, it was in practice placed under strong centralizing pressures from a number of sources. From 1935 to 1945 democratic self-government ceased altogether and was replaced by the *Führerprinzip*. Only after 1945, and especially with the founding of the Federal Republic in 1949, has there been unambiguous legal protection and support for both local self-administration and democratic self-government.

The Constitutional Protection of Local Governments

The Basic Law. In contrast to the United States Constitution, which is silent on the matter, the Basic Law, or constitution, of the Federal Republic contains provisions which are devoted to local government. Article 28, paragraph 1, requires that the constitutional order of the constituent *Länder* correspond to the principles of a republican, democratic and socially just state under the rule of law as provided by the Basic Law. In the *Länder* and in the counties and municipalities which form the territory of the *Länder*, the people must have representative institutions derived from general, direct, free, equal, and secret elections.[2]

Article 28, paragraph 2, provides a global institutional guarantee for local self-government. Municipalities are guaranteed the right "to regulate on their own responsibility all affairs of the local community within the framework of the law" (*Allzuständigkeit* or *Universalität des Wirkungskreises*). Counties and associations of municipalities also enjoy the right of self-government, but they do not have the same *Allzuständigkeit* that the individual municipalities enjoy. They must be given by law a sphere of activity to meet the institutional guarantee of article 28, and this sphere includes those tasks that are beyond the capacity of the smaller municipalities (*überörtliche Aufgaben*).[3]

The guarantee of self-government for local governments is an institutional guarantee, not one applied to them as individual corporations. Thus a municipal corporation is not protected against consolidation or annexation. On the other hand, *Land* constitutional courts may determine in a conflict situation whether the dissolution of a municipal or county corporation was in the public interest and according to established principles and procedures.[4]

Because of the developments toward the welfare state, increased planning, rising costs for local services and capital investment needs, the growing demands for services which only higher and larger units of government can provide effectively, and numerous technical changes which have affected local governments, increasing concern has been expressed regarding the meaning today of the constitutional guarantee of self-government. One reaction to the pressures noted above has been that a "modern" functional understanding of matters properly belonging to local governments requires a recognition of the complementary nature of local self-government and state administration. That is, there should be no separation of functions between levels but rather local participation in *Land* and national decision-making processes. This argument in favor of participation, which is sometimes made in the United States as well, appears to be rejected by leading legal scholars on the grounds that it is really a justification for a centralized unitary state with "deconcentrated basic units" and therefore not in conformity with article 28.[5]

Article 28 guarantees the local governments a set of tasks which they are to regulate on their own responsibility. These tasks can change with time, but a "core area" must remain. The Federal Constitutional Court has avoided any attempt to define abstractly the "core area of local government"; rather, it has insisted on a case-by-case determination based on the concrete situation. In the process the Court has made clear that it will protect "the essential elements which cannot be removed from an institution without changing its structure and type."[6]

To protect themselves against higher-level invasions of their "core area" of self-government as guaranteed in article 28, local governments have the right to bring constitutional complaints before the Federal Constitutional Court (article 93, paragraph 1, 4 b.). They also are guaranteed a proportion of the most important tax revenues raised by the national and *Land* governments (articles 106 and 107). Finally, article 115c requires the federal government to pay attention to the basic requirements of the *Länder* and of local governments in case of an impending military attack on German territory.

The Land *constitutions.* In all of the eight territorial states, local governments have been guaranteed the right of self-government by the *Land* constitution. In six of the *Länder* the constitution permits the municipalities to bring constitutional complaints regarding *Land* laws before the *Land* constitutional courts.[7] Local governments also may go before administrative courts in disputes which they may have with *Land* supervisory authorities.

Local Government Law

Excluding the three city states, there are eight sets of local government laws in the Federal Republic. Each of the eight *Länder* has a detailed general municipal charter (*Gemeindeordnung*) and a general county charter (*Kreisordnung*). In addition there are regulations for associations of municipalities in Lower Saxony, in the Rhineland-Palatinate and in Schleswig-Holstein; for higher level associations in Bavaria, North-Rhine Westphalia and the Rhineland-Palatinate; and for regional associations in Baden-Württemberg. Bavaria and Baden-Württemberg also have special laws concerning local cooperation, associations of municipalities and special associations. There are election laws for local governments and implementing instructions regarding budget matters, accounting procedures, etc. Finally, there are *Land* laws concerning the redistributions among local governments of revenue resources. In spite of the separate systems of local government law, the general outlines and in many cases the details of the laws are quite similar. The major differences are in the forms of local government (*innere Verfassung*).[8]

The municipalities. The constitutional guarantee of local self-government includes the determination that local governments are judicial persons with autonomous rights. They are not mere administrative units, even though the counties and county-free cities serve as the lowest level of administration for the *Länder*. The performance of tasks delegated by the *Land* in accordance with *Land* laws and instructions from supervising authorities present no legal problems so long as the local governments continue to regulate on their own responsibility a core area of local concern.[9]

Municipalities differ from other corporations of public law in that they are territorial corporations (*Gebietskörperschaften*). There are four characteristics of territorial corporations: first, they occupy a given territory; second, they articulate a legal basis for membership for all inhabitants of the territory; third, they maintain territorial autonomy, in some sense of *Allzuständigkeit* (the right to regulate within the law all local affairs on their own responsibility); finally, they provide for direct election of representative organs by the inhabitants of the territory. As territorial corporations the municipalities may engage also in business transactions, borrow money, make contracts, etc.

As we saw in chapter 2, large cities may be divided into districts (*Bezirke*), and in some of the *Länder* towns which have annexed surrounding villages may be divided into *Ortschaften*. The city states always had districts, but districts for the county-free cities and *Ortschaften* for towns were introduced during the era of territorial reforms in the 1960s and 1970s. These have created considerable legal and administrative difficulties, especially regarding the concept of local autonomy. In order to preserve the autonomy of the larger unit and to remain within the spatial administrative principle of unity of administration, the sub-local units have been given more the right to advise and be consulted than the power to make decisions on their own. The subunits of local government, the city districts and town *Ortschaften*, are not territorial corporations, since they have no autonomy vis-à-vis the parent municipality. As legally dependent organizational units of local government, they have no legal guarantee under article 28 of continued existence as institutions.

In order to promote the participation by all citizens in municipal representative bodies and to ensure the uniform application of laws concerning the distribution of revenue resources among local governments, the local government laws of all of the *Länder* require that all territory should be incorporated. There are some exceptions to this rule in five *Länder*, for example, in the case of land owned by the federation or *Land* consisting of uninhabited forests, lakes or rivers, swamps, mountains and military exercise areas. The relative unimportance of such areas can be seen in the fact that there are only eleven areas of unincorporated territory with a total of 7,571 inhabitants.[10] This stands in sharp contrast to the United States, where more than 90 percent of the land area of the country is unincorporated.

The counties. The German county satisfies also the four requirements of a territorial corporation. It differs from the municipality in that it is an association of municipalities (*Gemeindeverband*) and the lowest level of state authority (the county-free city is also a municipality, and, like the county, it serves as the lowest level of state authority). As such the county carries out the functions delegated by *Land* law to local governments, and its chief administrative officer exercises legal supervision over its member municipalities. Since article 28, paragraph 2, of the Basic Law mentions expressly *Gemeindeverbände*, counties also enjoy constitutional protection as institutions of local government.[11] As noted above, the subcounty municipalities enjoy the right of *Allzuständigkeit* for "all affairs of the local community." The counties' right of self-government extends to those matters that are beyond the capacity of the individual municipalities, such as county roads and hospitals.

The general legal position of local governments. German county-free cities and counties are a part of "the state" in a legal sense which is different from American theory and practice. These major local government units are tied organizationally to the *Land* executive — that is, they implement most state (*Land* and federal) laws. Thus the city hall and the county administrative building are a part of the state in the German spatial-federal system. Yet there is an important distinction between the state and the local governments at the fourth level of administration in Germany. The relationship between them is in part hierarchical, in part that of equal partners. Cities and counties are not mere creatures of the state as they are in the United States, but rather constitutionally protected institutions of local government with their own separate, democratic legitimization. Furthermore, the county-free cities as well as the towns and villages which belong to a county (and to some extent the county itself) enjoy their own discretionary powers or *Allzuständigkeit*. This is the "double nature" of German local government law, and it can lead to "constructive tension" between state and local governments.[12]

Whether the local governments in Germany therefore represent a "third column" next to the *Land* and federal governments is a point of controversy. From a legal perspective it is doubtful that the third column thesis is correct. While local governments enjoy an institutional guarantee, this guarantee does not apply to individual local units. There are no local government courts; lower level courts and the police are *Land* responsibilities. Local governments do not pass laws, only local ordinances, regulations and by-laws; and even here, flexibility is limited by higher-level law.[13] Local government structure is determined by the *Land* general charters. On the other hand the municipalities have the right of *Allzuständigkeit*, and in the subcounty municipalities there is little state administration other than the federal post office and the *Land* police. However, local governments are supervised by the state, both in order to insure that state-delegated tasks are performed correctly and that all functions are performed within the limits of the law. Qualifications and salary scales for local personnel are regulated by higher law, but the right of local governments to select their own civil servants belongs to the core area of local government. Finally, local governments have few revenue sources of their own and are dependent on the state for most of their funds; however, they are guaranteed by the Basic Law a proportion of important national and *Land* tax revenues. All in all, then, local governments are only in a limited sense a third column. They are rather in a middle position between a separate third column and dependency on the *Land*.[14]

If one places less emphasis on the legal relationships and focuses instead on administrative, economic and political practice, the third column thesis appears to be somewhat more accurate. Since most administration—some estimates are as high as 80 percent—takes place at the local level, local units of government enjoy a considerable degree of bureaucratic discretion in individual cases of rule application. Because of heavy capital investment and numerous public services provided by local governments, including utilities, local savings banks (*Sparkassen*), hospitals, transportation networks, etc., local governments are important factors in the local and regional economy. While all county-free cities and counties fall under the functional and legal supervision of the district officers (or *Land* Ministries of Interior), this supervision is only partially effective with respect to the larger cities and counties that have their own highly qualified professionals. Channels of communication between these local professionals and their state counterparts are more collegial than hierarchical, a relationship that may be encouraged by political party ties between levels of administration. Finally, local governments are organized in powerful lobbies that promote the interests, respectively, of county-free cities, counties and sub-county municipalities.[15]

German constitutional law and *Land* local government law have not made local governments equal partners with the national and *Land* governments, in spite of arguments such as those above. They are not an entirely autonomous third column of the political-administrative structure. On the other hand, local governments enjoy constitutional protection as institutions of self-government with a guaranteed core area for self-determination. In the spatial administrative system of West Germany, they occupy also a key role in the actual administration of national and *Land* laws and local ordinances. In theory and practice German local governments are in a position to defend themselves with formidable resources against the pressures of centralization and uniformity that have grown in strength in all democratic industrial states. How successful the local governments will be in their defense, however, remains to be seen.

Forms of Local Government

Even though each of the eight territorial states has its own local government law, there are more similarities than differences among the provisions of these laws. The major exception lies in the different forms of government for the municipalities and counties. As we saw in chapter 1, indigenous forms of local government competed with French influences throughout the nineteenth century, and after 1945 the impact of British reforms was felt in Northern Germany. Today four competing municipal forms are reflected in *Land* municipal government laws (*Gemeindeordnungen*): the *Magistrat* form, the strong mayor form, the South German council form, and the North German council form (figure 5.1).

The Municipalities

The Magistrat form. The *unechte Magistratsverfassung*, the origins of which go back to the Stein City Charter Law of 1808, is found today in Hesse and Schleswig-Holstein.[16] All municipalities in Hesse have two organs: the council and the *Magistrat* (called the *Gemeindevorstand* in the smaller municipalities). The council is the highest organ of the municipality. It decides all important questions and oversees the executive organ, the *Magistrat*, which is responsible for routine administration. Decisions of council are not subject to the approval of the *Magistrat* as they were in the *echte Magistratsverfassung* dating back to the 1831 revision of Stein's City Charter Law. On the other hand the *Magistrat* may delay the execution of council decisions it considers to be illegal or inimical to local interests. In the cities the *Magistrat* deputies are called *Stadträte*. In cities above 50,000 the chief administrative officer is called the "lord mayor" (*Oberbürgermeister*), the first deputy the "mayor" (*Burgermeister*).

The council elects from its own membership a chairperson and one or more deputies (*Beigeordnete*). The chairperson sets the agenda for council meetings in consultation with the *Magistrat*, he chairs the council meetings, and he serves as the legal and ceremonial head of the municipality.

The responsibilities of the council may vary somewhat depending on the size of the municipality. Council committees may be formed, and members of the *Magistrat* may participate in committee meetings. Local citizens also may be asked to participate as experts or group representatives.

The *Magistrat* is a collegial organ, consisting of the mayor as chairperson, a first deputy and other deputies. The mayor is a full-time professional, while the deputies may be lay persons. As a collegial organ, however, all members are equal and have one vote each. The number of deputies is set by the municipality and depends on the number of inhabitants, but there must be at least two. In any case the number of professionals may not exceed the number of lay persons.

1) *Magistrat* form

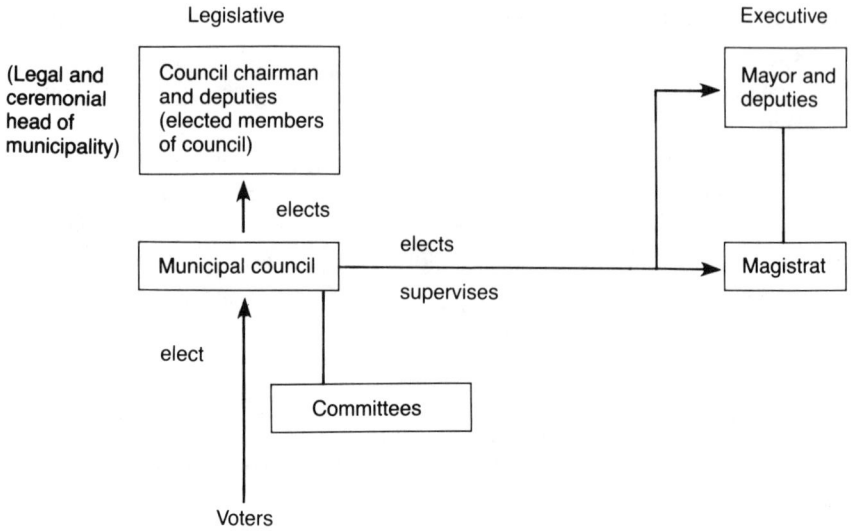

2) Strong mayor form (*Bürgermeisterverfassung*)

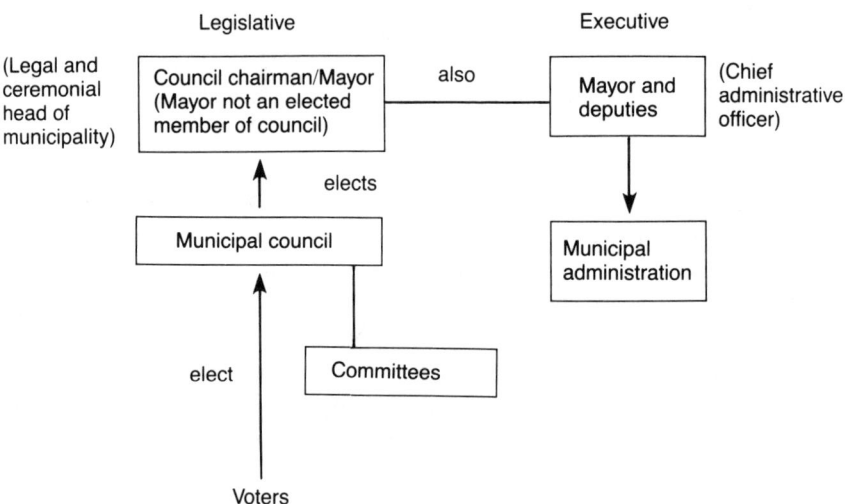

Figure 5.1. Forms of local government in the Federal Republic of Germany

5. The Legal Framework   75

3) South German council form

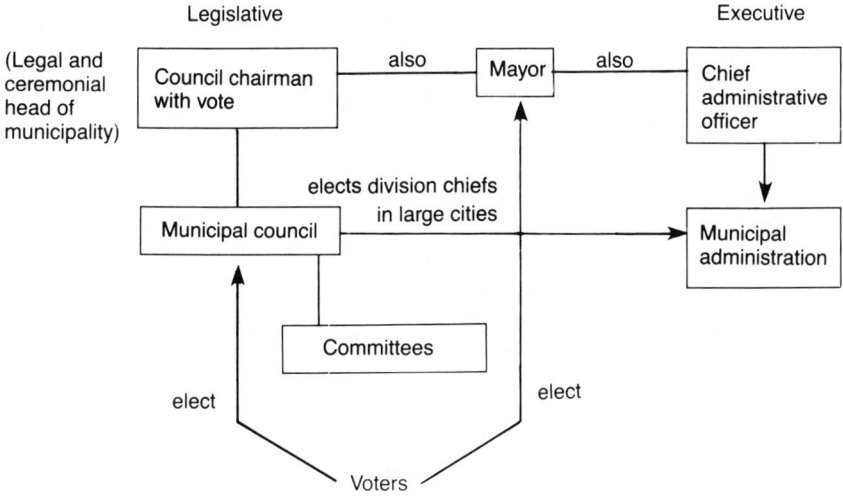

4) North German council form

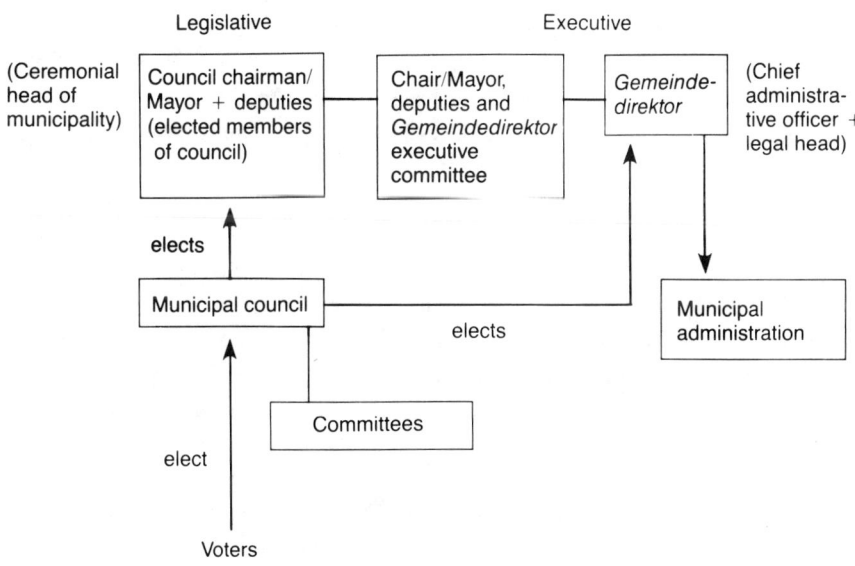

Members of the *Magistrat* are elected by the council for six- or four-year terms, depending on their professional or lay status. Members of the *Magistrat* may not be members of the council. The professionals may be removed by a two-thirds vote of council.

The mayor does not chair council meetings, but he does participate in them as a spokesman for the *Magistrat*. He prepares the decisions of council and executes them unless they have been delegated to a deputy for implementation. Under certain specified conditions he may challenge council decisions and delay their execution until an administrative court or the supervisory agencies have decided the issue. He shares ceremonial functions with the council chairperson. He is the head of all municipal employees except for the deputies, and he carries responsibility alone for the execution of certain state functions, for example, local police, elections, and so forth.

Schleswig-Holstein has the *Magistrat* form for its cities only; for its smaller towns and villages, it has strong mayor forms of government. In general outline, the *Magistrat* form in Schleswig Holstein is similar to the description above for Hesse; however, there are a number of differences. In larger cities the council must form an executive committee which coordinates the work of the other committees and oversees the work of the *Magistrat*. As in Hesse, the professional, full-time mayor is elected by the council. Though he is not a member of the council, he is the voting chairman of executive committee meetings. In cities of less than 7,000 inhabitants, the mayor may be a lay person. Members of the *Magistrat* that are responsible for functional areas are also members of the relevant council committee, but they have no vote. In contrast to Hesse, the number of lay and professional members is set by the *Land* Charter Law, and it ranges from six to nine lay members and one to six professionals. Lay members must always be in a majority.

The strong mayor form. The *Bürgermeisterverfassung* has its origins in the French *maire* system which was introduced in the Rhineland during the Napoleonic occupation. More democratic features, such as election of the mayor by the council rather than appointment by the state, have been introduced over the years. Even today the focus remains on the rule of the mayor, although recent revisions in the Rhineland-Palatinate have introduced *Magistrat*-like collegial elements.[17]

The Prussian City Charter Law of 1856 for the Rhineland called for a separation of the decision-making and executive organs, that is, between the council and the mayor. On the other hand, the mayor was not only the chief administrative officer but also the voting chairman of the council. Unlike the *Magistrat* form, the council was and is the only collegial organ. The mayor's deputies (*Beigeordneten*) enjoy little independence, and unlike the mayor they have only an advisory role in the council. In the place of the collegial *Magistrat* or

Gemeindevorstand, then, there is a single-person monocratic executive organ, the mayor. That the mayor is the voting chairman of the council, even though he is not a popularly elected member, is a major characteristic of the "genuine" strong mayor system.

In the Rhineland-Palatinate today the mayor is still elected by the council. Efforts to have him elected by popular vote have failed on the grounds that this would make the mayor too independent, thus weakening the council. In the larger unitary municipalities, the mayor is a full-time professional, and his term of office is ten years. In smaller municipalities lay mayors are elected for a term of office corresponding to the council term. The professional mayor may be removed, but only by a two-thirds vote of council.

The mayor chairs the council meetings and controls the agenda. One-fourth of the council may require that an item be placed on the agenda of the next meeting. The mayor calls for meetings of the council, of which there must be at least one every three months or whenever one-fourth of the members requests a meeting. The mayor has also the right to chair council committees, though he may delegate this responsibility to his deputies. In case of a need for urgent decisions, the mayor can act in consultation with his deputies without the council; however, the council must be informed of his actions, and it may overrule the mayor if it disagrees with him.

The mayor is the chief administrative officer, and he is the legal and ceremonial head of the municipality. He plans council actions, and he is responsible for their execution. He is responsible for the selection of municipal employees, except that the council must confirm higher-level public servants. He may challenge council decisions he deems to be illegal. If the disagreement persists, the supervising authority must decide the issue. If that decision is against the council, it may appeal to an administrative court. Such disputes rarely, if ever, occur in practice.

The mayor is supported by at least one and up to seven deputies, depending on the size of the municipality. Normally these are lay persons, but they are professionals in the larger cities. Lay deputies are elected by the council for five-year terms, professionals for ten years. As in the *Magistratsverfassung*, the first deputy is called the "mayor" in the larger cities, while the "lord mayor" is the chief administrative officer.

In 1973 a new organ was introduced which contradicts the principle of the genuine strong mayor form. The distinction which is made between this new *Stadtvorstand* and the *Magistrat* is that the former is not an autonomous organ but rather more of an internal administrative body. It was designed to spread responsibility for administration without becoming another *Magistrat*. The *Stadtvorstand*, or city executive committee, consists of the mayor and his deputies, both professional and lay, but the majority must be professionals. The *Stadtvorstand* has assumed many of the administrative responsibilities that used to belong to the mayor alone. Though the mayor chairs this committee, decisions are made by majority vote.

In the associations of municipalities in the Rhineland-Palatinate, the individual member villages (*Ortsgemeinden*) retain some degree of autonomy, but local administration becomes the responsibility of the association (*Verbandsgemeinde*). The head of the association is the *Bürgermeister*, while the head of the individual member villages is the *Ortsbürgermeister*. There is a considerable degree of cooperation between the *Bürgermeister* and the several *Ortsbürgermeister* regarding numerous local tasks.

The strong mayor form of government in the Saarland leans heavily on the Rhineland-Palatinate as a model. One of the few differences between the two *Länder* is that the mayor is the *nonvoting* chairman of the council. The Saarland, therefore, has what is called an "ungenuine" strong mayor form of government for its municipalities.

As we saw above, the cities in Schleswig-Holstein have the *Magistrat* form of government, while the towns and villages have either the ungenuine or the genuine strong mayor system. The first applies to towns with a professional mayor, the second to towns and villages with a lay mayor. For villages with fewer than seventy inhabitants, the town meeting replaces a council and mayor. As in the case of the *Stadtvorstand* in the Rhineland-Palatinate, a *Hauptausschuss*, or executive committee, is chaired by the mayor. If he is a full-time professional, however, he does not chair the council meetings. Instead, the council elects a lay spokesman.

In Schleswig-Holstein the local units headed by a lay mayor are mostly associations of municipalities (*Ämter*), where the genuine strong mayor form applies. Most of these associations have fewer than 5,000 inhabitants. The mayor is both voting chairman of the council and chief administrative officer, but local employees are hired by the association council.

South German council form. During most of the nineteenth century, the South German states adopted local government charter laws similar in essential respects to the Prussian *Magistrat* forms. On the other hand, French influences were also felt, especially in Baden. After World War I a modified council form of government was introduced in Bavaria which served as the model for the current *Süddeutsche Ratsverfassung* in that *Land* and Baden-Württemberg. Because of the strong position enjoyed by the mayor, it might be more accurate to speak of the "council form with mayorial supremacy."[18]

In this form of government the mayor is the *Gemeindevorstand*, or municipal executive. As such he is the voting chairman of the council and all of its committees, the chief administrative officer and the legal and ceremonial representative of the municipality. In Baden-Württemberg the municipal executive is called the mayor, in large cities the "lord mayor." In Bavaria he is called the "first mayor," in larger cities the "lord mayor."

As the chairman of the council, the mayor is a nonelected special member. He prepares council meetings and the agenda. In a few cities, where formed, a council of elders may consult with the mayor concerning such questions. If urgent decisions are required, the mayor may act on behalf of the council.

The mayor is the full-time chief administrative officer; however, in larger cities where functional division chiefs are elected by the council on the basis of proportional representation, the mayor and one or more of his leading civil servants may be of a different party. This can disturb the observed trend away from a monocratic leadership by the mayor toward a collegial relationship in the executive departments.

Perhaps the major characteristic of the South German council system is the popular election of the mayor. This strengthening of the mayor vis-à-vis the council is promoted even further by an eight-year term of office in Baden-Württemberg as opposed to a five-year term for the council; in Bavaria both terms are for six years. In Baden-Württemberg candidates for mayor appear on the ballot without party designations, while in Bavaria party or group membership is indicated. It is sometimes alleged that as a result party and mayor are more closely tied together in Bavaria than in Baden-Württemberg. It is possible also for the mayor to be of one party and the council of another.

Most mayors in towns and villages with fewer than 5,000 inhabitants are part-time, whereas they are normally full-time professionals in larger municipalities. Because Bavaria did not pursue village consolidation in its recent territorial reforms to the same extent as most other *Länder*, there are more part-time mayors in that *Land* than in Baden-Württemberg.

The North German council form. During the British occupation of northern Germany after World War II, three new territorial states were created in the British zone: North-Rhine Westphalia, Lower Saxony and Schleswig-Holstein. In each of these *Länder*, a council form of local government was introduced for which the English system served as a model. The mayor was elected by the council, and his major functions were chairing the council meetings and serving as the ceremonial representative of the municipality. The chief administrative officer, the *Gemeindedirektor*, was analogous to the English town clerk, and as such he was the mere instrument of the council. While North-Rhine Westphalia and Lower Saxony, the first and fourth among the eleven *Länder* in size of population, retained the English-influenced council form, Schleswig-Holstein adopted in the early 1950s the *Magistrat* form for its cities and strong-mayor forms for its smaller municipalities (see above).

Over the years the North German council form has undergone a number of changes, the most important of which has been the growing influence of the *Gemeindedirektor* to the point that one expert now suggests that the system should be called the "city manager form" of government (*Direktorialverfassung*).[19] Particularly in the larger cities the *Gemeindedirektor* is seen as posing a major challenge to the mayor and council for municipal leadership. Counterexamples, however, suggest that much depends on the personalities of the *Gemeindedirektor* and mayor.

Traditionally the *Gemeindedirektor* was elected by the council for a twelve-year term; however, in 1979 the term was reduced to eight years in North-Rhine Westphalia. In Lower Saxony the first term can be for six rather than twelve years. Because of this option, the *Gemeindedirektor* in Lower Saxony may not be removed before his term expires, while he may be removed by a two-thirds vote in North-Rhine Westphalia. The eight-year term in North-Rhine Westphalia and the six-year first-term option in Lower Saxony are reflections of the political — even partisan political — role that the *Gemeindedirektor* has tended to assume in the last few decades. This, of course, is a development that does not fit the British model of a low-profile, nonpartisan town clerk.

In the larger cities the *Gemeindedirektor* is called the *Oberstadtdirektor*; in other municipalities his title is *Stadtdirektor*. In contrast to the South German council system, he is not a member of council. He prepares the decisions of council, which normally means working closely with the executive committee (*Verwaltungsausschuss*), a separate organ of local government. In North-Rhine Westphalia the *Gemeindedirektor* does not have legal authority for preparations of the council agenda; that is done by the mayor in consultation with the *Gemeindedirektor*. In Lower Saxony the *Gemeindedirektor* can demand that certain items be placed on the agenda, but he may not force the removal of any item from the agenda. The *Gemeindedirektor* must participate without a vote in council meetings and, if asked, in committee meetings. He implements all council decisions and is responsible to the council for his actions. He has the right to challenge council decisions which he deems to be illegal.

The ceremonial head of the municipality is the mayor; however, he usually is forced to share the spotlight with the *Gemeindedirektor*. As the chief administrative officer, the *Gemeindedirektor* is the legal representative of the municipality. As the chief administrative officer he is, of course, responsible for the selection and supervision of local government employees.

A major distinction between North-Rhine Westphalia and Lower Saxony can be found in the executive committee (*Verwaltungsausschuss*). The executive committee in Lower Saxony, unlike executive committees in other *Länder*, is not a committee of council. Rather, it is a separate organ of the municipality with its own set of responsibilities. Voting members include the mayor as chairman and at least two and no more than ten deputies (*Beigeordnete*) selected by proportional representation from the council membership. The *Gemeindedirektor* has an advisory vote.

The focus of the work of the executive committee is the preparation of council decisions and the making of decisions on matters falling outside the responsibility of either the council or the *Gemeindedirektor*. Before any final decision is reached by council, the matter must have been considered in the executive committee. The executive committee has a suspensive veto against decisions of council it deems to be illegal or improper. As chairman of the executive committee, which under certain circumstances may review actions of the *Gemeindedirektor*, the mayor is in a stronger position than otherwise would be the case vis-à-vis the *Gemeindedirektor*.

The Counties

A brief decade (1935–45) saw a uniform charter law for all German municipalities, but there has never been a uniform charter law for all German counties. The closest attempt was the Prussian County Charter Law of 1872 which did not become uniform even for all eight Prussian provinces until the 1880s and was adopted only by some of the other German states. The major common thread today among the county charter laws (*Kreisordnungen*) of the eight territorial states is the designation of the county council, called everywhere the *Kreistag*, as the highest organ of the county. Each county charter law provides also for a county executive committee (*Kreisausschuss*), although its membership and functions vary among the *Länder*. Otherwise there tends to be a strong similarity between the municipal and county forms of government in each *Land*.[20]

As could be expected, then, there are similarities in the county charter laws of Hesse and Schleswig-Holstein, where the county executive committee as the collegial administrative authority is analogous to the *Magistrat* in the larger municipalities of these *Länder*. In Schleswig-Holstein the *Landrat* (chief administrative officer) selected by the county council must be confirmed by the *Land* Ministry of Interior; in Hesse the *Land* authorities are involved in the recruitment of the *Landrat*.

In both the Rhineland-Palatinate and the Saarland, the chief county administrative officer (*Landrat*) is a *Land* rather than a county official, that is, he is actually selected by the *Land*; however, he must be confirmed by the county council. In both *Länder* the *Landrat* chairs the county council and the county executive committee meetings. Until recently he was a voting member of each in the Rhineland-Palatinate.

In Bavaria and Baden-Württemberg the *Landrat* enjoys a strong position, but the county councils also are strong. The council committees function alongside

(Bavaria) or in place of (Baden-Württemberg) the county executive committee. The elimination of the executive committee in Baden-Württemberg and the popular election of the *Landrat* in Bavaria are the two major differences between the *Länder*. In Baden-Württemberg the *Land* participates in the recruitment of the *Landrat*.

In North-Rhine Westphalia and Lower Saxony, the major similarity is in the position of the chief administrative officer who is called the *Oberkreisdirektor* rather than the *Landrat* as in the other *Länder* (the *Landrat* in these two *Länder* is the lay chairman of the county council and is the ceremonial head of the county). He does not chair either the county council or the county executive committee, which functions as a kind of miniature council in both *Länder*. There are a number of differences, however, in the functions of the executive committee and the *Oberkreisdirektor*. In North-Rhine Westphalia the county council's selection of an *Oberkreisdirektor* must be confirmed by the Ministry of Interior, since he serves also as a lower-level state authority in that *Land*.

In spite of numerous similarities between the forms of government in the counties and municipalities of the *Länder*, there also are several functions which distinguish the two. In order to provide for more democratic representation, the county councils are quite large bodies. Their size and the distance between the county seat and the town or village of residence of the individual councillor may make it impractical or inconvenient at times to call meetings quickly or for mere routine matters. The traditionally strong ties between the county and the higher *Land* administrations also separates the counties from the subcounty municipalities. These differences are seen especially in the positions of the county executive committees and the chief administrative officers.

The county council is the highest county organ in all the *Länder*, and it is provided with very similar responsibilities in all of the county charter laws. It has the decision-making authority everywhere over important local matters and can delegate certain functions to the chief county executive officer or to the county executive committee. The county executive committee, which has been eliminated in Baden-Württemberg, does not enjoy a uniform position. In some *Länder*, for example, the executive committee makes urgent decisions, but in others these are made by the chief executive officer; in some *Länder* the executive committee may challenge council decisions which it considers to be illegal, but in others this is the responsibility of the chief administrative officer. The chief officer is involved everywhere in the preparation of council decisions, which he also implements. He is responsible for routine administration, and he supervises the county employees. Except in Lower Saxony, he administers both local government functions and those functions delegated by the *Land* authorities for implementation at the local level.

Conclusion

In spite of the stresses and strains that have confronted German administration in five changes of regime since 1870, local government administration has been influenced strongly by historical patterns. Many changes have been brought about, especially since 1945, by the introduction of more democratic features, by the centralizing pressures of the welfare state, by demands for more equality and thus uniformity, and by far-reaching territorial reforms in the 1960s and 1970s. All of these have led to large increases in the number of local government personnel. Nevertheless, it could be argued that in terms of many administrative principles local governments today are not strikingly different from their predecessors of one hundred years ago. This could be said even of the forms of local government, which have been influenced by traditional German and French but also, after 1945, British forms. It is well within the German tradition that these forms vary today. On the other hand, the brief review presented in this chapter has demonstrated that in spite of the different forms of government, certain features seem to be characteristic of all of them. The popularly elected council is the main organ in all municipalities and counties, and it is responsible for all important decisions. At the same time, a powerful executive, whether the *Bürgermeister*, the *Gemeindedirektor*, the *Landrat*, or the *Oberkreisdirektor*, directs the administration and implements the decisions of council. In each form of government, the chief administrative officer of larger municipalities is a professional, whose qualifications (and frequently his party orientation as well) for office are normally undisputed. Regardless of form, the system of council control and highly professional administration, under the functional and/or legal supervision of *Land* authorities, is the major general characteristic of German local government.

6

Local Government and

the Distribution of

Administrative Responsibilities

In the preceding chapters we have seen that the German *Länder* (states) are responsible for the administration of most national laws. Furthermore, we have seen that most—approximately 80 percent—of the national and *Land* laws are actually implemented at the local level. The administration of state (both federal and *Land*) laws at the regional and local level is a characteristic of the spatial administrative system described in chapter 3, and it can be traced back to the Prussian administrative reforms of the early nineteenth century.

Local governments in Germany are, of course, responsible also for the administration of their own local sphere of activities. But this sphere is not constrained by a local charter or state constitution as is typically the case in the Anglo-Saxon countries. Thus a second important and distinctive characteristic of German local government which has its origins in the Stein City Charter Law of 1808 is the concept of *Allzuständigkeit*, also known as *Universalität des Wirkungskreises*. This means that German municipalities may offer any service, construct any facility, or perform any other function that is within the law and not already regulated by the state. At least in theory this right, guaranteed by article 28, paragraph 2, of the Basic Law, stands in sharp contrast to the English and American doctrine of *ultra vires*, according to which local governments may engage only in those activities which are permitted by their charter (of course home rule provisions in the United States may modify this doctrine). Indeed, an English student of local government has described the general power of German local governments in rather glowing terms:

> What is the effect of the possession of a general competence and how does it compare with the operation of local government under the rule of *ultra vires*? Undoubtedly there are substantial advantages. The local authority is encouraged to regard itself as responsible for the well being of the community as a

whole and not as a provider of specified services. Its attitude is less likely to be negative. A proposal to undertake a new function entails not a search for an enabling power, but a check to ensure that it is not already the duty of another authority. Central supervision tends to be altered for the better. Superior authorities look broadly at the local authority's performance as a whole rather than scrutinise individual functions, whereas dependence upon separate statutory power for each function, as in England, invites regulations, detailed scrutiny, consents, returns, inspections and the like.

Moreover, a general competence ministers to the pride of the authority. Germans set great store by its possession, and books on local government make much of the merits, contrasting the freedom it confers with the limitations of Anglo-Saxon practice. Finally there is the practical value of the freedom to expand activities. Local authorities can look for additional ways in which to serve the public, either by providing new services or by participating in the efforts of other bodies. It is significant that German authorities have an exceptional variety of joint arrangements, financial and otherwise, with public and private organisations. Housing for example can be assisted in many ways. In short, to allow general competence to local authorities, as is done in Germany (and also in other countries, e.g., Sweden), is to embrace a more flexible form of government, one which, being founded on trust in the local authorities' wisdom, promotes a sense of responsibility.[1]

How does this general power of local governments work not just in theory but also in practice? How much room for maneuver do local governments really have in a spatial-federal system in which they serve as main field agencies for both the federal and *Land* governments? How flexible are the authorities which supervise the local governments on behalf of the *Land* governments? Given the highly developed welfare state which has emerged in Germany during this century, and given the tendency in the last century and a half toward a detailed, almost perfectionist legal regulation of virtually every activity, behavior and right in the social system, what activities have been left to the local governments to regulate on their own responsibility? These are the questions we will explore in this chapter.

There are numerous threats and challenges to local self-government everywhere, including the perennial problem of local finances. Another major threat in Germany is seen by many observers to lie in the large and increasing number of laws which local governments are expected to carry out on behalf of the state. It is not a little ironic that precisely the efforts to perfect the principles of the social welfare state under law (*sozialer Rechtsstaat*) run the danger of undermining the constitutional protection of local self-government.

Federal and *Land* Administration

As indicated in chapter 3, not all laws and activities are administered or carried out at the regional or local level in a spatially administered system. Some functional administration exists both in the German spatial-federal and in the French spatial-unitary systems.

Federal administration. In the spatial-federal system of the Federal Republic, administration by the central government is the exception to the rule. Indeed, article 83 of the Basic Law states explicitly, "The *Länder* execute the federal laws as matters of their own concern unless this Basic Law provides otherwise." Such provisions are found primarily in articles 87–89. Activities of the federal government are not merely a matter of Basic Law provisions, but these are the most important guidelines available.[2]

First of all, of course, the central government is responsible for the administration of the sixteen federal ministries, which are involved especially in political planning. A second category is foreign affairs, and, of course, external security forces. Internal security is primarily a responsibility of the *Länder*; however, the federal government does provide central data collection facilities which serve the *Länder*, and the federation is responsible for the border patrol forces, which include anti-terrorist units. In the general area of transportation and communications, the federal government administers with its own field agencies the federal railways, the postal service, including telephone and telegraph services, and navigable waterways and canals. The federal government is responsible for the weather service, for the regulation of such activities as long-distance trucking, and for the control of air transportation. Federal roads, including the *Autobahnen*, are administered by the *Länder* for the federal government.

A variety of ministries and offices are responsible for economic regulation and development, including the federal bank. More recently, since 1969, the federal government "participates" with the *Länder* in the promotion of so-called "joint tasks" (*Gemeinschaftsaufgaben*) with the overall goal of "improving living conditions" throughout the country (article 91a). These joint tasks include public investments for the promotion of the economic and agricultural structure of a region and for the protection of coastal areas (see table 6.1). The federal government also may provide the *Länder* and local governments (but only through the *Länder*) a variety of categorical grants for the improvement of local and regional economic structures (article 104a, paragraph 4).

In the general area of social welfare, the federal Ministry of Labor and Social Welfare is very important; however, even it is concerned primarily with legislation. The various social insurance programs, including the sickness funds, accident insurance, old age security and so forth, fall under the general supervision of this

Table 6.1. Administrative tasks at the federal level (Federal Republic of Germany)

Planning responsibilities	Service delivery responsibilities	Regulative responsibilities
Budget	Federal railways	Foreign affairs
Medium-range financial planning	Post office	Defense
	Federal waterways	Federal criminal office
Major highway planning	Foreign aid	Federal border patrol
Multilevel educational planning (GemA)	Agricultural improvements (GemA)	Federal trust office
		Federal health office
Planning within the framework of the joint tasks (GemA)	Public housing (GemA)	German patent office
	Urban development (GemA)	Federal airways office
	University facilities improvements (GemA)	Motor transportation office
	Promotions of improvements in economic structure (GemA)	Office for constitutional protection
		Private data protection
	Local transportation improvements	
	Hospital construction (GemA)	
	Research promotion (GemA)	
	Resource storage	
	Federal bank	
	Federal employment office (U.K. = Labour Exchange)	
	Federal employee social insurance office	

Source: Frido Wagener, "The Functions and Services of German Public Administration," *International Review of Administrative Sciences* 49 (1983): 189.
GemA = *Gemeinschaftsaufgabe* (Joint task)
Italic type indicates legally autonomous activities.

ministry, but they are basically administered by autonomous, self-governing agencies. The federal employment office has field agencies throughout the country that serve both as employment agencies and unemployment offices. There are federal ministries also for youth and family affairs and a federal health office with a variety of responsibilities.

While "culture" is generally a sphere of activity belonging to the *Länder*, the federation is involved here through archeological research and cultural activities abroad, the latter of which are administered by the foreign office. Most cultural and scientific activities of the federation are administered by the Federal Ministry of Education and Science. General educational policy questions require the cooperation of the federal and *Land* governments, a cooperation which, especially for ideological reasons, is not always easy to secure. A federal science council is concerned with scientific planning at the federal level, a federal planning committee exists for the "joint task" of university building construction, a German

Research Council is responsible for research support activities, etc. The federal government is involved directly and indirectly in numerous research activities and facilities.

This brief discussion of federal administrative activities is designed to provide the reader with a general impression only; a detailed description is beyond the scope of this book. Table 6.1 is incomplete also in some details, but it does provide another perspective on federal responsibilities in the administration of public affairs. It should be noted again that the federal government has relatively few field agencies for the functions listed in table 6.1. These are indicated in tables which follow, and they include *Land*-level field agencies for the federal bank, employment office, and military administration; regional-level field agencies for the railway, post office and finance offices; county-level field agencies for the employment office, customs office, and military administration (for example, the military draft); and municipal-level field agencies for the post office, railway and employment office.

Land *administration.* As noted above, administration in the German spatial-federal system is the responsibility primarily of the *Länder*. Since the *Länder* are organized also according to spatial principles, however, *Land* administration does not exist at the municipal level. Rather, the municipalities carry out *Land* administrative responsibilities as delegated functions.[3] On the other hand, there is some *Land* administration at the county level, which will be described in a later section.

The general internal administration of the *Länder* is the responsibility of the *Land* Ministry of Interior. This ministry has four classical tasks: general administration and constitutional issues, the civil service, local governments, and public security. The last responsibility includes various police forces, fire protection, civil defense and protection against catastrophies as well as supervisory administrative responsibility for matters such as building codes, health regulations, water purity, and economic regulation. Other classical tasks of internal administration include residency registration, marriage licenses, personal identification and pass documents, and, of rapidly growing importance, matters concerning nationality and foreign residents. Emerging internal issues of importance, which are not only the responsibility of Ministries of Interior, include land-use planning, sports, the mass media and the environment.

The *Länder* have numerous responsibilities in the general area of economic regulation. A responsibility with a long tradition is the licensing and regulation of business activities. Of increasing importance today is the licensing of enterprises that pollute the atmosphere or water system. Special *Land* authorities exist for weights and measures, while numerous other activities related to the economy are regulated by self-governing chambers of industry and trade. Today activities of economic promotion have been added to the general area of economic regulation, including various subsidies for the encouragement of certain kinds of growth. The *Land* governments are not involved in providing transportation, but they do exercise supervision over private touring companies and over the local governments that have bus and streetcar services. The *Länder* are involved also in road construction, in part on behalf of the federal government, automobile and driver licensing, road signs, and transport regulation.

A third major area of activity for the *Länder* is agricultural administration. The federal government and the European Common Market are responsible for the most important questions of general policy, but the *Länder* are very much involved in promoting their agricultural products and in improving and advancing various agricultural activities. Land-use planning and the rearrangement of agricultural fields are important policy instruments in the general area of agricultural structure, as are water policies, including the construction of dams, dikes, pipelines, etc. About one-third of the forest land in the Federal Republic is owned by the *Länder*, and *Land* ministries of agriculture are responsible for their economic use, care, and maintenance. The *Länder* also carry certain administrative responsibilities for forest lands owned by the local governments and by private persons.

The *Länder* enjoy an important degree of autonomy in the general area of culture. In the past this concerned primarily matters affecting the church, whereas today it involves especially schools and universities. Indeed, these have become so important that some *Länder* have separate ministries for them. A distinction is made in Germany between internal and external school administration. The *Länder* are responsible for the internal administration, which includes all matters concerning teachers and their qualifications, the curriculum, and educational materials. *Land* supervision over the largely autonomous universities, including their financing and matters concerning their professors and other personnel, has assumed considerable importance over the past two decades. The growth in the number of universities and other institutions of higher education and the expanded educational opportunities for German youths have been accompanied by sometimes bitter ideological disputes over teaching and research as well as over student participation in general university self-governance. School reforms and school curricula also have been the subjects of bitter political and professional disputes in recent years, so that it would be fair to say that educational policy in general has been and continues to be one of the most controversial areas of *Land* politics since about the late 1960s. The *Länder* are involved in other cultural activities as well, including adult education, correspondence courses, libraries, and museums. Furthermore, they support theaters, orchestras, the protection of monuments, and the promotion of artists and filmmakers.

In matters of social welfare policy, the *Länder* are responsible for executing federal laws regarding employee safety regulations and the protection of youths

Table 6.2. Administrative tasks at the *Land* level (11 *Länder* including 3 city-states)

Planning responsibilities	Service delivery responsibilities	Regulative responsibilities
Budget	Universities, higher education	Police
Medium-range financial planning	*Land* roads	*Land* youth office
Land planning, regional development	Forest administration	Historical monuments
Multilevel educational planning (GemA)	*Land* survey office	Agricultural field rearrangement
Planning within the framework of the joint tasks (GemA)	Federal highways, autobahnen (AV)	Mining and natural resources
	Airports (GemA)	Office for protection of the constitution
	Public housing (GemA)	**Regional military administration**
	Urban development (GemA)	
	Hospital financing (GemA)	
	University facilities construction (GemA)	
	Economic structural improvements (GemA)	
	Agricultural improvements (GemA)	
	Land central bank	
	Land employment office (U.K. = Labour exchange)	
	Radio and television stations	
	Land banks	
	Land insurance offices	

Source: See table 6.1.
GemA = *Gemeinschaftsaufgabe* (Joint tasks)
AV = *Auftragsverwaltung* (Delegated tasks)
Boldface indicates federal agencies.
Italic type indicates legally autonomous activities.

and expectant mothers. Environmental protection is a growing area subject to federal law and *Land* regulation. Public housing, rent controls, and so forth are administrative concerns of the *Länder*, as are numerous questions of health care and health facilities. Family and youth policies and care of those affected by the war are also within the administrative sphere of the *Länder*. Of these items, public housing and health facilities are legislative responsibilities of the *Land* and local governments.

While the courts do not belong to the area of public administration, there is an overlapping of responsibilities between these two general areas that makes a neat separation difficult to maintain. It should be noted also that only the *Länder* have a court system; the federal courts are courts of appeal except for the Federal Constitutional Court which hears cases as a court of first instance. There are no courts under the responsibility of local governments.

Table 6.3. Administrative tasks at the government administrative district (*Regierungsbezirk*) and regional level (26 government administrative districts and 14 regional authorities)

Planning responsibilities	Service delivery responsibilities	Regulative responsibilities
Regional planning	Special schools for the deaf	*Police
Budget (for regional administration only)	Special schools for the blind	*Appeals regarding building code supervision
	Psychiatric clinics	
	Reform schools	*Matters regarding eminent domain, state sovereignty
	Mental hospitals	
	Specialized hospitals	*Local government supervision
	Regional public assistance	
	Nature parks	*School supervision
	Regional airports (GemA)	*Coordination of development funds
	Federal highways, autobahnen (AV)	
	*Special care offices (war disabled, physically disabled)	*Scenic protection
		*Civil defense
	Electricity production	**Regional finance and revenue office** (in part *Land* authority)
	Gas production	
	Water procurement	
	Chambers of industry and commerce	
	Chambers of crafts	
	Major regional offices of the federal railroad	
	Regional offices of the post office	

Source: See table 6.1.
* = *Land* agency
GemA = *Gemeinschaftsaufgabe* (Joint tasks)
AV = *Auftragsverwaltung* (Delegated tasks)
Boldface indicates Federal agencies.
Italic type indicates legally autonomous activities.

Taxes and most other revenues are collected by the finance offices in the *Länder*; to the extent that the federal government is involved in tax collecting, it is concerned primarily with customs duties and alcohol taxes. *Land* finance offices are responsible as well for *Land*-owned property and *Land* shares in business enterprises, the administration of public debts and other matters concerning finances, including state lotteries.

Table 6.2, like table 6.1, provides a simplified but useful general picture of administrative responsibilities. Perhaps most apparent in this table is the number of activities shared financially between the federation and the *Länder* through the joint tasks programs.

Regional administration. The administrative districts (*Regierungsbezirke*) represent a third level of administration in the six larger territorial states of the Federal Republic, but they are not politically autonomous, self-governing units (Bavaria represents a somewhat different case) as are the other four administrative levels in Germany. Instead, the district officer (*Regierungspräsident*) and his staff (*Bezirksregierung*) serve as key spatial coordinating instruments for *Land* administration. At the same time the district territory is a convenient geographic area of administration for certain federal and *Land* functional agencies. Table 6.3 provides a representative listing of administrative tasks that are performed at the regional administrative district level.

For our purposes the most important function of the administrative district staff is the supervision of local governments. To those accustomed to a functional administrative system, and in particular perhaps to Americans, the general state supervision over local governments in a spatial administrative system suggests a lack of local government freedom, an institutionalized means by which the state may interfere in local government matters.[4] That a possibly even stricter but different kind of fragmented supervision by function may exist in Great Britain or the United States is frequently ignored or not even recognized.

The German view is that supervisory authorities perform two important functions: first, they ensure the enforcement of state (federal and *Land*) laws and the proper administration of state functions that have been delegated to local governments for implementation; second, they protect the local governments from invasions of their responsibility and authority.[5] It is perhaps tempting to associate the first function with control or even repression. There is some historical justification for this view, especially from the perspective of much of the nineteenth century (see chapter 2). Today, however, repression exists only in extreme cases, if at all. State supervision operates on the principle of as little interference in local decision-making as possible. When interference does occur, its purpose is usually to protect the interests of the whole against the special interests of an individual municipality. A common example is the refusal of the district officer to accept an illegal promotion of local personnel into higher civil service ranks for which they do not qualify.

The second function, the protection of local governments, has assumed greater importance in recent years. Whether this function can be described as supervision is a controversial question, since it involves primarily consultation and advice. If consultation, advice, and encouragement of local governments by the supervisory authorities occur, then interference by these authorities should be unnecessary. Thus consultation is perceived by some observers to be the major function of the supervisory authorities, a preventive measure ensuring cooperation in place of conflict. Even after the local reforms of the 1960s and 1970s, some local governments lack the necessary expertise and personnel to deal with the often complex laws and regulations which they are to administer. The responsibility of the supervisory authorities is to help, but not to act in place of the local unit. The goal is to develop a relationship of cooperation and trust. Some experienced observers suggest that the supervisory authorities may dominate the relationship with smaller local units, whereas there is more of a partnership with the larger units; indeed, the local units may dominate the relationship in the case of the largest cities, since their administrative personnel are at least as well qualified as those of the supervisory authority.[6]

There is some controversy over the question whether supervisory authorities must intervene when they detect irregularities at the local level (there is rarely a systematic effort to do so). While the means of intervention may remain flexible, according to the legal principle of proportionality, the prevailing view seems to be that the state has an obligation to ensure that local governments act according to the law. Individual citizens have the right to challenge local government actions in the administrative courts, but this does not relieve the supervisory authorities from the responsibility to ensure that the laws are administered properly. On the other hand, individual citizens do not have the right to demand intervention by the supervisory authorities.[7]

Not all regional administration in Germany is at the level of the administrative district. As indicated in chapter 3, there are a number of higher-level local government associations above the county level that are responsible for a variety of activities. Probably the best known of these are the *Landschaftsverband Rheinland* and the *Landschaftsverband Westfalen-Lippe*, which together cover the entire territory of North-Rhine Westphalia. Their administrative functions include the provision of specialized hospital services, special schools for the handicapped, and special welfare programs; the construction, maintenance and administration of federal and *Land* highways and, upon request, of county roads; the maintenance, care and construction of monuments, museums, archives, etc., and the encouragement of scenic planning; participation in a variety of economic activities, including public banks, insurance companies, housing enterprises, and transportation services and promotion of certain water and forestry activities; and participation in *Land* planning, support of vocational schools, and management of certain social insurance programs.[8]

The *Landeswohlfahrtsverband Hessen*, the boundaries of which are coterminous with those of the *Land* Hesse, is concerned primarily with the provision of numerous specialized hospital services, special education for the handicapped and disturbed youth, and youth vacation homes.[9] The *Ostfriesische Landschaft* is concerned primarily with promoting the traditions, culture and scenery of the islands and coastal area in the northwest corner of Lower Saxony. The *Oldenburgischer Regierungsverband*, also in Lower Saxony, is responsible for a home for the elderly, two homes for children, and a home for transients, for an insurance program covering local civil servants of Oldenburg, for animal disposal, and for the training of midwives.[10]

In Southern Germany the *Bezirksverband Pfalz* in the Rhineland-Palatinate is responsible for a number of activities and facilities concerned with health, vocational schools and adult education, historical preservation, culture, tourism and economic development.[11] The *Landeswohlfahrtsverband Baden* and the *Landeswohlfahrtsverband Württemberg-Hohenzollern* in Baden-Württemberg are involved primarily in the provision of welfare services. The first association is responsible for three institutions which provide services and care for disturbed youth. The second administers fifteen homes for the handicapped or mentally disturbed, three youth vacation homes, three youth consultation centers, and two facilities each for war-injured and other disabled persons.[12]

While all of the six larger territorial states of the Federal Republic have administrative districts, only the seven Bavarian districts are semiself-governing associations of local governments (*Gemeindeverbände*) with their own sphere of activities set by law. (Since their administrative personnel are *Land* civil servants, the districts are not self-governing in the normal sense of the term.) As such they represent a third level of local government, legally equal to the municipalities and counties, with a popularly elected council and a *Präsident* elected by the council. Within their own sphere of activities (*eigener Wirkungskreis*), the focus of the Bavarian districts is on the promotion of the economic, social and cultural well-being of their inhabitants. Their mandated or obligatory functions (*Pflichtaufgaben*) include social welfare programs for general welfare, psychiatric care, handicapped persons, TB care, the homeless, etc., programs for those affected by the war, youth programs, special education programs, and programs concerning water conservation and environmental protection.[13]

Local Government Functions:
Delegated and Self-Government

The responsibility for public administration in Germany is divided between the state (federal and *Land* governments) and local governments. Most state administration is the responsibility of the *Länder*, which distribute their administrative tasks (*Aufgaben*) among the *Land* (central) level, regional (middle) level and local (lower) level. For the three city states, there is the city-wide (central) level and the "local" district level. Local (*kommunale*) administration is the responsibility of the municipalities and counties.[14] Indeed, as was noted in chapter 5, the local governments are guaranteed the right "to regulate on their own responsibility all affairs of the local community within the framework of the law." While oversimplified, it can be said that local governments (1) execute on the basis of instructions state laws delegated by the federal and *Land* governments, (2) administer on their own responsibility local programs and activities mandated, that is, made obligatory, by state laws, and (3) implement on their own responsibility local programs and activities which they have decided voluntarily to provide. The complexity of the distinctions among the three basic categories of public functions and the different terms used in the various *Länder* to describe these functions make a sober foreign observer tremble at the thought of explaining these to others without hopelessly confusing both them and himself. Nevertheless, I shall attempt to do this in the discussion that follows.

Origins and development. The idea that local governments should carry out most state as well as local administrative tasks and also enjoy a general power to act in matters of local concern appears to go back to the French Revolution and the Constitution of 1789; however, the *pouvoir municipal* which this constitution granted local governments was short-lived. After 1800 French municipalities came under the prefects' control and became mere administrative units of the central state.

Whether Baron vom Stein was influenced by the French developments became a point of bitter scholarly dispute in Germany in the latter half of the nineteenth century.[15] In any case the dualism between state and local self-government matters was a characteristic of the Stein reform of 1808, and the local government laws in Prussia and in other German states built upon the Stein foundation in the course of the nineteenth century.[16]

The traditional legal distinction which has been made in German local government has been between matters of local self-government (*Selbstverwaltungsangelegenheiten*) and delegated functions (*Auftragsangelegenheiten*) or, from the perspective of the local governments, matters of their own concern and delegated matters (*eigener und ubertragener Wirkungskreis*). Even though the state could require local governments to perform certain functions which belonged to the first category of tasks (*Pflicht-Selbstverwaltungsaufgaben*), the state supervisory authorities could interfere in this "obligatory" sphere of local self-government only in case a law had been broken (legal supervision, that is, *Rechtsaufsicht*). In the case of delegated state tasks, on the other hand, the state could exercise legal supervision *and* issue instructions for the administration of the particular function or activity (functional supervision, or *Fachaufsicht*). This simple separation between the two categories of functions has been made more complex since 1945 with the addition of new functions, interpretations, concepts and terms. Unfortunately, legal scholars disagree among themselves on the terms and the appropriate description of the current relationships.[17]

Four of the territorial states, Lower Saxony, the Rhineland-Palatinate, the Saarland and Bavaria, still follow the traditional dual system of task distribution according to which the supervisory authorities exercise legal supervision over the self-government activities (those made obligatory by the state as well as those assumed voluntarily) and functional supervision over delegated matters. General laws grant extensive powers to the *Land* supervisory authorities to issue instructions to the local governments which carry out the delegated functions.

In Baden-Württemberg, Hesse, North-Rhine Westphalia and Schleswig-Holstein the situation is more complicated. These *Länder* followed a recommendation made at a conference of local government experts in Weinheim in 1948 according to which local governments were to possess exclusive authority for all public administration activities in their territories. Any exceptions would have to be regulated by individual laws. This concept of local government authority rejected the idea of delegated functions as a general category of activities to be performed by local governments acting as agents of the state. With the local governments assuming responsibility for all functions of public administration, a distinction was made, first, between voluntary and obligatory functions (*freiwillige-* and *Pflichtaufgaben*) and, second, within the category of obligatory functions, between those that are executed with or without instructions (*Weisungs- und weisungsfreie Pflichtaufgaben*).

Whether the "obligatory functions with instructions" (*Pflichtaufgaben nach Weisung*) are merely a new term for the older "delegated functions" (*Auftragsangelegenheiten*), a "new type of self-government function" or an "ungenuine self-government function" is a point of dispute among legal scholars. There appears to be a consensus that matters delegated by the federal government for execution at the local level are legally the same under either system of classification, that is, in implementing federal laws, *Pflichtaufgaben nach Weisung* are the same as *Auftragsangelegenheiten*. In other cases of obligatory or delegated functions, however, there are certain legal differences between the two systems.[18] These can be seen, for example, in the supervision of the local governments by state authorities.

State supervision of local government functions. Supervisory authorities in the German *Länder* are involved in two forms of supervision: legal supervision limited to ensuring that the activities, procedures or purposes are within the law (*Rechtsaufsicht*), and functional supervision, including the right to issue instructions and ensure that implementation of a function occurs in a certain manner (*Fachaufsicht*). Legal supervision extends to all matters within the area of responsibility of the local government (*Angelegenheiten des eigenen Wirkungskreises*), that is, it covers self-government functions made obligatory by *Land* law *and* those assumed voluntarily by the municipalities.[19]

Legal supervision over the municipalities that are part of a county is the responsibility of the chief administrative officer of the county in his capacity as lower-level state authority (except in Lower Saxony, where the county administration is the responsible authority). The county-free independent cities, most of the larger nonindependent municipalities, and the counties are supervised by the administrative district officer (*Regierungspräsident*) in the six larger territorial states; however, in Schleswig-Holstein and the Saarland supervision over these local government units is performed directly by the Ministry of Interior. The means of enforcement range from the right to information (which alone is usually sufficient to ensure compliance) to the dissolution of a local council or, in a few *Länder*, the calling of new local elections. Only North-Rhine Westphalia provides for the cutting off of funds. Local governments may, on their part, challenge the supervisory authority in an administrative court.[20]

There is less uniformity among the *Länder* in the area of functional supervision. In the traditional dual system of functional distribution, according to which the local governments are responsible for their own sphere of self-government activities on the one hand and for activities delegated by the state on the other hand, there is a simple rule that the self-government activities are subject to state legal supervision only and the delegated activities to state legal *and* functional supervision. General laws grant extensive powers to state supervisory authorities (the functional supervisory authorities are determined by law and are not always the same as those that exercise legal supervision) to issue instructions to the local governments, which carry out the delegated functions in the capacity of lower-level state authorities or on the state's behalf.

In Baden-Württemberg, Hesse, North-Rhine Westphalia and Schleswig-Holstein, the situation is more complicated. As noted above, these *Länder* have rejected the idea of delegated functions in favor of the concept of obligatory functions (*Pflichtaufgaben nach Weisung*) which can be imposed only by individually applied laws. A separate law is supposed to indicate whether each function is to be carried out with instructions under state supervision and, if so, describe the limits of the instructions; however, in practice there are few such laws even in the *Länder* mentioned above. Some observers doubt, therefore, whether there is very much difference in practice between these *Länder* and those that retained the traditional dual system of task distinction.

In most cases the local governments do not have the right to challenge in the courts instructions for functions carried out on behalf of the federal and *Land* governments. An exception would include instructions perceived to be invasions of the right of self-government. In the case of the *Länder* that have rejected the concept of delegated functions, another exception might be the question whether the state authority has the right to issue instructions in a particular case or whether a particular instruction is within the law.[21]

In addition to exercising legal and functional supervision over local governments, supervisory authorities are involved also in approving a number of actions which local governments intend to pursue, for example, local land-use plans. More important, however, is the function that the legal supervisory authorities perform as the first instance in deciding citizen complaints against certain administrative acts of local governments. (In Bavaria a distinction is maintained between legal and functional supervisory authorities.) Decisions concerning citizen complaints against local government actions are among the most important and frequent activities of the supervisory authorities. Since these authorities focus increasingly on consultation, intervention now occurs almost exclusively in response to citizen complaints. The local governments on their part may challenge such intervention in the administrative courts, but only if it concerns a matter within the sphere of local self-government, not generally if it involves a delegated function.[22]

The Counties as Lower State Administrative Authorities and as Units of Self-Government

In carrying out state functions, two basic models of administration can be followed by local governments. Under one model, the local government establishes separate administrative facilities (for example, separate buildings) for those personnel administering state tasks and for those administering local affairs. In the first case the personnel are *Land* employees working in a state-owned building, in the second case local employees working in a county or municipal building. Under the second basic model, local government employees alone administer in their locally owned building both categories of tasks, state and local, the first as delegated responsibilities with instructions from above, the second as matters of local concern without instructions. The second model is the one applied in the county-free independent cities, and to a lesser extent but also in the larger non-independent municipalities which form part of a county. It is also the model that has been accepted (quite possibly as an oversight) for the counties of Lower Saxony. The first model, on the other hand, is applied in a variety of highly modified forms in the counties of the other seven territorial states.[23]

The modified model of separate administration. In all of the eight territorial states of the Federal Republic, the counties represent the level of general, all-purpose *Land* administration. Since the counties are also units of local government, a distinction is made in seven of eight *Länder* between the administration of state and local government matters as called for in model one. In contrast to model one, most *Länder* attempt to make this distinction without creating two separate administrative structures; however, they differ in their organizational solutions to this problem.

In Southern Germany—Bavaria, Baden-Württemberg and the Rhineland-Palatinate—the county administration serves also as the lower state administrative authority, so that for the outside observer there is no distinction between local government and state administration. In fact, however, the county administration is a "double authority" (*Doppelbehörde*).[24] In German legal terms, there is a "borrowing" (*Organleihe*) of the county administration by the *Land*. The *Land* governments provide the higher-ranking personnel (*Beamte*) for the administration of state matters, even though these are handled along with local matters in functionally organized divisions or offices. The chief administrative officer of the county can move his *Land* and county personnel from one category of administration to another, although in Baden-Württemberg he needs the approval of the Minister of the Interior if the switch is to be for a longer period.

In Hesse, North-Rhine Westphalia, Schleswig-Holstein, and the Saarland, it is the chief administrative officer alone who serves as the lower state administrative authority. In Schleswig-Holstein the *Landrat* as the chief administrative officer of the county serves as a double authority, legally comparable to the county administrations in Southern Germany. In his capacity as an administrator for state functions, he is a county organ borrowed by the *Land*.

Like Schleswig-Holstein, the *Länder* Hesse and North-Rhine Westphalia have designated their chief administrative officers of the counties as lower state authorities; but unlike the South German *Länder* and Schleswig-Holstein, the county administration and the lower state authority are organizationally separate. This means that when the chief administrative officer is administering state laws, he is acting as a borrowed *Land* authority; when he and his staff perform local county functions, they are acting in a legally separate local government capacity. There is, then, no double authority in these *Länder*.

A separation between state and local government functions exists in the Saarland as well. Indeed, the personnel for the administration of county and state functions are separate, the personnel for state functions even being provided by the *Land*. Only in the Saarland is the separation so strict that personnel cannot be moved from one category of administration to another. In theory the situation is similar in Hesse, but in practice the *Land* no longer provides the personnel. In contrast to the above two *Länder* and to the three South German *Länder*, all personnel in the county administrations of Schleswig-Holstein and North-Rhine Westphalia are county employees; support by *Land* civil servants is permitted under certain conditions, but it is rarely given except in practical apprenticeship supervision for young lawyers.

Another major difference between the Saarland and all other *Länder* except the Rhineland-Palatinate is the French tradition of appointment of the chief administrative officer of the county by the state rather than election by the county council. In spite of his method of appointment, the chief administrative officer of the county in the Saarland is primarily a local organ of the county, so that one can still speak of the *Land* "borrowing" a local official.

The model of delegated administration. In Lower Saxony, in the Saarbrücken municipal association, in all county-free independent cities (that is, city-counties) and in the larger non-independent municipalities in all of the *Länder*, there is no lower *Land* administrative authority and, therefore, no borrowing of local officials by the *Land*. Rather, in accordance with model two, the local administrations carry out state functions as delegated tasks with instructions.

Unlike the requirements of model one and in contrast to the traditional pattern before 1945, administration buildings in all of the counties are the property of the counties. Direct costs of administrative supplies for both categories of administration are the responsibility of the counties. Indirect costs (for example, court costs resulting from challenges to the administration of state laws) are the responsibility of the *Land*. Personnel costs are covered at least in part by the *Land* in the South German states and in the Saarland and Hesse, although the *Land* civil servants that are provided are rarely sufficient in number to do the job. In several *Länder* revenue-sharing funds or special grants are available for helping to defray personnel costs. In some *Länder* certain fees also may be used for this purpose. In general the *Land* is liable for the actions of its personnel in the county, while the county is responsible for all other employees.

In addition to acting as lower state administrative authorities in the German spatial-federal system, the counties serve as convenient geographic areas for the field agencies of a number of separate, functional state authorities. These include in most *Länder* health offices, veterinary services, land-registry and survey offices, school supervisory authorities and police forces. Their area of operation does not always correspond to the territory of the county, but a concerted effort is made to avoid overlapping of boundaries. They are not found generally in the municipalities below the county level.

The tasks of the lower state administrative authorities. In the three North German territorial states there are a number of parallels regarding the state functions performed by the chief administrative officer of the county, especially with respect to the legal and functional supervision of the municipalities that compose the county, to matters concerning military and civil defense, and to other matters involving danger to the population. Chief officers in Schleswig-Holstein and North-Rhine Westphalia have been given a number of mostly supervisory functions in addition.

In the central and South German *Länder*, the lower state authorities have been given more tasks to perform for the *Land*. These include legal and functional supervision over the county's municipalities, municipal auditing, supervision over various other public corporations, and the administrative regulation of business enterprises, firearms possession (allowed for hunting and target practice only), hunting and fishing, nationality and foreign resident law, catastrophy protection, and civilian defense. They also carry administrative responsibility for the lower-level traffic authorities, rent assistance, insurance, war burden sharing, meat inspection, monument protection, price control, and supervision over fire protection services. With the exception of Hesse, the lower state authorities in these *Länder* are responsible for important functions concerning construction and planning, building code enforcement, the approval of zoning plans, traffic regulation, and the promotion of public housing. In most of these *Länder*, the lower level authorities are responsible also for such matters as emergency rescue and ambulance services, the promotion of vocational training, basic welfare services, and pollution control. In Hesse and the Rhineland-Palatinate the lower state authorities have been given the responsibility for county police forces.[25]

The lower state authorities can issue instructions to the county's municipalities in those few instances in which a further subdivision of administration may be called for. With the exception of Bavaria, the chief administrative officer of the county, who is either the head of the lower state authority or is identical to that authority, has the task of coordinating the special state functional authorities in his county.

The functions of the lower state authorities are not immutably fixed. They can be changed in scope and number, or they can be transferred to the county administrative authorities as delegated or obligatory functions (according to model two, above). Such a transfer has already taken place to a certain extent in most *Länder* with respect to the functions given to the semi-independent larger municipalities in the counties. Finally, functional state special authorities may serve to limit the competence of lower state authorities. These include, with some *Länder* excepted in each case, state health offices, veterinary offices, land registry offices, school authorities, and police authorities. Other relevant examples include state offices concerned with water management, road construction, business regulation, culture, and agriculture.[26]

In the past the proportion of state to county personnel was generally in favor of the state. Today it is probably about even, if one excludes county employees working in county operations such as hospitals, homes for the aged or youth, schools, public transportation, equipment parks, housing enterprises, utilities, etc. Since these activities are so important for county administration today, their employees should be included in a comparison of county versus state employees at the county level. In this case the conclusion might be permitted that local county functions have a weight which is several times that of the state functions.

The distinction between state and local government tasks. As indicated in the section above, the number of state tasks assigned to the lower level state authorities in Schleswig-Holstein and North-Rhine Westphalia is considerably less than the number assigned to these authorities in the Central and South German *Länder*.

This suggests that there can be some disagreement over the question of what functions belong appropriately to these authorities. Given the fact that the county-free independent cities and the counties of Lower Saxony do not have lower state authorities, the more fundamental question is whether such authorities are even necessary.

While all of these questions are controversial, there appears to be general agreement that such authorities are necessary for the counties, if for no other reason than that the chief administrative officer of the county must exercise legal and functional supervision over the municipalities which belong to the county in order to ensure that local administration is in conformity with *Land* policy. What responsibilities these authorities should carry in addition to such supervisory functions can be debated; most observers appear to be persuaded that there is a core area which includes police, municipal auditing (*Gemeindeprüfung*), and school supervision. In other words, the responsibilities of the lower state administrative authorities in Schleswig-Holstein and North-Rhine Westphalia (where these authorities consist of one man only) constitute core responsibilities, while the more numerous state tasks of the authorities in the Central and South German *Länder* are in addition to such a core.[27] In any case the number of local government functions administered in the counties far exceeds the number of state tasks assigned to the lower state administrative authorities (see table 6.4, below).

All state tasks, whether implemented by lower state administrative authorities or given to the counties and cities as delegated functions, have in common the assessment by the respective parliaments that they must be administered uniformly under central direction. Local government functions, in contrast, whether made obligatory by the *Land* or assumed voluntarily, are those "affairs of the local community" guaranteed by article 28, paragraph 2, of the Basic Law.[28]

The Distribution of Functions between Counties and Municipalities

In the preceding section we saw that there are differences among the *Länder* in terms of the organization of the lower state administrative authorities in the counties and in the number and scope of state tasks that they have been given to administer. Of course not all state administrative functions have been given to the lower state authorities. Indeed, even in the South German *Länder*, most state functions are delegated to the county administrations for execution by instructions. In addition to these delegated functions, the counties also have to administer with limited instructions or without instructions from the supervisory authorities (but often with detailed written regulations) numerous local government tasks which the state has made obligatory, and, finally, they are responsible for those tasks they have assumed voluntarily.

Within the area of local government tasks, both those made obligatory and those assumed voluntarily, how is the division of responsibility determined for those tasks administered by the county and those administered by the municipalities belonging to the county? As in the case of the distinction between state and local government matters, the answer varies according to different legal, economic and political influences which are themselves not static. Nevertheless, in part due to the territorial and administrative reforms of the 1960s and 1970s, there is considerable uniformity in the pattern of task distribution at the county level in the German territorial *Länder*. There is less uniformity at the municipal level. Legal differences, the disparities among the *Länder* in municipal size and area (for example, North-Rhine Westphalia vs. Bavaria) and differences with respect to unitary municipalities (*Einheitsgemeinden*) vs. associations of villages (*Verbandsgemeinden, Samtgemeinden*, etc.) make comparisons among *Länder* somewhat difficult. In addition the semiautonomous status of larger, nonindependent municipalities in the counties complicates any attempt to make generalizations about the quality, scope and number of typical municipal tasks.[29]

Constitutional aspects of task distribution. One of the important legal distinctions between state and local government functions is that only the latter enjoy constitutional protection. This means that state parliaments are free of constitutional limitations in their assignment of state tasks to be administered by local governments. It could be argued that this leaves the *Länder* free to overburden their local governments with state administration, thus limiting the scope, flexibility or effectiveness of self-government at the local level. There are, however, persuasive arguments against such fears. First, the state must usually provide the local governments with the necessary funds to carry out delegated functions, and, second, administration of state tasks at the local level gives the local governments an opportunity to exercise some influence in the actual application of many rules. This is made possible by the fact, first, that local council decisions may affect the manner in which delegated tasks are implemented and, second, that autonomy of local government personnel (those who execute the laws) and organizational form are core areas of local government that enjoy constitutional protection. Of course the decisions of the local councils and local personnel are subject to legal and functional supervision in delegated matters, but in fact this supervision is not very strict, especially in the case of larger municipalities.

Legal controversies over the meaning of the constitutional guarantee of municipal self-government for "all affairs of the local community" and over the question of where this guarantee ends and the rights of the counties begin are more difficult to resolve. It is generally agreed that the municipalities enjoy a general competence (*Allzuständigkeit*) to act regarding all "local affairs" (*örtliche Angelegenheiten*), while the counties have the right to assume responsibility for all matters that are essentially local but beyond the capacity of individual municipalities to handle (*überörtliche Angelegenheiten*). Other considerations of constitutional relevance may include matters such as decentralization or citizen participation.[30]

Both of the concepts applied above, *örtlich* and *überörtlich*, have been changed somewhat by the results of the territorial reforms of the 1960s and 1970s. In the five *Länder* that have associations of villages, *örtlich* now refers to the administrative level of the association. The enlarged counties also perform more today than before the reforms the function of a service community for the *örtliche* and *überörtliche* needs of its various kinds of municipalities, for example, unitary and associated, structurally weaker and stronger, larger and smaller.[31]

A potentially serious issue of constitutional relevance is the increasing trend toward transforming voluntary local government tasks into obligatory tasks. This is a result of many factors, including the increasing regulation by the federal and *Land* governments of the expanded sphere of local activities and the precedence given to federal and *Land* political priorities. These were based in part on the demands of citizens regarding local services, including expectations of equality among local government units. Such expectations were encouraged strongly by *Land* and federal politicians who turned increasing numbers of local tasks into obligatory tasks. In order to ensure as much uniformity and equality as possible, these were then regulated to the last detail. Examples include zoning, sewerage and waste disposal, street cleaning, adult education, hospital facilities, nursery schools, and scenic and monument protection. Combined with categorical grants from the federal government, this trend could raise the question whether the core area for which the local governments enjoy constitutional protection has not been invaded. Local governments may not, after all, be reduced merely to implementing *Land* and federal laws.[32]

The distribution of local government functions between counties and municipalities. It is not possible to provide a valid list of county functions which can be compared to municipal local government functions because of differences both among the *Länder* and among municipalities within the *Länder*. Nevertheless, one can make certain generalizations about the kinds of tasks that counties and municipalities can be expected to implement.

Municipalities, as noted above, are guaranteed self-government responsibility for "all affairs of local concern" (*örtliche Angelegenheiten*). Counties, in contrast, have the "above-municipal" (*überörtliche*), "complementary" (*ergänzende*), and "equalizing" (*ausgleichende*) local government functions. *Überörtliche* functions are those that by their nature are beyond the capacity of individual municipalities, for example, county roads, intermunicipal public transportation, and hospitals. Certain tasks, such as indoor swimming pools, are not necessarily *überörtlich* if administrative responsibility is shared by two or three municipalities via a special-purpose authority (*Zweckverband*). Complementary functions are local (*örtliche*) tasks that the municipality cannot perform due to insufficient administrative capacity; neighboring villages are likely also to lack the capacity to perform such a function, even as members of a special-purpose authority. Examples of complementary tasks that the county might assume would include homes for the aged or youth, libraries, and schools. Complementary tasks have been reduced as a result of the territorial reforms. Finally, the equalizing tasks involve financial and administrative support for municipalities in order to ensure an equal level of services for all county residents. Examples of financial support would include the promotion of voluntary associations (for example, sports and music), while administrative support might be provided for zoning, health care, or monument protection.[33]

Table 6.4 provides a listing of local government functions based on the division found in North-Rhine Westphalia. It reveals clearly that the municipalities are responsible for most local government functions in spite of the tendency of the county to assume ever more functions. Differences among counties which the table cannot show may result from historical tradition, geographic-economic structure of the county, the size of the municipalities in the county, the degree of intermunicipal and county-municipal cooperation in certain matters, etc. Cooperation is encouraged through the planning process for a variety of areas, through information flow between municipal and county officials, through supervision of municipalities by the chief administrative officer, who is more interested in consulting than in controlling, and through the dual membership of many councillors in municipal and county councils.[34]

The distribution of state administrative functions between counties and municipalities. As we saw in a previous section of this chapter, state functions are not executed in a uniform manner in the eight territorial *Länder*. In seven of the *Länder* they are implemented in part by lower state administrative authorities. In addition some county administrations carry out delegated functions, while in others these are in effect obligatory functions with instructions. In Lower Saxony, where there are no lower state administrative authorities, the county administrations implement all state tasks as delegated functions.

In spite of the different organizational patterns in the various *Länder* at the county level, there are strong similarities in the blocks of functions that counties everywhere perform on behalf of the state. Table 6.5 shows the distribution of delegated or obligatory functions with instructions. It is based on the practice found in North-Rhine Westphalia. According to table 6.5 it is clear that most state functions are performed at the county level. In many cases where municipalities also administer certain state tasks, they must exceed certain minimum popula-

Table 6.4. Distribution of local government affairs (*Selbstverwaltungsaufgaben*) between municipalities and counties (based on the example of North-Rhine Westphalia)

Administrative area	Municipality	County
General administration	Town hall and special purpose offices Statistics Data processing Public relations Auditing	County hall and special purpose offices Statistics Data processing Public relations Auditing
Schools and education	Nursery schools	—
	Elementary schools (*Grund- und Hauptschulen*)	—
	Middle schools	Middle schools
	Advanced high schools	Advanced high schools
	Integrated schools (*Gesamtschulen*)	Integrated schools
	—	Vacation homes for schools
	Special education schools	Special education schools
	—	Vocational schools
	—	Advanced vocational schools
	Pupil promotion	Pupil promotion
	Adult education	Adult education
	Youth music schools	Youth music schools
	School development planning	School development planning
	—	Audio-visual aid library
Culture	Municipal library	County mobile library
	Cultural productions, e.g., concerts, theater	—
	Local history and museum	Local history and county museum
	Municipal archives	County archives
	Monument maintenance	Monument maintenance
	Partner cities	Partner cities

tion size requirements. Differences among the *Länder* in the distribution of certain state functions and differences within the *Länder* among counties of different size are not, of course, indicated in the table.

The administrative reforms and changes in the distribution of functions. As we saw in chapter 4, one of the goals of the local government reforms of the 1960s and 1970s was the redistribution of tasks from higher to lower levels, for example, from counties to municipalities. Those tasks that involved close contact with the public were specifically to be given to the newly enlarged municipalities. Another

Table 6.4 (continued)

Administrative area	Municipality	County
Social welfare	Homes for the aged	Homes for the aged
	Nursing homes	Nursing homes
	Home care for the aged	Home care for the aged
	Housing for the homeless	—
	Youth vacation homes	Youth vacation homes
	Youth promotion activities	Youth promotion activities
	Welfare payments	Welfare payments administration
	—	Child rearing consultation
	—	Vacation home for children
Health care	Home care for sick mothers, etc.	—
	Hospitals	Hospitals
Veterinary care	Slaughterhouse	—
Sports and recreation	Athletic fields	—
	Athletic halls/centers	—
	Outdoor and indoor swimming pools	—
	Playgrounds	—
	Facilities for special events and lectures	—
	Camping grounds	—
	Youth hostels	Youth hostels
	Subsidy and promotion of local clubs	Subsidy and promotion of local clubs
Public utilities	Heat and electricity (in regional association)	—
	Waste collection	Waste disposal
	—	Animal disposal
	Water supply	Water supply
	Sewerage	—

goal was the further integration of *Land* special authorities into the county administration (*Bündelung*).

Some observers argued that administrative reforms were no longer necessary after the territorial reforms had been completed, since the latter had in effect brought about the former. Others insisted that the territorial changes had been merely a preparatory first phase in the administrative reform process. In practice, of course, there was a considerable degree of overlap between the territorial and administrative reforms.[35]

Unfortunately, the creation of larger local units and the elimination of hundreds

Table 6.4 (continued)

Administrative area	Municipality	County
Construction	Municipal land-use planning (*Bauleitplanung*)	—
	Municipal development	—
	Land development preparation	—
	Land acquisition and sale	Land assessment
	Property administration	Property administration
	Construction and maintenance of municipal streets and places	Construction and maintenance of county roads
	Underground and surface engineering	Underground and surface engineering
	Equipment park	Equipment park
Economy and transportation	Attraction of industry and business enterprises	Economic promotion
	Tourist promotion	Tourist promotion
	Municipal or association savings banks	County savings banks
	—	Public commuter transportation
	—	Domestic airports
Environmental protection	Parks and gardens	—
	Hiking and horse paths	—
	—	Nature parks
	Recreation facilities	Recreation facilities
	Scenic care	Scenic care
	—	Scenic planning
	Cemeteries	—

Source: Heinz Köstering, "Das Verhältnis zwischen Gemeinde- und Kreisaufgaben einschliesslich der Funktionalreform," in *Handbuch der kommunalen Wissenschaft und Praxis*, 2d ed., ed. Günter Püttner (Heidelberg and Berlin: Springer-Verlag, 1983), 3:51–52.

of counties and thousands of small municipalities led to the loss of a significant proportion of local councillors. On the other hand, it can be argued that losses would have occurred also if the territorial reforms had not been carried out. An administrative reform without boundary changes would have led to a redistribution of functions that would have given most tasks to higher levels. The result would have been a significant weakening of local self-government.[36] Some observers would suggest that precisely this process of giving state and especially federal authorities responsibility for a wide variety of tasks that are in large part local in nature has occurred even more in the United States. The practical impossibility of implementing large-scale boundary or territorial reforms in the United States, especially in metropolitan areas, can be seen as a contributing cause of this transfer of responsibility from lower to higher levels.

There were certain limitations on the administrative reform process in Germany worth noting. In the first place the focus of reform had to be on delegated state functions and on local government tasks made obligatory by law, since the *Länder* have no legal authority over that sphere of voluntary activity (*freiwilliger Wirkungskreis*) which the municipalities and counties control by constitutional right. On the other hand there were also federal limitations on the redistribution of federal functions. In spite of a federal law that loosened these restrictions, there are still numerous federal laws that specify which units of administration are to be given the responsibility for implementation.[37] It also made little sense to enlarge the counties on the grounds that often they were too small to implement many of the functions of local government that were beyond the capacities of the municipalities, and then to give such functions to the reformed municipalities.[38] Therefore many of these functions, as well as the local field agencies of certain *Land* special authorities, were retained at the county level.

The Functions of the "County-Free" or Independent Cities

While the counties and their constituent municipalities share local government functions, both those made obligatory by law and those assumed voluntarily, the county-free cities are responsible for these functions as well as for the delegated state tasks. Of course all county-free cities, most of which have at least 100,000 inhabitants, have a general power to act (*Allzuständigkeit*) regarding all affairs of the local community, according to article 28, paragraph 2, of the Basic Law. Thus, whether regulated by state law or not, all local government matters are the administrative responsibility of the city and, to a considerable extent, the legislative responsibility of the elected city councils.[39]

In part for historical reasons, the county-free cities do not have lower state administrative authorities for certain state tasks at the local level (Hesse is at present an exception to the rule). Instead, all state tasks are executed by the city administrations as delegated functions. In theory the cities fall under the functional and legal supervision of the administrative district officers (or *Land* Minister of Interior) in their administration of these delegated functions. In practice the highly qualified civil servants in the supervisory agencies and cities have a more collegial than hierarchical relationship, and the actual supervision which takes place may be minimal at best. The city administrations are, nevertheless, bound by instructions in the execution of delegated tasks, and they must conform to the law in carrying out all local government functions.

Because the independent cities administer all delegated state functions and all

Table 6.5. Distribution of delegated functions (*Auftragsangelegenheiten* or *Pflichtaufgaben nach Weisung*) between municipalities and counties (based on the example of North-Rhine Westphalia

Administrative area	Municipality	County
Public security and order	Regulative activities	Regulative activities
	Foreign residents[a]	Foreign residents
	Nationality matters[a]	Nationality matters
	Passport and registration	Passport and registration
	Marriage offices	Supervision over marriage offices
	Fire protection	Technical services for fire protection
Transportation	Parking regulation, parking meters, etc.	Traffic regulation
	—	Automobile registration
	Traffic control and safety[b]	Traffic control and safety
	—	Motor vehicle driver licensing
	—	Supervision over municipal street maintenance
Construction	Supervision of construction	Supervision of construction
	Monument protection	—
Nature conservation, scenic preservation and water protection	—	Nature conservation and scenic preservation
	—	Hunting and fishing
	—	Water supervision
Economy	Business law	Business law
	Price controls	Price controls
Implementation of state transfer payments	—	War burden sharing
	—	Compensation for maneuver damage

Source: See table 6.4.
a. Found only in cities of more than 60,000.

local government functions, both regulated and voluntary, a complete listing of typical city tasks would be quite formidable. It would vary also among the cities, in part as a result of size differences, and there would be some variation according to the *Land*. Nevertheless, a general sketch of normal city activities will be presented below.[40]

Voluntary functions would include cultural activities and facilities such as theaters, operas, orchestras, and museums. Of sixty-seven cities with more than 100,000 inhabitants, fifty-two have their own professional theater, many with more than one stage. Twelve cities have opera houses, and many more have orchestras. All of these activities are subsidized heavily by the city at a high total

Table 6.5 (continued)

Administrative area	Municipality	County
	Supplementary payments to families with provider in military service[a]	Supplementary payments to families with provider in military service
	—	Promotion of occupational training
	Subsidies for home construction[a]	Subsidies for home construction
	Rent subsidies	—
	—	Refugee and expellee affairs
Insurance	Insurance office	Insurance office
Civil defense	—	Civil defense
	Catastrophy protection[a]	Catastrophy protection
State supervision	—	Supervision over the municipalities which constitute the area of the county
State special authorities located at the local level (examples vary somewhat among *Länder*)	—	Health office
	—	Pharmacy supervision
	—	Foodstuffs supervision
	Ambulance service[b]	Ambulance service
	Emergency rescue service[b]	Emergency rescue service
	—	Veterinary office
	—	Local registry and survey office
	—	School office
	—	County police authority

b. Found only in cities of more than 25,000.

cost. Museums are subsidized also, but these may be aided by private collectors. Other voluntary activities related to the general category of culture include libraries and adult education centers. In some *Länder* the latter have become an obligatory function regulated by law. Another major area of voluntary activity is sport and recreation. All cities today have added indoor swimming pools to their improved network of outdoor (often heated) pools. The subsidies for such pools are also quite high, and in some cities they are becoming a serious burden. Other sport-related activities and facilities include stadiums, other competitive arenas, athletic fields, and subsidized sport clubs.

Self-government functions that have been made obligatory by law and state tasks delegated to the cities for administration are far more numerous than the voluntary functions. In the general area of "safety and order," the cities must approve assemblies and demonstrations, issue licenses to businesses and restaurants, control pollution and noise levels, issue automobile tags and drivers' licenses and regulate commercial transport. Each city also has an office for the registration of all inhabitants (*Meldewesen*) and for the issuing of identification cards and passes. Of increasing importance is the administration of matters concerning foreign inhabitants. Another important office is concerned with marriages and the registration of births and deaths. The fire department is responsible for a variety of emergency situations and is not limited to fighting and preventing fires.

Schools of all kinds, from elementary to advanced high schools (*Gymnasien*) and to schools for special education, are a responsibility of the cities, but not with respect to curricula or teachers. The latter internal school matters are the responsibility of the *Länder*.

In the general area of social welfare, the cities have a traditional responsibility for the care of the poor and needy. Today this obligatory local government function involves primarily welfare assistance (*Sozialhilfe*) for those whose various insurance benefits are inadequate or who do not qualify for such benefits. It can be provided for support of the handicapped, blind persons, old people, etc., as well as for those whose unemployment benefits have been exhausted. Related to *Sozialhilfe* are facilities and services for the aged. Other and similar private facilities may be subsidized by the city. *Sozialhilfe* is now the largest item in the city budget.

Youth services are another example of an obligatory local government function provided by the cities, and they include special assistance for problem children as well as aid to young people in general. The latter might consist of vacation camps or youth centers, but the focus is likely to be on the promotion of youth group activities. Publicly run nursery schools as well as nursery schools run by churches and other groups and subsidized by the city are also examples of youth services.

In the general area of health, the cities carry the responsibility for hospitals. Cities and *Länder* decide together whether and where and how to build. Once constructed with the help of the federal and *Land* governments, the hospital's personnel and administration become the responsibility of the city. In northern Germany the cities are also responsible for public health, providing for hygiene, prevention of epidemics, vaccinations, and the supervision of regulations concerning foodstuffs; in the South, these activities are the responsibility of health offices which are special state authorities.

Cities are responsible for disbursing federal and *Land* funds to housing firms and individuals for the purpose of constructing public housing, and they may themselves become active in building and operating public housing units. They also approve the applications and disburse funds for rent subsidies. They enforce building codes, which are similar in each *Land*. A very important activity of local government which is required by law is land-use planning and zoning. Land-use plans cover the entire city area except for federal property, for example, railways, and they serve as important instruments for center city development programs.

Another traditional responsibility of the cities is the construction of streets, bridges, and canals, and the construction and maintenance of sewage disposal facilities. Trash disposal and street maintenance services, like sewage disposal, are city activities that are financed normally by user fees and assessment of property owners. Public utilities, that is, water, electricity, gas, and piped heat, are city responsibilities, but they are not always handled in the same manner. Special-purpose authorities (*Zweckverbände*) and to an even greater extent nonprofit corporations are common instruments in the provision of such services.

A network of public transportation facilities is found in all German cities. Not only busses but also streetcars and subway systems are common features of larger cities. Though highly subsidized, the transportation system is operated usually by a nonprofit private corporation.

Cities engage voluntarily in economic promotion activities designed to attract business to the city for the creation and retention of employment opportunities as well as for the additional revenue and purchasing power they represent for the city. Cities are engaged themselves in numerous economic activities, examples of which include airports, exhibition and convention halls, restaurants that are located in such facilities, and local savings banks.

Finally, like most cities elsewhere, German cities are responsible for the city forests, parks, gardens and cemeteries. In addition, German cities rent to the public small plots of land for the purpose of vegetable and flower gardening and weekend leisure activities. Large colonies of such garden plots, most of which have small cabins and patios, can be seen on the outskirts of most German cities. Foreign observers occasionally mistake these for the modest homes of low-income persons.

Land-Use Planning and Zoning

In part as a negative reaction to the planned economies of Eastern Europe, German public authorities did not engage in systematic planning until the mid-1960s. By the late 1960s and early 1970s, however, attitudes toward planning had changed dramatically, and self-confident planners appeared to have convinced themselves and many others that it was not only desirable but also possible to direct and control economic, social, and political developments at all levels through rational planning procedures.[41] Today a far more sober view prevails.[42] It has become clear that many past assumptions on which plans were based were incorrect and that even the best data can prove to be inadequate for future projections. Population decline, economic stagnation and recession, structural changes in the economy, and the growing problems associated with a large foreign population have made a mockery of some of the best plans of a decade ago.[43]

Nevertheless, there appears to be a consensus in Germany today that planning is necessary.[44] What is less clear is how much planning is possible at each level, to what extent fundamental planning goals may be in conflict, how planning in different functional and geographic areas at different levels is to be coordinated and conflicts resolved, and whether certain planning procedures and goals will weaken federalism and local self-government in the long run.

Federal planning. The Federal Land-Use Law (*Bundes-Raumordnungsgesetz* —BROG) was passed in 1965, and shortly thereafter was supplemented in all of the *Länder* by *Land* planning laws. The BROG was conceived as an organizational framework for land-use (*räumliche*) planning at all levels, including local governments. The BROG requires that local governments adapt their plans to land-use principles and plans for the surrounding area as determined in the *Land* regional plans. Local planning is also regulated to some extent by the Federal Construction Law (*Bundesbaugesetz*) of 1960 and 1976. In spite of these two important federal laws, the role of the federal government in the planning process remains limited generally to planning coordination among government levels, whereas the actual conception and administration of land-use planning is the responsibility of the *Länder*. Since 1975 the federal government, with only limited success, has attempted to come up with an integrated development framework plan for the federal and *Land* levels that would promote "equivalent living conditions" throughout the country (article 72, paragraph 2, and article 106, paragraph 3, of the Basic Law) while maintaining environmental standards. For this purpose the territory of the Federal Republic has been divided into thirty-eight "territorial units."[45]

The responsibility for federal planning was taken from the Ministry of the Interior in 1973 and given to the Ministry for Planning, Construction and City Development. This ministry has little authority to implement rules and regulations; rather, it is involved in collecting data, providing information, engaging in research, and persuading others to take or desist from certain actions. Due to the actual weakness of this federal ministry in enforcing or implementing planning decisions, it is not unfair to assume that land-use planning is of limited importance at the federal level.[46]

Land planning. At the *Land* level a distinction is made between planning for the *Land* as a whole (*Landesplanung*) and for a part of the *Land* (*Regional-*

planung).⁴⁷ While planning laws among the *Länder* differ, they all call for *Land* development plans or programs which contain information about areas that are below the federal average in a number of respects, categories for land-use planning, and directives concerning fundamental measures that should be taken in order to meet the goals of land-use planning. Coordination among the *Länder* and between these and the federal government is secured at least in large part via a planning conference consisting of the responsible federal and *Land* planning ministers. The success of these general land-use plans depends to a considerable extent on the ability of the *Land* planning agencies to defend their planning concepts against the demands of the functional ministries and agencies. Since the latter are responsible generally for execution of specific measures with planning relevance, the *Land* planning agencies are said to suffer from a certain "implementation deficit."

The difficulties of integrating areal and functional considerations is reflected in the organizational structures of *Land* planning agencies. Thus in some *Länder*, *Land* planning is the responsibility of the Office of the Minister-President (*Staatskanzlei*); in others it is located in a ministry, usually the Ministry of Interior; in still other *Länder* there is a special planning ministry. Each alternative is designed to strengthen the planners against the functional ministries.

Regionalplanung, which is required by the BROG, is designed to provide more detailed information concerning land-use, functional needs, and cost estimates for a particular region or area of the *Land*. This detail is needed not only by the *Land* planning agencies but also by the local governments. The responsibility for regional planning varies among the *Länder*: in four *Länder* it is shared by the local governments and state authorities; in the two smallest *Länder* it is a state function; in one *Land* it is shared among several counties; in Lower Saxony responsibility for regional planning lies with the individual counties. In part as a result of these different structures, regional plans can vary considerably among the *Länder* in their coverage and detail. What they appear to share in common is a lack of power behind them to impose a regional perspective, especially given the increased temptation on the part of local governments to pursue a strategy of self-interest in a time of economic stagnation or even decline.⁴⁸

Local government planning. Land-use planning at the local level is called *Bauleitplanung*. Local planning is made obligatory by the Federal Construction Law, but as a local government function it is carried out by local governments "on their own responsibility." Indeed, local planning is a core area protected by article 28 of the Basic Law.⁴⁹

Bauleitplanung consists of two sets of plans. The *Flächennutzungsplan*, or, literally, land area-use plan, is the general plan for the entire municipal area. It serves as a basis and framework for the *Bebauungspläne*, the specific zoning and building plans for the various parts of the municipality. Only the more specific *Bebauungspläne* are legally binding on public and private persons. The Federal Construction Law requires that both kinds of plans in local *Bauleitplanung* consider a number of factors in the planning formulation process,[50] but these are general enough to give the local governments some room for interpretation.

The larger municipalities may engage also in "development planning" which attempts to integrate land-use planning with functional planning. In part because of the differences between plan expectations and actual developments which many cities have experienced, such development planning does not appear to be an important activity in most cities today.[51]

Federal law requires that the *Bauleitpläne* must be accommodated to the planning goals of the *Land*. This can, of course, lead to conflict, since local, regional and *Land* planners are looking at the same territory. In legal terms conflict can and does occur on the one hand over the guarantee of local self-government and on the other hand over the constitutional requirement of the socially just state to promote to the extent possible "equivalent living conditions" in the country. One means of coming closer to the latter goal is, of course, through a planning process that binds local governments.

That *Land* plans can place limitations on local governments is clear; however, a distinction needs to be made between the municipal-wide *Flächennutzungsplanung* and the specific *Bebauungsplanung*. The latter belongs to the core area of local government and cannot be removed by a simple law. For the *Bauleitplanung* in general it can be said that *Land* plans can provide only framework goals which leave the local governments as much room as possible for developing their own plans. The goal of the state to promote equivalent living conditions is in principle no higher—some would argue that in fact it is lower[52]—than the right of local self-government, and *Land* plans can supersede local plans only if it can be demonstrated that there is an urgent federal or *Land* interest at stake. Even then the local governments must be given an opportunity to be heard by higher planning authorities.[53]

Local government *Bauleitplanung* must be coordinated not only with regional and *Land* plans but also with the specific plans of functional authorities for activities such as highways, hospitals, schools, adult education centers, power plants, etc. "Joint task" (*Gemeinschaftsaufgaben*) planning, especially between the federal and *Land* governments, for regional economic development, agricultural development, and university facilities construction, are additional examples of functional planning that may affect local governments. On the other hand the local governments that are affected by these plans have a right to be heard in the functional planning process, and recent court decisions have made it clear that this right is not a mere formality.[54]

Planning and recent local government reforms in Germany are closely related.

The initial proposals for local reforms were motivated in large part by planning considerations, and the trend toward increased planning and the local government reform movement took place together in the 1960s and early 1970s. It can be argued that only because of the territorial reforms are the local governments in a relatively strong position in the total planning process—federal, *Land*, regional and local—which, in effect, covers the entire area of the Federal Republic. Having been enlarged and placed in a better position to assume planning reponsibilities, local governments have been able to make a more convincing case than before that they deserve to be protected against attempts by the state to interfere in their own plans, organization and activities.[55]

Local government planning is complicated, however, not only by the need to reach an accommodation with higher-level land-use and functional planners but also with the citizens who are affected directly by the municipal *Bauleitplanung*. Local planning procedures are regulated in considerable detail by the Federal Construction Law. The plan draft must be coordinated with other public authorities and with neighboring municipalities, and public hearings must be held to enable public participation at an early stage of plan formulation. Once the plan has been formulated, it must be approved by the district officer or chief county administrative officer. The plan is then placed on public display as it goes into effect. In addition to public hearings, citizens may challenge *Flächennutzungspläne*, and, especially, the more specific *Bebauungspläne*, in the administrative courts. In the 1970s the federal law was changed to allow the municipality to make specific changes resulting from challenges which before had led to a rejection of the entire plan.[56]

Conclusion

In the German spatial-federal system, public administration is the primary responsibility of the *Länder*. While the federation has a number of functionally organized services and authorities, only a few of these have their own field agencies down to the local level. The *Länder* have more functional bureaucracies than the federation, and some *Land* special authorities—varying in number and kind among the *Länder*—can be found at the local level. Certain state functions also are carried out by lower state administrative authorities in the counties of seven of the eight territorial *Länder*, but the largest proportion of state tasks is delegated to the counties and county-free independent cities for these to administer according to instructions under *Land* supervision. Therefore local governments, not the *Land* governments, are the most important instruments of state administration.

Local governments are not, however, mere agents of higher authorities. They administer "on their own responsibility all affairs of the local community within the framework of the law." Affairs of the local community—local government functions—can be tasks made obligatory by the *Länder* or functions assumed voluntarily by the local governments on the basis of their general competence (*Allzuständigkeit*).

While both counties and their constituent municipalities are local governments (*Kommunen*), a further distribution of functions is made between these two levels of local government. In seven of the eight territorial *Länder*, there is a lower state administrative authority "borrowed" by the *Land* for the purpose of carrying out certain state functions, such as the supervision of the municipalities of the county. Most state functions, however, are delegated or made obligatory with instructions from supervisory authorities to the county administrations. While some of these may be delegated further to the municipalities, most are retained by the county for execution. On the other hand, the municipalities carry the major responsibility for most local government functions, both those that are obligatory without instructions from supervisory authorities (though regulated by law) and those that are voluntary.

The county-free cities in the Federal Republic (excepting those in Hesse) and the counties in Lower Saxony differ from the counties in the other seven *Länder* in that they do not have lower state administrative authorities. Rather, they administer state tasks as delegated functions. Only a very rough analogy exists between the cities and counties in the distribution of tasks between the city and its districts (which are not protected by article 28) and the county and its municipalities (which are protected). In the case of the cities it is generally the city council, rather than *Land* law, that determines task distribution. Nor does the chief administrative officer of the city have any supervisory responsibilities that conform to the supervision of county chief administrative officers over the county's municipalities.

Whether the local governments are being undermined in their autonomy by the increasing delegation of state tasks, the continuing trend toward obligatory local government functions often accompanied by detailed regulations, limitations on local initiative by regional and *Land* planning goals, and the practice of "cooperative federalism" in general are questions that have generated considerable controversy in recent years. They have not been answered in this chapter, and we will have to return to them in the final chapters.

7
Local Government Finance

It has been noted on a number of occasions in previous chapters that article 28, paragraph 2, of the German Basic Law guarantees the municipalities and counties self-government within the law. Article 28 is silent, however, on the question of the financial foundation of local autonomy. Since local self-government could hardly exist without some degree of financial autonomy, the Basic Law does include the local governments in its financial provisions and ensures that they have adequate resources (from the perspective of the local governments, of course, their resources are never "adequate"). It is the *Länder*, however, that have the primary responsibility for their local governments, the revenues and expenditures of which are considered to be a part of *Land* finances. As a result there is no direct financial relationship between the federal government and local governments.

General Overview of Fiscal Relationships in the Federal Republic

In contrast to the Constitution of the United States, the German Basic Law contains an entire section devoted to the financing of federal, *Land* and local governments. Section X, articles 104a to 115, provides a detailed outline of fiscal responsibilities, respective tax sources, tax sharing among government levels, tax collection and administration, budgeting procedures, fiscal reporting and credit limits.

In general terms much of section X provides for a distribution of financial resources, and therefore of responsibilities, between the national government and *Land* governments, among *Land* governments, between *Land* governments and local governments, and among local governments. This is referred to in German as the system of *Finanzausgleich*, or fiscal equalization. Fiscal equalization in the Federal Republic is achieved by allocating certain taxes to each level of government;

by sharing the most important taxes; and through federal grants, state grants and assessments of municipalities for the fiscal support of the counties.

A financing system which would give each level of government its own separate tax resources would guarantee the most autonomy among the levels; however, such a system suffers from several disadvantages. It is hardly possible to assign taxes to different levels in such a manner that each has adequate revenues. It practically eliminates the possibility of economic regulation or planning. In its purest form revenue sources are tapped unevenly by the different levels, and the taxpayer must pay taxes to different levels at different rates, depending on location. Some taxes are also more sensitive to economic cycles than others, and reliance on a sensitive tax in a period of economic downturn can cause local governments severe stress and strain in meeting public obligations.[1]

An alternative model of financing is a shared system of taxation,[2] according to which each level has a claim on a certain proportion of the individual taxes collected. The tax yield can be distributed in a variety of ways, for example, on the basis of the contribution made by the various units of government, or on a principle of redistribution designed to overcome differences in local tax potential. In the first system the lower level raises the taxes and transfers a proportion to the next higher level. In the second system of "centralized tax administration,"[3] the central government raises the taxes and distributes them to lower levels by some formula, for example, one based on population. This system allows for a uniform, efficient, and productive tax policy, but it tends to reduce the autonomy of the local level.

Funds can be distributed under the centralized shared model of taxation with or without strings. If provided without strings, a formula for distribution must be found that considers both population and needs. On the other hand categorical grants with strings may be received by government units that are fiscally strong. Categorical grants tend to weaken the receiving unit's decision-making autonomy.

Most modern tax systems today are mixtures of these two basic models. In the Federal Republic certain taxes are reserved for each level; other taxes are shared among the national, *Land* and local levels according to proportions set by law; and still other taxes are shared through general-purpose or special-purpose grants. This system of vertical relationships is known as vertical fiscal equalization (*vertikaler Finanzausgleich*), and it is designed to distribute revenue among the three basic levels of administration according to their respective public service responsibilities. Thus the local level is supposed to be placed in a position to meet its local government obligations from the revenues received from its own separately assigned taxes and from its set proportion of important common taxes and to carry out delegated and obligatory functions with general purpose and categorical grants received from *Land* governments.[4]

In the Federal Republic fiscal equalization is seen not only as a means of sharing public service burdens but also of providing citizens everywhere with an equal level of public facilities and services, in spite of a federal structure and decentralized administration. The result is that the principle of equivalent living conditions contained in article 72, paragraph 2 (3) and article 106, paragraph 3 (2) and the guarantee of local self government contained in article 28, paragraph 2, can be and are in a state of tension and conflict. Much of the debate about regional and local government autonomy in federal systems everywhere revolves around this conflict.

Tax Resources in the German Federal System

The system of taxation in the Federal Republic is outlined in considerable detail in section X of the Basic Law.[5] During the 1950s and the 1960s a number of changes were made in the system, including the allocation in 1956 of the business tax (*Gewerbesteuer*) to municipalities. Dissatisfaction with the distribution of tax resources continued, however, and in 1969 a major reform of the tax system was introduced by a significant revision of the provisions of section X. The only modifications made since that time have been in the proportionate share of common taxes received by the federal, *Land* and local levels and in the elimination of the local payroll tax in 1979.

Separate taxes. The federal government has exclusive claim to the government monopolies for matches and brandy; customs duties, most of which are transferred to the European Common Market; consumer taxes (excluding those reserved for *Land* and local governments), such as tobacco, liquor, and gasoline taxes; transport taxes; taxes on stock market transactions and insurance; one-time wealth taxes for postwar burden-sharing payments; special supplementary income and corporation surtaxes; and taxes raised for the European Common Market. The *Länder* have the right to raise taxes on wealth and inheritance, automobiles, land acquisition, betting on races, and for the purpose of fire protection; they may also sponsor lotteries. Taxes on beer and gambling casinos also belong to the *Länder*. The most important tax for the municipalities is the business tax (*Gewerbesteuer*). Until 1969 it accounted for 85 percent of the total municipal revenue. Since 1969, however, 40 percent of the locally collected business tax has been transferred to the *Land* and federal governments (in return the municipalities received a share of the income tax, as described below), and now this tax makes up around 40 percent of local tax revenues. Other municipal taxes include the property tax on both urban (*Grundsteuer B*) and rural (*Grundsteuer A*) property (together with the business tax called the *Realsteuer*), local consumer or user taxes, depending on *Land* law, such as taxes on entertainment, non-alcoholic drinks, dogs, hunting and fishing, and licenses for the sale of beer. These latter taxes provide generally a very small proportion (3–5 percent) of municipal tax revenues. Fees collected for various services are important sources of income, but they are not taxes. In spite of their general authority to act (*Allzuständigkeit*) in matters of local concern, local governments do not have the right to raise taxes other than those provided by law.[6]

Common taxes. The federal government has exclusive jurisdiction over the monopolies (matches and brandy) and customs duties. It has concurrent powers over all other taxes; however, the *Land* governments are in fact responsible for the laws concerning traditional local taxes. Taxes shared by the different levels are regulated by the federal government, but they require the approval of the *Bundesrat* which represents the eleven *Länder*.

In contrast to the United States, it is a general principle of German tax law that two levels may not tax the same source of revenue (*Gleichartigkeitsverbot*). Instead, the German solution has been to provide for sharing the most important taxes among the levels of government (see especially article 106 of the Basic Law). These are the income, corporation and value-added (sales) taxes—together called *Gemeinschaftssteuern*—which account for more than two-thirds of the total tax revenues in the Federal Republic. Since January 1980 the municipalities have received 15 percent (from 1969–79, 14 percent) of the income taxes based on the total income tax payments made by their own local citizens. The remaining 85 percent of the income tax and all of the revenues from the corporation tax are divided equally between the *Land* and federal governments. Since the revenues from income and corporation taxes are dependent to a significant extent on economic conditions, the less sensitive value-added sales tax was added to the shared taxes in 1969 in order to provide an element of stability (the value-added tax was raised from 13 to 14 percent in 1983, and to 15 percent in 1986). In contrast to the provisions of article 106 concerning income and corporation taxes, there is no constitutional rule concerning the division of the value-added tax between the federal and *Land* governments. Instead, the proportion to be received by each level (as of 1986 the *Länder* will be given 35 percent) is set by federal law and reviewed annually to take account of federal and *Land* fiscal needs. As a result this tax has become the keystone of the system of vertical fiscal equalization.[7]

In the distribution of revenues from the value-added tax between the federal and *Land* governments, both levels have the constitutional right to have their necessary expenditures covered (article 106, paragraph 3). The scope of expenditures is to be ascertained from a long-range fiscal planning process; however, integrated planning has never been achieved, and the separate fiscal plans of the federal and *Land* governments have not made it easy to balance the revenue supply with the expenditure demands of the two levels. Needs of each level are also to be balanced so that taxpayers are not overly burdened due to regional differences in tax potential and in order to preserve the "unity of living conditions" throughout the country. In practice, of course, the distribution of value-added tax revenues between the federal and *Land* governments is a result of political compromise.

Although the business tax (*Gewerbesteuer*) is a municipal tax, about 40 percent of its proceeds are shared equally with the federal and *Land* governments. In addition to the business tax on capital and profits, many municipalities—especially in North-Rhine Westphalia—imposed a business payroll tax which was abolished by federal law in 1979. The loss of revenues from this tax was made up by increasing the municipal share of the income tax from 14 to 15 percent in 1980. The municipalities set their own business (and property) tax rates (*Hebesatz*) within a range permitted by *Land* law. Because the business tax is now shared with the *Land* and federal governments (all business tax revenues went to the municipalities between 1956 and 1969), it has become a part of the system of shared taxes, even though it is not considered to be a *Gemeinschaftssteuer*.

Federal Aid to the *Länder*

Special grants. In addition to changing the proportion of the value-added tax received by the federal and *Land* governments when there is a significant new development in the relationship between their revenues and expenditures, the federal government is obligated by article 106, paragraph 4, to provide the *Länder* with financial grants to compensate them for any loss of revenue or increase in expenditure brought about by federal law. These grants are to be made only for the purpose of meeting temporary burdens imposed by the federal government.[8] Furthermore, article 106, paragraph 8, requires the federal government to compensate the *Länder* and local governments for any special activities (for example, a census) or facilities (for example, military bases or research centers) which impose an unusual burden on these government units. Thus the city of Bonn receives federal compensation for the burdens imposed on it as the capital city of the Federal Republic.

"Joint tasks." One of the most important changes made in the Basic Law as a result of the finance reform of 1969 was the insertion of a new section (VIIIa) and two new articles (articles 91a and 91b) concerning "joint tasks" (*Gemeinschaftsaufgaben*) involving both the federal and *Land* governments. This section on joint tasks has legally formalized the system of "cooperative federalism" that now exists in the Federal Republic.

According to article 91a the federal government is to participate in the completion of certain *Land*-level functions when these are important for the public at large and when federal assistance is required in order to make improvements in living conditions. These functions include the expansion of old and the construction of new institutions of advanced education (not just universities) and university medical clinics; the improvement of regional economic structures; the improvement of agricultural structures; and the improvement of coastal protection measures. These provisions do not permit the federal government to interfere in the traditional *Land* responsibility for the internal structure, personnel, curricula or research activities of the advanced schools and universities, and the *Länder* remain responsible for the maintenance and upkeep of facilities once constructed with the assistance of the federal government. All federal laws regarding these joint tasks require the approval of the *Bundesrat*.

Article 91a provides also for a system of common framework planning of joint tasks. Federal law has implemented this provision by setting up planning committees of which representatives from the federal and *Land* executives are members. This reflects the view that planning is an executive function. Individual plans contain data concerning the projects to be supported and the estimated costs for the federal and *Land* levels. To the extent possible, these plans are to contain longer-range future projections as well as short-range initiatives. Plans are implemented by the *Länder*, which must approve any project carried out within their territory.

The federal government assumes responsibility for 50 percent of the expenditures for the construction of institutions of advanced education, university clinics, and improvements in the regional economic structure; it assumes at least half of the costs for agricultural and coastal improvements. The federal share of costs for joint tasks is the same for all *Länder*.[9]

Article 91b, the second of the two articles which deals with joint tasks, authorizes the federal and *Land* governments to cooperate in the promotion of facilities and activities involving scientific research. Unlike the provisions of article 91a, the proportionate share of costs between the two levels for scientific research is not regulated in article 91b.

Grants for delegated functions. According to article 104a, the federal and *Land* governments are responsible financially for their respective public tasks; however, if the federal government delegates certain tasks to the *Länder* for these to administer, the federal government must compensate the *Länder* for all nonadministrative costs. The federal government provides the funds for a number of distributive functions administered on its behalf by the *Länder* and their local governments, including compensation for maneuver damages, rent subsidies, home construction support, individual savings account subsidies, support for vocational training, and gasoline subsidies for agriculture. If the *Länder* are to carry at least 25–50 percent of the financial burden, approval by the *Bundesrat* is required. If the federal government is responsible for half or more of the costs, the activity becomes a delegated function (article 104a, paragraph 3).

Federal aid for investments. Since the *Land* and local governments are responsible for about 80 percent of all public investments, these can have considerable impact on the economy of the Federal Republic. Therefore the finance reform of 1969 gave the federal government the right to give aid to the *Land* and local governments for investment projects which are designed to counter a disturbance in the economic balance, to contribute to an equalization of economic differences in the federal territory, or to promote economic growth. Federal grants for investment purposes are program-oriented, and they are directed especially at important investment initiatives considered essential by the federal government but which could probably not be completed without federal assistance. The federal government may not itself assume responsibility for the program; the program and all costs which follow completion remain the responsibility of the *Land* or local government. Federal support for investments by local governments is given to these units through the *Länder*, not directly.[10] The American practice of direct aid to local governments is seen as a violation of *Land* autonomy.

Grants designed to counter a disturbance in the economic balance of an area are a means by which the federal government can influence economic developments by providing counter-cyclical aid. While not restricted to certain areas of investment, such grants must be directed at activities that will help to overcome an economic disturbance. Grants must also be limited to temporary measures.

The obligation that article 72, paragraph 2, and article 106, paragraph 3, place on the federal government to promote uniform living conditions is underlined further by article 104a, paragraph 4, which authorizes the federal government to aid the *Länder* in their efforts to equalize the economic potential of the regions of their territory. Fiscal equalization as described earlier is supposed to be the primary means by which this problem is handled. Federal grants are seen, however, as an important complementary device for aiding economically weaker regions, especially by promoting improvements in the infrastructure of such regions. The authorization which article 104a, paragraph 2, gives to the federal government to help equalize regional economic potential overlaps with the very similar authorization of article 91a, paragraph 1 (2), to participate in joint task projects for improvements in regional economic structures. Either authorization can be used as a basis for granting assistance, depending in part on the local circumstances.[11]

The right of the federal government to provide grants for investments that promote economic growth is a virtually open-ended authorization, since almost any investment can be interpreted as contributing to economic growth. In sharp contrast to the United States, however, federal grants for these various investment purposes have been focused on only a handful of areas. Throughout the 1970s the most important of these were urban development projects, municipal transportation, hospital, public housing and student dormitory construction.[12]

Fiscal Equalization among the *Länder*

Discussion of the German tax system up to this point has concentrated on the separate taxes of each administrative level, the common taxes shared by the three levels, and federal aid to the *Länder* and through these to the local governments. Since it is primarily this "vertical tax equalization" which provides the *Länder* with their share of the common taxes raised within their territories, inequities are inevitable due to the differences among regions within the Federal Republic in terms of economic development and potential. In order to ensure a more equitable distribution of tax revenues than vertical equalization alone can produce, a "horizontal tax equalization" among *Länder* and municipalities has been added as an important second keystone of the *Land* and local tax systems. A by-product of this form of equalization is the strengthening of *Land* and local autonomy vis-à-vis the federal government.

The Land *share of common taxes.* As noted in an earlier section, the *Länder* share equally with the federal government 85 percent of the personal income taxes, two-thirds of the value-added tax, and 40 percent of the business tax. The federal and *Land* governments receive half each of the corporation tax. With one exception the *Länder* retain their share of the above taxes from the revenues collected within their boundaries. Only in the case of the value-added tax is the *Land* proportion distributed largely (three-fourths) on the basis of population. One-fourth of the *Land* proportion of this tax is distributed according to financial need; however, these need-based funds are provided only up to the point at which the receiving *Land* has reached 92 percent of the average *Land* revenue per inhabitant.[13] If, after all of the equalization procedures have been effected, there are *Länder* that still need financial aid, the federal government may give additional grants from its share of the value-added tax. Only the *Länder* with below-average revenue receive such aid.

Fiscal equalization procedures among the Länder. Given the relatively large populations of the eight territorial *Länder* in the Federal Republic and the virtually uniform tax system, differences among the *Länder* in tax potential are small in comparison to the United States. In 1978, for example, the range in the ratio of tax potential was only 1.24 to 1.[14] Nevertheless, article 107, paragraph 2, of the Basic Law calls for the differences in revenue potential among the *Länder* to be "adequately equalized." The means by which equalization among the *Länder* is to be accomplished are contained in the Fiscal Equalization Law of 1969 (rev. 1977). This law provides for a calculation of *Land* fiscal potential, including the fiscal potential of its municipalities, together with the tax needs of both levels of government.[15]

The first goal of the fiscal equalization procedures among the *Länder* is to increase the tax need indicator of the deficit *Länder* to 92 percent of the average for all of the *Länder*. The remaining deficit of 8 percent is supplemented only up to 37.5 percent. Therefore, the actual equalization process provides an increase in revenue of deficit *Länder* to at least 95 percent of the average tax revenue of all *Länder*. For the surplus *Länder*, the surplus between 100 and 102 percent is disregarded, whereas 70 percent of the surplus between 102 and 110 percent and all of the surplus above 110 percent is contributed to the equalization fund. In 1978 the result of this equalization process was that the 1.24 to 1 range in the tax revenue potential was reduced to 1:1.07,[16] which means that actual differences among the *Länder* in their per capita revenues became insignificant after equalization was completed.

During the 1970s four surplus *Länder*—North-Rhine Westphalia, Baden-Württemberg, Hesse, and Hamburg—contributed roughly equal amounts to the equalization fund. Due to growing structural problems with its smoke-stack industries, North-Rhine Westphalia dropped out of this foursome in the 1980s, while Baden-Württemberg became the chief "paymaster." By the mid-1980s this economically dynamic state was furnishing more than two-thirds of the equalization funds, with Hesse and Hamburg sharing the remaining 30 percent at a 60:40 ratio. The result has been serious disenchantment with the fiscal equalization procedures, not only on the part of the three remaining surplus *Länder* but also on the part of *Länder* such as Bremen and the Saarland that are experiencing especially serious economic problems and receiving far too little aid.

Fiscal Equalization within the *Länder*

Land fiscal equalization goals and methods. Horizontal fiscal equalization takes place not only among the *Länder* but between the *Land* and its local governments. The concerns of the *Länder* in their equalization policies include the maintenance and strengthening of local self-government, the supplementation of local resources, the equalization of fiscal differences among municipalities, the consideration of structurally conditioned needs and the activation of the local government budgets for economic stabilization policies.[17]

While all of these goals are important, most attention in recent years has probably been focused on structural differences and needs within the *Länder*. The provisions of the Basic Law concerning "unity of living conditions" (article 72, paragraph 2 [3] and article 106, paragraph 3 [2]) have been used by all the

Länder as an authorization for creating a system of "central places," that is, larger towns or cities serving other municipalities in the area as centers of social services, economic institutions, recreation, culture, and general public administration. These central places can be categorized further by size and importance. Both *Land* categorical grants for infrastructure investments and the more general formula grants have been important sources of income for central places in recent years.[18] It might be noted at this point that some of the theories and assumptions of the public choice school in the United States are of limited relevance in a society that places so much attention on equality in the provision of public services.

In principle, *Land* equalization policies are simply a means of supplementing local government income. The manner in which this is done, however, is left up to each *Land*, which is legally responsible for its local governments. It can be argued that in spite of some differences, the fiscal equalization policies in all of the *Länder* represent a compromise between the goal of strengthening local government and the goal of reducing inequalities in the infrastructure and the public services which the local governments provide their citizens. Local governments with insufficient funds cannot maintain the autonomy guaranteed them by article 28, paragraph 2, of the Basic Law. On the other hand, too much *Land* influence or direction in the process of promoting equality can also weaken local autonomy.[19]

Fiscal equalization between Land *and local governments*. According to article 106, paragraph 7, of the Basic Law, the *Länder* are to provide their local governments with a certain percentage of their income from the common taxes. *Land* laws are also to determine whether and to what extent the *Land* taxes are to be shared with the localities. From 1970 to 1977 the *Länder* made available to their local governments one-third of their tax revenues for local government fiscal equalization (*kommunaler Finanzausgleich*). Since this equalization is a *Land* function, however, differences can and do exist concerning the amounts of *Land* revenues that are shared with local governments. In 1977, for example, Lower Saxony shared 37.8 percent of its tax revenue with its local governments, while the figure for the Saarland was only 27.7 percent. The per-person average for the fiscally stronger set of *Länder* was 506 DM, for the fiscally weaker *Länder* 490 DM.[20]

Given the different distribution of tasks in the eight territorial *Länder*, it is difficult to make comparative generalizations about the net effects of *Land* aid to German local governments. A study conducted in 1977 by officials in North-Rhine Westphalia showed that when the differences in tasks are considered, Lower Saxony provided aid amounting to almost 450 DM per person, while Bavaria provided less than 225 DM per person. When all forms of aid, federal and

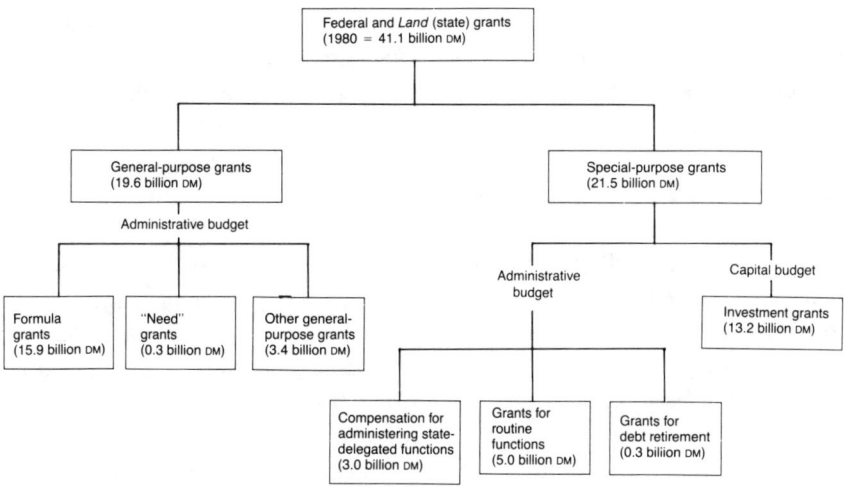

Figure 7.1. Distribution of federal and *Land* grants
Source: Bundesfinanzministerium, *Finanzbericht 1984*, 131.

Land, were considered, the fiscal ranking of the local governments by *Länder* was as follows: Lower Saxony, North-Rhine Westphalia, Saarland, Schleswig-Holstein, Bavaria, Rhineland-Palatinate, Baden-Württemberg, and Hesse. On the other hand, when all forms of aid plus net local tax revenues were taken into account, the ranking of local governments by *Land* in terms of their total financial resources was as follows: North-Rhine Westphalia, Baden-Württemberg, Lower Saxony, Hesse, Bavaria, Rhineland-Palatinate, Schleswig-Holstein, and Saarland.[21]

Forms of Land *aid to local governments.* In most of the *Länder* a distinction is made between two forms of aid: general-purpose formula grants and special categorical or project grants. Since the terms are not all the same in all of the *Länder*, Voigt has suggested that aid be divided into three general categories: general-purpose grants (*allgemeine Finanzzuweisungen*), special-purpose grants, and infrastructure investment grants (see figure 7.1).[22]

Most general-purpose grants are provided in the form of formula grants, distributed primarily on the basis of population; however, some general-purpose grants are provided on the basis of need. Formula grant proportions vary among the *Länder*, ranging in 1977 from about 55 percent of total aid in the Saarland to about 28 percent in Bavaria. The formula grants have the double purpose of providing all local governments with additional revenues—and are thus similar to American revenue-sharing and bloc grants—and of helping further to equalize revenues. Calculation formulas for meeting these twin purposes vary among the *Länder*, but the similarities are strong. In all *Länder* the tax potential of the municipalities is determined by adding the property taxes for urban and rural real estate, 60 percent of the business tax on profits and capital, and the municipal share of the income tax. The relatively insignificant municipal taxes on beverages, dogs, etc., are not considered. Differences, on the other hand, can be found among the *Länder* in the rates applied to various taxes for the measurement of tax potential.

Need for the formula grants to the local governments is calculated by adding population size (*Hauptsatz*) and special needs not met by population (*Nebensätze*), for example, compensation for being a "central place," for serving as a location in which foreign troops are stationed, or for being a health spa. Educational or social service needs may also be considered. It is interesting to note that the population factor in the formula is affected by municipal size in such a way that additional weight is given to higher size categories. Thus a municipality in Bavaria, for example, receives a weight of 100 percent for 3,000 inhabitants, 110 percent for 10,000 inhabitants, 125 percent for 25,000 inhabitants, etc., up to 150 percent for 500,000 inhabitants. The reasoning behind these progressive rates lies in the experience that the larger the municipality, the higher the costs of government per person. For the counties, on the other hand, a progressive increase is given on the basis of the number of small villages, since administrative costs in small units are also higher. The final calculation combines the *Hauptsatz* and the *Nebensatz* into the *Gesamtsteuer*, which then is multiplied by a basic sum (*Grundbetrag*) set annually by the *Land* parliament.[23]

Special-purpose grants are designed to finance all or part of certain functions. Special-purpose grants include grants that compensate the local government for carrying out delegated tasks, grants for direct transfer payments (for example, rent subsidies), and grants for certain functional areas, such as schools, welfare payments for those who do not qualify for unemployment compensation, war burden sharing, streets, and especially commuter transportation.[24]

Infrastructure investment grants, like project grants in the United States, are awarded on the basis of application from the local units of government. They do not normally cover all of the costs of the investment. They are frequently criticized for distorting the priorities of local governments and thus limiting to some extent local autonomy.[25]

Fiscal equalization within the counties. In contrast to the federal, *Land*, and municipal governments, the counties have few taxes of their own; indeed, only about 3 percent of their income is from their own tax sources.[26] They do not receive a share of the income tax or value-added sales tax as do the municipalities as a matter of constitutional right, nor do they participate in the business tax, real estate tax or the other municipal taxes. On the other hand article 106, paragraph 7, of the Basic Law requires the *Länder* to provide their municipalities *and* counties with a proportion of their income from the common taxes, the percentage to be determined by each *Land* parliament. In addition article 106, paragraph 8, requires the *Länder* to compensate their municipalities for any special burdens placed on them by *Land* law (nevertheless, the municipalities complain that *Land* compensation does not cover all costs).[27] For most of their revenue, then, the counties must rely on the formula grant, project grant, and infrastructure investment aid from the *Land*.

Another important source of income for the counties is the county assessment (*Kreisumlage*), which amounts to about one-third of the counties' revenue.[28] The county councils assess each municipality within the county a certain proportion of their income from the real-estate and business taxes (*Realsteuern*), from formula grants and from the income tax. The assessment rate—which the *Land* supervisory authorities must approve—depends on the needs of the county, which are determined largely on the basis of the number and intensity of county tasks. These in turn are affected by the number and size of municipalities within the county. The larger municipalities generally pay more in assessment costs than they receive in return, while the small villages receive more from the county than they pay. The effect is a rough equalization or fiscal strength among the county's municipalities.[29]

It is generally agreed that the county assessment may not exceed 50 percent of the municipal tax revenue, since a higher rate would undermine municipal autonomy. The methods used to calculate the average county assessment produce significantly varying results, but it can be said that in 1978 the municipalities paid an average nationally of about one-third of their tax income to the counties. These in turn were required to pay an assessment to the administrative districts (*Regierungsbezirke*).[30]

Conflict and tension over the county assessment tend to persist between the municipal and county councils for two general reasons. Since the larger municipalities generally pay more than they receive from the county in return, they are likely to feel that their assessments are too high. The increase in county functions in recent years and the concern shared by municipalities and counties that they have too few funds to meet their myriad needs have, of course, exacerbated somewhat the relations between these units of local government.[31] If the *Land* supervisory authorities—normally the *Bezirksregierungen*—approve the assessment rate, the only legal recourse remaining is for the municipal government to take its complaint to an administrative court; however, the administrative courts will disallow assessment rates only in extreme cases.[32] The municipalities would probably be more successful in the political arena, since most members of the rate-setting county council are also members of municipal councils.

A second area of controversy is the issue of county equalization aid to financially weak municipalities. Equalization is supposed to be accomplished in the county assessment process, and a second round of equalization by the county is said to undermine the autonomy of the recipient municipalities. Others point out that much of the county equalization aid is designed to help certain municipalities meet the costs of special projects, such as schools and streets. So long as the aid is designed only to meet special circumstances in individual counties, it should not be considered inappropriate.[33]

Trends and Controversies in Local Government Finance

The finance reform of 1969 created a system of financing that contained even more tax-sharing features than had existed before, thus making local governments less dependent on any one tax source and providing more stable and reliable income flows. In addition, measures providing for more equalization among the *Länder* and among local governments within the *Länder* were included in the constitutional and legislative changes brought about by the reform. A third element of the reform was a clarification and rationalization of the system of financial grants that had grown up since the 1950s without a clear constitutional basis. These changes were to make possible more and better financial planning for all levels of government, including counter-cyclical measures that would, for example, increase investments in periods of economic stagnation or decline. In the most general sense, of course, the finance reform of 1969 was supposed to meet the demands of the various associations representing local governments for a fair and efficient system of local government financing that would provide adequate revenues for active and progressive councils and administrations.

It is perhaps not surprising that the goals of the finance reform of 1969 have not been met in full. Revenues did increase, but expenditures increased even more. To some extent these expenditures were the result of the high and growing expectations of both citizens and local government officials regarding the quality and quantity of public services and facilities, expectations which are certainly higher than in the United States. In any case the reforms of 1969 have disappointed those who had hoped that the perennial problems of municipal finance had been solved. In another respect the reforms of 1969 have exacerbated the problem of local autonomy in the German federal system. The influence exercised indirectly by the federal government and directly by the *Länder* through special grant programs and "joint tasks" have led to a growing criticism of "cooperative federalism" as it is now being practiced in the Federal Republic.

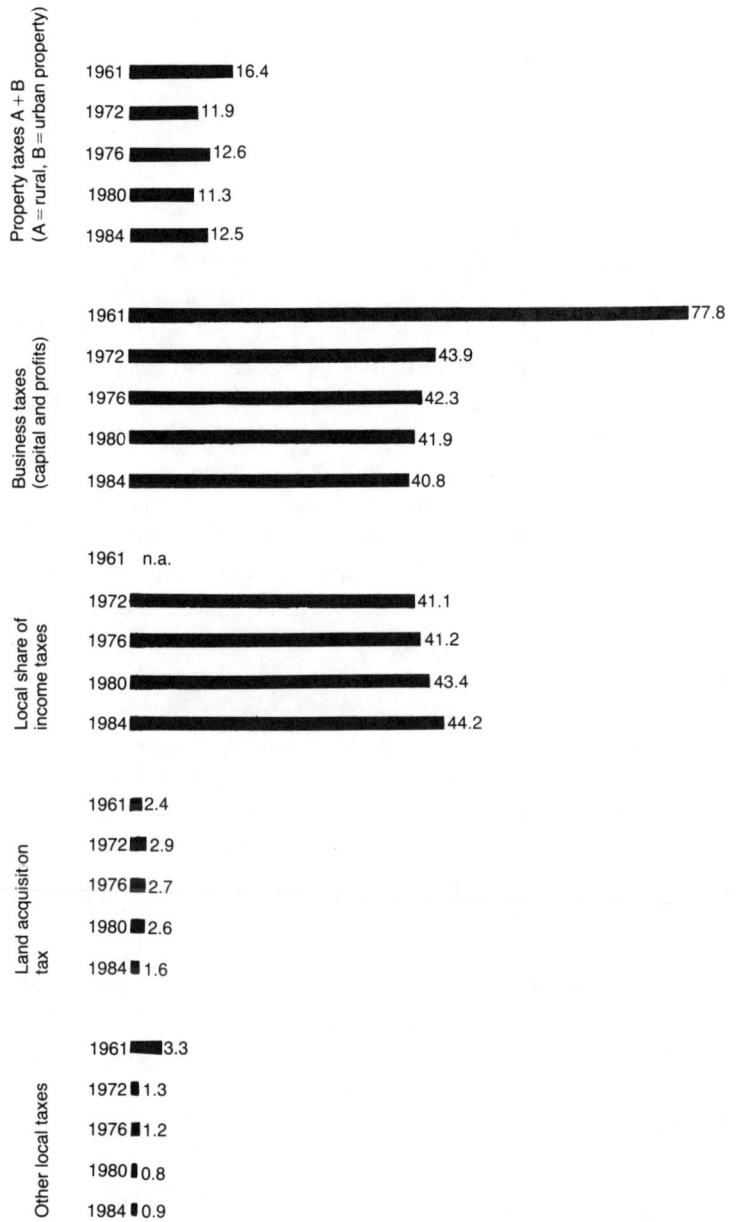

Figure 7.2. Make-up of local government tax revenues by source, 1961–1984 (in percent)

Source: Adapted from Hanna Karrenberg and Engelbert Münstermann, "Gemeinde-Finanzbericht 1984," Der Städtetag (February 1984): table 4b.

Trends and developments in local government income. From 1950 to 1984 the total income of German local governments increased more than 21 times. Nevertheless, the proportion of this income to total revenues for all levels has remained almost constant (for example, 1975 = 26.8 percent, 1982 = 26.4 percent). The proportion of local tax revenues to total tax revenues for all levels has not varied significantly over the years, either. In the 1960s the local tax proportion began to decline, for example, from 12 percent in 1962 to 11.1 percent in 1968. In the 1970s, following the finance reform of 1969, the proportion of local tax revenue increased from 12.3 percent in 1970 to 12.5 percent in 1975 and to a high of 13 percent in 1980. By 1982 it had declined to 12.4 percent.[34] Local tax revenue as a proportion of all local income has also varied only slightly, from 34.7 percent in 1950 to 33.6 percent in 1984.

The contributions to local tax revenues made by the various local tax sources are reflected in figure 7.2. As indicated in section II above, the major source of local tax revenue before the finance reform of 1969 was the business tax. Though sharply reduced, the business tax remained the most important single tax even after 1969 until 1979, when it was replaced in importance by the local share of the income tax. This shift can be explained in large part by the elimination in 1979 of the payroll tax as a part of the business tax and the increase in the local share of the income tax from 14 to 15 percent. The property taxes have varied only slightly since 1969, while other local taxes were declining until recently.

As noted above, the proportion of local government tax revenue to total tax revenues has declined in recent years, from 1977 to 1984 by about 0.6 percent. For the large cities, however, the decline has been from 5.9 to 5.0 percent, in part because of the process used for distributing the income tax.[35] This proportional reduction in local income is the result of several factors, including the effects on the income tax of the economy in general and lower wage and salary increases in particular, reduced revenues from the business taxes as a result of a weaker economy, and federal tax policies which have direct and indirect effects on local revenues. An example of federal tax policy is the Tax Reduction Act of 1984, which not only reduced the tax burden for business and individuals but also brought about or will bring about a loss of revenue for the local governments amounting to about 435 million DM in 1984 and to more than 700 million DM in 1985 and 1986. These losses take account of revenues received from the increase in 1983 of the local government share of the sales tax.[36]

Because economic conditions relevant to tax revenues vary by region and city, there are significant differences among the *Länder* in trends in tax revenues derived from the local share of the income tax and the business tax. In the latter case the local governments set the rates, but these, too, are influenced by general economic developments. Revenues from the business tax have declined about 8 percent between 1980 and 1984, with wide variations in the range.[37]

As shown in table 7.1, total income for local governments has increased only modestly in recent years, often failing to keep up with inflation. Since tax revenues were virtually stagnant from 1980 to 1984, federal and *Land* grants actually declined both in absolute numbers and in percentage from 1980 to 1983, and borrowing has been sharply reduced since 1982. In the meantime, local governments have been looking—like their American counterparts—at various fees as a means of collecting more revenue. In part because of the nature of newer services, fees have tended to increase over the decades; however, the most dramatic increases have been taking place since 1980. As shown in table 7.2, these recent increases still do not cover actual costs for services, and in many cases the subsidies continue to make up a dominant proportion of the expenditures. Since about one-fourth of the operating budget is made up of fees, increases in the fee structure can have an immediate effect on municipal revenues. Concern is now being expressed, however, that fees cannot be raised further without making the service prohibitively expensive for too many citizens. The alternative of discontinuing the service altogether is generally considered to be a measure of last resort at best, even though a few theaters, pools and nursery schools have been closed or hours sharply reduced. Turning the service over to the private sector is also done occasionally; for example, there are a number of cities that now provide private garbage collection, building clean-up, etc. On the other hand, there is serious opposition to privatization on ideological, political, legal and practical grounds, and it is safe to predict that the private sector will never become as important in Germany as in the United States in providing local services.

Reductions in *Land* financial grant programs have also had an adverse effect on local government finances (see table 7.1). The *Länder* have reduced their grants in the process of consolidating their finances. The local governments, however, complain that the *Länder* have made these reductions vis-à-vis the local governments since 1980 while actually increasing their own total expenditures; meanwhile, the local governments have been forced to consolidate their finances and cut total expenditures. Thus the *Länder* are accused of viewing their local governments as a kind of reserve fund for their own finances.[38]

As shown in table 7.1, local government borrowing has varied widely over the years. Local governments were in debt 34.6 billion DM in 1970, 67.7 billion DM in 1975, 86.9 billion DM in 1980 and 99.5 billion DM in 1982. This represents 617 DM per resident in 1970 and 1,732 DM per resident in 1982.[39] Indebtedness grew especially rapidly in the early 1960s and 1970s. In 1960 the municipal proportion of total public debt was 23.1 percent, and in 1973 it reached a high of 39 percent. In 1979 it had declined to 22.2 percent, as a result of even heavier federal and *Land* borrowing. Because of the need to invest more for reasons of their importance as "central places," large cities have borrowed more heavily

Table 7.1. Local government income (all municipalities and counties), 1950–1985

	Total		Taxes and other income	
	Billion DM	Percentage	Billion DM	Percentage
1950	7.2	100	2.5	34.7
1955	12.8	100	5.0	39.0
1961[a]	23.4	100	9.5	40.5
1965	34.7	100	11.8	34.2
1970	50.8	100	16.7	32.8
1975	92.2	100	30.3	32.9
1980	139.8	100	47.5	34.2
1981	141.5	100	46.1	32.5
1982	144.9	100	47.0	32.4
1983	150.6	100	49.4	32.8
1984	154.4	100	51.9	33.6
1984[c]	154.7	100	52.4	33.9
1985[c]	160.0	100	55.1	34.4

Sources: Statistisches Bundesamt, *Wirtschaft und Statistik 1982*, p. 32; Bundesfinanzministerium, *Finanzbericht 1984*, pp. 129, 132, 133 and 135; Hanns Karrenberg and Engelbert Münstermann, "Gemeindefinanzbericht 1984," *Der Städtetag* (February 1984): 84, 105.

than other local governments. Since borrowing is reviewed by supervisory authorities on the basis of revenue surpluses over expenditures for the administrative budget, it has been difficult for the cities and other local governments to invest counter-cyclically, as is frequently demanded of them. It seems doubtful that even without restrictions on borrowing, one could seriously expect the local governments to act in terms of national economic policy.[40]

Table 7.1 does not contain data concerning "other" sources of local government income. These include income derived from economic enterprises, interest, and other routine payments. Rental income and leasing of public property, for example, brought in 1.9 billion DM in 1980. In the same year profits from enterprises accounted for 500 million DM, and concession licenses for 2.3 billion DM. Other income was derived from the sale of land owned by the local governments and other capital transactions. These amounted to 4.3 billion DM in 1982.[41] Concerns are now being voiced that too much land is being sold by local governments to raise revenue, and that this will seriously handicap these governments in their efforts to plan future economic and residential development.[42]

Because of the continuing dissatisfaction expressed by the German associations of cities, towns and counties with the present state of local government finances, considerable discussion has taken place in recent years concerning new tax distribution formulae or new tax sources for local governments. One proposal

Table 7.1 (continued)

Fees and dues		Federal, Land- and municipal grants		Loans	
Billion DM	Percentage	Billion DM	Percentage	Billion DM	Percentage
0.9	13.0	2.1	28.8	—	
1.9	14.8	3.0	23.7	—	
3.5	15.0	5.9	25.4	—	
5.6	16.2	11.3	32.9	—	
9.4	18.2	15.5	29.8	6.0	11.8
16.8[b]	18.3	28.5[b]	30.9	12.4	13.4
25.9[b]	18.6	41.1[b]	29.5	9.9	7.1
27.7	19.6	41.7	29.5	13.0	9.2
30.0	20.6	41.0	28.3	14.3	9.9
32.5	21.5	40.2	26.7	12.2	8.1
33.6	21.8	41.5	26.9	10.5	6.8
33.7	21.8	41.0	26.5	10.2	6.6
34.7	21.7	43.1	26.9	10.0	6.3

a. The budget year was changed in 1960.
b. These figures are from the 1984 report of the BFM; they are significantly different from those in the 1982 report of the Statistisches Bundesamt.
c. Estimates from Hanns Karrenberg and Engelbert Münstermann, "Gemeindefinanzbericht 1985," *Der Städtetag* (February 1985):73, 112.

is to eliminate the business tax and raise the value-added tax (*Mehrwertsteuer*) by 2 or 3 percent. Another is to eliminate the business tax and to introduce a new local government tax on the value increases which result from almost all economic activities in the community (*Wertschöpfungssteuer*). In both cases the proposal calls for elimination of the business tax, because of the many exceptions made in its application (only about one-third of all businesses now pay the tax), the wide variations in revenue that it produces from year to year, and the uneven distribution of tax potential among the municipalities. One of the difficult questions which a possible reform of local taxes raises is whether local autonomy would be weakened or strengthened by the change.[43]

Trends and developments in local government expenditures. While revenues, grants and other income sources increased dramatically between 1950 and 1985, expenditures more than kept up with income. Local government expenditures accounted for 24 percent of all public expenditures in 1950, for 25 percent in 1975 and for 24.6 percent in 1982. Even in the best years—one might say especially in the best years—local governments borrowed large sums to cover the costs of investments (they are not allowed to borrow to meet expenditures from the administrative budget). With the assistance of investment grants from the *Länder* and indirectly from the federal government for joint tasks, their own

Table 7.2. Cost coverage of user fees for selected services and fee increases, 1982–1983

Service	Proportion of service costs covered by fees 1982	Proportion of service costs covered by fees 1983	User fees, 1983 (in percent)	Expenditures from budget 1982 (in percent)	Expenditure for service to total for all selected services (in percent)
Sewerage	83.4	85.1	+13.3	+11.0	42.3
Waste disposal	93.0	91.4	4.5	6.3	26.9
Retirement homes	74.3	75.6	7.8	5.8	8.9
Cemeteries	55.0	57.8	9.1	3.8	6.0
Street cleaning	59.2	63.2	10.4	3.5	4.4
Swimming pools	18.2	20.0	13.0	2.4	3.0
Theater	11.3	11.8	8.6	4.0	1.5
Slaughterhouses	52.4	52.5	0.2	0.0	2.3
Nursery schools	10.9	11.9	14.3	4.2	2.0
Music schools	25.5	27.0	12.4	6.2	1.5
Adult education centers	18.8	20.1	9.9	2.7	1.1
Libraries	1.1	1.9	19.3	3.6	0.0
Museums	8.1	8.7	11.0	3.0	0.2

Source: Hanns Karrenberg and Engelbert Münstermann, "Gemeindefinanzbericht 1984," Der Städtetag (February 1984):98.

funds and borrowing, local governments have accounted over the years for about two-thirds of all public investments in Germany. About 80 percent of these investments have been for the construction of streets, schools, sewerage facilities, hospitals, etc.[44] As table 7.3 shows, investments as a percentage of expenditures reached a peak around 1970, while the largest expenditures in amount were made in 1980. During this decade local investments more than doubled, increasing especially between 1977 and 1980. With the economic downturn of the 1980s, higher interest rates, reduced borrowing, and reduced Land grant aid for investments, investment activity has declined sharply. Indeed, by 1985 municipal investments reached their lowest level since 1963.[45]

Given the feverish construction activities of the 1960s and 1970s, combined with the implications of a sharp decline in the school-age population, some questions have been raised about the real need for much additional investment in terms of construction. Complaints can be heard that too many administrative buildings, schools, and, especially, swimming pools and convention centers, have been built too luxuriously and with too little thought given to maintenance costs. By international standards, it is doubtful that one can speak of an investment crisis in Germany; however, this is not to say that individual cities do not have serious problems in some areas or that investments in environmental protection and maintenance of existing facilities are not highly desirable. It should be noted also that another complaint which is made especially by young environmentalists is that far too much construction of new buildings and streets has destroyed numerous older buildings and formerly green areas.

As can be seen in table 7.3, dramatic increases in the number of personnel in the 1970s, higher pay scales, and inflation have made personnel costs, not investments, the greatest single item of expenditure for local governments. Given the current problems of local government finance, numerous positions have been eliminated in recent years; however, in contrast to a number of American cities, where large-scale lay-offs have taken place, personnel reductions in Germany have been made by nonreplacement and the elimination of positions. This, of course, has been an especially bitter measure to take at a time of high unemployment (around 9.0 percent in 1983 and 1984). Local governments in general, but especially the larger cities, had lower increases in personnel costs in 1983 than did the *Länder* and federal government, and the average annual increase in the period 1981–84 was only 2.3 percent, that is, a rate below inflation. The significance of this low average annual increase can be seen in comparisons with previous years, when the annual increase in personnel costs ranged from 20 percent in 1971 to 5 percent in 1976. A number of cities have actually reduced their personnel costs, in spite of numerous barriers to such reductions. These barriers include factors over which local governments have little control, such as the result of wage and salary negotiations with public service unions and the salary increases determined by the federal government for higher-level civil servants at all levels of government (*Beamte*).[46]

In other areas too, for example, in reductions of expenditures for materials, supplies, maintenance, and certain routine costs (*laufender Sachaufwand*), which increased above the average of other expenditures from 1975 to 1981, the local governments have been more successful than the *Länder* and the federal government. For some services, however, the local governments have had to absorb rising costs. Here the best example is social support services of various kinds. The most important cause of these increases is without doubt the high unemployment of the 1980s. Social welfare (*Sozialhilfe*) is the responsibility of the independent cities and counties, and social welfare payments are made to those who do not qualify for federal unemployment benefits (for example, unemployed teacher-candidates from the universities) or whose benefits have run out after one year of unemployment. Only by cutting in other social support areas over which the local governments have more control could even more dramatic increases in total social support expenditures be avoided.[47]

Local government finance and local government autonomy. The right of local governments to determine their own budgets is one of the core areas of self

Table 7.3. Local government expenditures (all municipalities and counties), 1950–1985

	Total		Personnel		Materials, supplies, maintenance, routine expenditures	
	Billion DM	Percentage	Billion DM	Percentage	Billion DM	Percentage
1950	7.4	100	2.1	28.4	2.0	27.0
1955	13.8	100	3.7	26.8	2.9	21.0
1961[a]	24.2	100	6.2	25.6	4.6	19.0
1965	39.0	100	9.2	23.6	6.8	17.4
1970	56.7	100	15.2	26.8	10.8	19.0
1975	101.2	100	30.4	30.0	16.1	15.9
1980	145.5	100	42.9	29.5	26.4	18.1
1981	152.5	100	45.8	30.8	28.2	18.5
1982	152.5	100	47.0	30.8	29.0	19.0
1983	151.6	100	48.0	31.7	29.0	19.1
1984	156.4	100	48.9	31.3	29.9	19.1
1984[b]	154.7	100	49.3	31.0	31.5	20.4
1985[b]	160.5	100	51.0	31.8	33.1	20.6

Source: See table 7.1.
a. The budget year was changed in 1960.

government protected by the Basic Law and *Land* constitutions. On the other hand the local governments are financed in a national system in which they share important tax revenues with other levels. Local governments have no major taxes over which they exercise complete control. Even the business tax, the rates for which are set by the municipalities, is now shared with the *Land* and federal governments.

More problematic is the responsibility of the *Länder* for the fiscal equalization that takes place within their borders. The *Länder* determine the total amount to be distributed, the distribution scheme among the county-free (independent) cities, counties, and municipalities that belong to the counties. They determine the range within which rates for the property and business taxes may be set, and they provide the funds for activities and services which they delegate to the local governments.[48]

Above all, however, there is the problem of federal "joint task" financing and *Land* special purpose grants and their effect on local government autonomy. The finance reform of 1969 was supposed to help clarify the responsibility for certain grant programs and to limit their effects on local autonomy. Instead, mixed financing (*Mischfinanzierung*) programs grew to the point that there are now very few functions for which some funds from a special grant are not available.[49] This increased sharing of responsibility for functions at the local level was promoted even more by the local government reforms of the 1960s and 1970s

Table 7.3 (continued)

Investments		Social services		Debt service	
Billion DM	Percentage	Billion DM	Percentage	Billion DM	Percentage
1.4	18.9	0.9	12.2	—	—
3.3	23.9	1.5	10.7	—	—
6.8	28.1	2.1	8.7	—	—
12.4	31.8	3.7	9.4	—	—
20.2	35.6	4.4	7.8	2.4	4.2
29.6	29.3	10.5	10.4	5.3	5.2
41.3	28.4	15.4	10.6	6.6	4.5
39.5	25.9	17.0	11.2	7.6	5.0
34.5	22.6	18.3	12.0	8.7	5.7
31.4	20.7	19.4	12.8	10.0	6.6
32.5	20.8	20.3	13.0	9.0	5.7
30.5	19.7	20.4	13.2	8.9	5.8
31.5	19.6	21.6	13.5	9.0	5.6

b. Estimates from Hanns Karrenberg and Engelbert Münstermann, "Gemeindefinanzbericht 1985," *Der Städtetag* (February 1985): 73, 112.

which were oriented strongly toward considerations of efficiency in the creation of larger units of local government. In the 1970s the view seemed to prevail that all levels should cooperate in implementing activities of common concern. *Land* legislatures also tended to interpret—some would say thoroughly misinterpret—those provisions of the Basic Law calling for "maintaining the equivalency of living conditions" by introducing numerous programs for which the *Land* and local governments could share the costs.[50]

Five federal grant programs provide for mixed financing among levels of government. Two of these programs, one of which deals with money transfers (for example, housing subsidies, savings bank account subsidies or occupational training), and the other, which deals with educational planning and research, have only a limited effect on local government autonomy. Of greater concern is a third block of joint tasks regarding the construction of higher-education facilities, regional economic structure, agricultural structure, and coastal protection measures. The *Länder* can hardly refuse the funds for these activities, yet the resultant binding effect on *Land* budgets is clear. Of more concern still is a fourth block, which provides funds for investments. These are used especially for urban development, transportation, and hospitals, but the general authorization contained in the provisions of the Basic Law for joint tasks permits much more federal involvement. Finally, a fifth "miscellaneous" block has emerged, which grants federal funds based on pragmatic considerations and unwritten authorizations derived from past practice. By the end of the 1970s more than 10 percent of the federal budget was designated for joint task financing.[51]

More problematic than all of the five federal blocks, however, are the special-purpose grants of the *Länder*. In 1981 in North-Rhine Westphalia, for example, there were 134 grant funds available to local governments for mixed financing purposes. Even the funds with small amounts of money carried with them provisions and regulations that interfered seriously with local autonomy.

By the end of the 1970s, *Land* grants of all kinds provided on a national average 30 percent of the revenues of local governments. One-half of these funds were from special-purpose grants which provide detailed instructions for their use. Special-purpose grants for investment have become so important that by the end of the 1970s North-Rhine Westphalia was able to control to some degree 60 percent of all local investments made within its borders.[52]

Criticism of the system of mixed financing is based on a number of considerations: the Basic Law provisions according to which each level of government is independent of the other in financial matters are weakened; local government autonomy is undermined, in part through the common interests of functional authorities to strengthen their relations at varying levels at the expense of the spatial-administrative organization of *Land* and local governments; decision-making is made less transparent; decision-making is made unnecessarily complicated and lengthy; establishing political responsibility is made difficult; maintenance costs for investments are not covered by grant assistance, thus placing a sometimes unanticipated burden on local governments; local priorities are manipulated by the availability of grant funds; and administrative and personnel costs are increased significantly by the red tape inherent in mixed financing schemes.[53]

Thus a finance reform in 1969 that was to provide for cooperation between the federal and *Land* governments in a few selected areas has been used as a device for introducing a system of cooperative federalism that threatens to turn the traditional spatial-federal system into a modified functional-federal system of intergovernmental relations along current American lines.

The question of local government finance, federal "joint task" funding support and *Land* grants-in-aid has become part of a broader discussion of German federalism today. It is a discussion with many parallels in the United States. It involves issues which ultimately go to the core of the question of the nature of modern federal systems. Because of its importance, we will return to this subject in a later chapter.

8

The Public Service and the Organization of Local Bureaucracies

As in so many other respects, German federalism differs significantly from the American model in the national rules and regulations that apply to local public servants and in the degree of uniformity in the administrative organization of local governments. National laws that regulate the training and status of higher-level civil servants in the cities and counties have a long tradition in Germany, and more recent rules affect even the number of leading civil servants that local governments may employ. On the other hand German local governments have a long tradition of selecting their own personnel and of exercising almost complete independence in the handling of middle- and lower-level public servants. While there are no national or *Land* rules requiring the local governments to adopt any standardized scheme of administrative organization, most of the larger units have accepted voluntarily a model of organization which has led to a considerable degree of uniformity among and within the *Länder*.

Public Servants at the Local Level

General. In 1980 there were about 4.4 million public servants in the Federal Republic, not including military personnel, in a working population of about 26,276,000 (including military). The public servants represented 16.8 percent of the working population and 19.2 percent of those not self-employed. Excluding both military and railroad personnel, the proportion of public employees to the total working population was 15.5 percent. As shown in table 8.1, the number of persons working actually declined from 1965 to 1980, due to a significant reduction in the number of self-employed persons and family operations. On the other hand the number of public servants increased by more than one million during the same period.

Of the 4.4 million public servants in 1980, 3.8 million were employed full

Table 8.1. Proportion of public servants to total working population, 1965–1980

Year	Total working population (in thousands)	Nonself-employed (in thousands)	Public service (in thousands)	Public servants As percent of total working population	As percent of nonself-employed
1965	26,887	21,758	3,351[a]	12.5	15.4
1970	26,668	22,246	3,644[a]	13.7	16.4
1975	25,810	22,014	4,184[a]	16.2	19.0
1980	26,276	22,960	4,418[a]	16.8	19.2
1980	26,276	22,960	4,078[b]	15.5	17.8

Source: Adapted from Statistisches Bundesamt, *Wirtschaft und Statistik* 12 (1982): 920.
a. Without military.
b. Without military *and* railroad employees.

time. Almost 4.2 million (95 percent) were in the direct (*unmittelbar*) public service, that is, the federal, *Land*, or local governments, federal railways, and postal/telephone/telegraph services. The largest component was employed by the *Länder* (1.82 million), followed by the local governments (1.2 million), the postal service (500,000), the railways (340,000), the federal government (330,000), and various special-purpose authorities (40,000). Only in the railway system has there been a decline in personnel between 1965 and 1980. The *Länder* increased their personnel by 60 percent, the local governments by 40 percent; the federal government employed only 13 percent more personnel in 1980 than in 1965. These trends are similar to developments in the United States during the same period.

Around 230,000 persons were employed in the indirect (*mittelbar*) public service in 1980. This area includes the Federal Labor (Employment/Unemployment) Office with 57,000 employees, the federal social insurance offices (77,000) and the *Land* social insurance offices (92,000). Other indirect public servants include those working in research centers and similar institutions.

About 70 percent of all public servants employed by the three levels of government are in the areas of education, political leadership and central administration, health and recreation, and public security and order. The largest increases in personnel since 1965 have been in the areas of education and health.

Most federal employees (54 percent) are in military administration, while about one-fourth (23 percent) are in the general area of political leadership and central administration. At the *Land* level most public servants are in education (47 percent). Political leadership and central administration (14 percent) and public security and order, mostly police (13 percent), follow in importance. At the local level public servants in health and recreation make up about 29 percent of the total, while 20 percent are employed in general administration.[1]

Table 8.2. *Beamten* categories, pay scales, and educational requirements

Category	Pay scale range	Educational requirements (degree)
Higher service (*Höherer Dienst*)	A13–B11	University
Intermediate[a] or executive service[b] (*Gehobener Dienst*)	A 9–A12	"Higher school" (*Oberschule/Gymnasium*)
Medium[a] or clerical[b] service (*Mittlerer Dienst*)	A 5–A 8	High school (*Realschule/Mittelschule*)
Lower[a] or basic[b] service (*Einfacher Dienst*)	A 1–A 4	Junior high school (*Hauptschule*)

Source: Adapted from David Southern, "Germany," in *Government and Administration in Western Europe*, ed. F. F. Ridley (Oxford: Martin Robertson and Co., 1979), 137.
a. The terms used by Renate Mayntz and Fritz W. Scharpf, *Policy-Making in the German Federal Bureaucracy* (New York: Elsevier, 1975), 51.
b. The terms used by Southern, "Germany," 137.

The classification of public servants. The public service (*öffentlicher Dienst*) in Germany consists of three general classes of employees: *Beamten, Angestellten* and *Arbeiter*. Since this classification scheme is different from that of English-speaking countries, a completely satisfactory translation of terms is difficult to make.

The first and generally most prestigious class of public servants are the *Beamte*, that is, "civil servants"[2] or "officials."[3] *Beamte* make up about 45 percent of the full-time public service employees, but this proportion is higher in the *Länder* (55 percent—most of whom are teachers), the federal railways (55 percent), and the postal/telephone/telegraph services (58 percent).[4] *Beamte* have been traditionally the backbone of German officialdom, and they have a special status with regard to the state. As explained by David Southern, "the official alone is entrusted with the exercise of sovereign powers of the state, enjoys a special position in public law, is required to have a special loyalty to the constitutional order, must obey orders from his service superior, cannot lawfully strike, and is entitled to non-contributory pension and social insurance rights. The official alone is subject to disciplinary law and claims which he has against his employer are referable to the Administrative Courts."[5] *Beamte* are divided into four categories, according to the degree of complexity and responsibility of the service performed (see table 8.2). Pay scales, annual salary increases, benefits, etc., are set by the federal government, sometimes after consulting with the civil servant union, the DBB—*Deutscher Beamten Bund*. Regardless of the quality of performance, a *Beamter* cannot generally be promoted from one category to the next without having completed certain educational requirements. In the past these requirements were quite rigid. Today they apply largely to *entrance* into the service; promotion to higher categories from ranks within the public service is not only possible now, it is becoming quite common.

The second class of public servants are the *Angestellten*, or salaried employees. This class makes up about 34 percent of all full-time public servants; however, their numbers and percentages have been growing over the years at the local level, where they make up about 52 percent of all local personnel.[6] Like the *Beamten*, *Angestellten* are represented by a powerful separate public employee union (DAG —*Deutsche Angestellten Gewerkschaft*). Unlike *Beamte*, however, they may strike, and salary and benefits are negotiated between representatives of the three levels of government and union officials. Though *Angestellte* are not divided into categories as are the *Beamte*, they do perform services and receive salaries that make them increasingly difficult to distinguish from most *Beamte*. Only *Beamte* in the higher service category (*höherer Dienst*) are a relatively distinct group, since these include professors, teachers, and upper-management-level officials.

The third class of public servants are the *Arbeiter*, or blue-collar workers, who make up about 21 percent of all full-time public servants. Their numbers are higher than average in the federal railways (42 percent) and postal/telephone/telegraph services (32 percent), and they are strongly represented at the local level (36 percent).[7] They are organized in a powerful union (ÖTV—*Öffentlicher Dienst, Transport und Verkehr*), which negotiates contracts with representatives delegated for the purpose by the local governments, and they have the right to strike.

Recruitment and training. As indicated above, there are certain educational requirements for entry-level positions in each of the *Beamten* categories, and there are certain educational requirements for *Angestellten* positions as well. For some positions, especially for workers, some degree of technical or occupational training is usually required. For *Beamte* of the higher service (*höherer Dienst*), the basic requirement is a university degree. A two-year preparatory service (*Vorbereitungsdienst*) is usually a prerequisite to official acceptance into the higher service. Law students, who must visit a variety of legal and administrative stations during their two-year apprenticeship or residency (*Referendarzeit*) between the first and second bar examinations, are considered to have met this prerequisite upon completion of the second bar examination. Lawyers, or, in the more general German sense, "jurists," are often said to have (or are accused of having) a monopoly in the higher service. This was a more accurate observation in the past than it is today. Jurists are more likely to be found in *general* administration, and therefore their numbers are higher at the federal and *Land* levels.[8] At the local level the proportion of jurists in the ranks of the *Beamten* is much smaller. In a study conducted in North-Rhine Westphalia in the early 1970s, jurists were found to represent only 14 percent of the *Beamte* in independent cities (35 percent were engineers and 31 percent had moved up through the ranks), 16 percent in towns belonging to the counties (where 60 percent had moved up from the ranks), and 22 percent in the counties (where 30 percent were engineers and 22 percent were in health professions). On the other hand jurists were in a large majority of the leading positions at all levels of government.[9] Another study in 1980 showed that in nine cities the proportion of jurists among all *Beamten* and *Angestellten* in the higher service ranks was only 6.5 percent. Jurists did make up almost half of the highest leadership positions, but they occupied only a little more than 5 percent of the second-level leadership positions.[10]

To the extent that jurists do continue to occupy a large proportion of leadership positions, the monopoly myth does have some basis; however, whether a legal education in the past or today was and is really the best preparation for leadership at the local level is a controversial question. Ernst Pappermann, a leading official of the influential German Association of Cities, argues that a legal education is and has been an excellent preparation for service with local governments. He notes, however, that jurists are now being challenged increasingly by those coming up from the intermediate (*gehobenen*) ranks, who today have completed not only a more practical and relevant training program (see below) but who also have had at least five years' experience on the job by the time a jurist takes his first appointment. Without a reform of the lengthy legal education system (few students complete the second and final bar examination before the age of 28), Pappermann sees a steady erosion of the position of the jurist in local government and, by implication, elsewhere in the public service.[11]

Training for the intermediate service (*gehobener Dienst*) has changed considerably in recent years from a kind of practical internship with formal instruction in schools of administration to an integrated program of instruction in theory and practice at newly established schools of public administration (*Fachhochschulen*). Candidates are selected from an increasingly large pool of applicants, 70–80 percent of whom today have the "higher" school degree (*Abitur*) required for admission to a university. According to Pappermann, there are now 10–20 applicants for each opening in North-Rhine Westphalia, a large majority of whom are graduates of the higher schools who have decided not to go on to a university. Those not accepted may enter the university and take up legal studies![12]

Those candidates who are accepted are simultaneously guaranteed a position in the intermediate service upon the successful completion of the training program. There are also some who transfer from the medium or clerical service ranks into the training program for the intermediate service. If they should fail, they would return to their previous position. For three years the candidates are in the paid preparatory service ranks, during which time they alternate between formal instruction in the *Fachhochschulen* and internships with various offices. Federal regulations require that at least 18 months of the instruction should be theoretical and 12 months practical training. The distribution of the remaining six months varies among the *Länder*.

There are, then, significant differences between the trainee for the intermediate service and the university student who might have aspirations to enter the higher service. The trainee is guaranteed a position, which today is a very important advantage over the large surplus of university graduates; he is already considered to be a temporary public servant and is paid; however, class attendance is mandatory, and he has little selection in the courses he takes.[13] Perhaps of more importance is the fact that the trainee will begin his public service three to six years before the university graduate. As indicated above, this may give him a crucial advantage over the university graduate—even the jurist—in future competition for higher service positions.

For the middle service (*mittlerer Dienst*), candidates are generally required to have a high school degree (*Realschule*). While in some respects (age of students), the *Realschule* is not quite comparable to an American high school, in terms of subject matter and demands made upon the students it is quite comparable to a general high school education (advanced courses for preparation for college would be found in the German *Oberschule/Gymnasium*; industrial arts and other vocational programs would follow completion of the *Hauptschule*). For the technical services at this level of the public service, vocational training is required. For the nontechnical service, the *Realschule* plus one and a half to two years of preparatory service, which includes 600–900 hours of instruction in theoretical and practical subjects, are required.[14]

For the *Angestellten*, the salaried employees who make up the largest proportion of local government public servants, there was no uniform training program in the various *Länder* until the federal government issued a set of regulations in 1979. Since that time a uniform three-year training program has been instituted, with the *Länder* having the right to design the program in the third year. The minimum requirement is a junior high school education (*Hauptschule*). The three years of training take place over a period of six half-years. Practical training in the first four half-years is followed by two half-years of more general subject-matter training. There are two major examinations, at midterm and at the end of the six years.[15]

Programs of continuing education and advanced training are offered for higher service *Beamten* at the national Post-Graduate School of Public Administration in Speyer, for example, and for *Beamten* and *Angestellten* within the various *Länder* at their schools of public administration. There is no uniformity among the *Länder* in their programs, however, and even within the *Länder* much appears to depend on the individual program director.[16]

Legal regulation. All laws concerning civil servants or officials (*Beamte*) in Germany are federal and *Land* laws (local government ordinances and regulations are not laws), and with few exceptions they apply to all *Beamte* at all levels of government. On the other hand *Personalhoheit*, the right to act autonomously in matters of personnel, is one of the rights enjoyed by local governments that belongs to the core of local self-government. How is this contradiction resolved in German law?

In the historical development of the concept of *Personalhoheit*, a distinction came to be made between "normative" and "administrative" aspects of local personnel management. Normative aspects are those concerning general decisions regarding civil service status, that is, career regulations, salary and benefits, and disciplinary procedures. These areas belong to the state, which today means especially the federal government. The administrative aspects concern the selection, appointment, placement, promotion, firing, etc., of personnel, and this area is reserved for local government decision-making. The state may exercise some influence in this area as well, but this is an exception to the rule. A recent example of such an exception was the requirement by the *Länder* that the enlarged local governments hire those personnel whose positions were lost due to the territorial and administrative reforms of the 1960s and 1970s.[17] An example of federal interference in this area is the recent regulation of the number of leading *Beamte* that the local governments may employ (see below). Nevertheless, since the ratio of *Beamten* to salaried employees and blue-collar workers is about 1:6 or 1:7 at the local level, it can be argued that federal or *Land* regulations concerning *Beamte* have only a limited effect on local autonomy.[18]

Local governments exercise more autonomous decision-making powers in dealing with the two non-civil servant classes of public servants. Salaries, wages and benefits are negotiated between separate public employee unions for salaried employees and workers and a local government employer association with headquarters in Cologne. As members of this association, individual local governments agree to accept the conditions met by the association's negotiating team, as approved by a representative assembly of member governments. The local government employer association maintains close contacts with the *Land* government employer association and with the federal government in its dealings with the public employee unions. But even here the *Länder* have laws ensuring that uniformity is maintained between local and *Land* levels in pay and benefits for salaried employees and blue-collar workers.[19]

In spite of the federal regulations concerning *Beamte*, there were some differences in pay scales and benefits among the *Länder* until 1978, when federal regulations approved by the *Bundesrat* were issued which brought about uniformity in the treatment of *Beamte* and established maximum proportions of *Beamte* for different classes of local governments. This uniformity was deemed necessary in order to prevent one local government or *Land* from attracting highly qualified personnel from financially weaker governments of the same size. It was also considered necessary to prevent municipalities from rewarding their local civil servants with unjustified promotions, thus bringing pressure on other local governments to escalate their promotions. The price paid for this uniformity was, of course, the loss of some local flexibility in personnel management.

The civil servants at the local level who carry the most responsibility and, as a result, enjoy the highest status, are the elected civil servants (*kommunale Wahlbeamte*). Election is generally by the local council, but it may be by popular vote in the case of the mayors in Bavaria and Baden-Württemberg. Civil servants elected by the councils include mayors in Schleswig-Holstein, Hesse, Rhineland-Palatinate, and the Saarland, the city and county managers in North-Rhine Westphalia and Lower Saxony, *Landräte* in all other *Länder*, and the department heads in the larger local governments. Local *Personalhoheit* is maintained, then, in the selection of these civil servants, in the decision whether to reelect after the set term of office (from six to twelve years) or, in unusual circumstances, in the right to fire them. On the other hand local governments are bound to rules that regulate pensions and other rights, even for those not rehired or fired. After five years of service, for example, an elected civil servant has the right to receive a pension at 35 percent of his salary. After twenty-four years, he receives 75 percent of his salary.[20]

Federal law sets the maximum pay scales for elected civil servants as a guide for the *Länder*. According to this law, the chief administrative officer may not be placed in a higher salary category than A 15 for cities of 10,000 or less, B 3 for cities with 10,000 to 30,000 population, B 6 for cities with 30,000 to 100,000 inhabitants, and B 9 for cities between 100,000 and 500,000. The few cities above 500,000 may set their own pay scales. The person second in rank to the chief administrative officer is placed one step below the chief officer, other elected civil servants at least two steps below. For the counties the pay scales are B 4 for 75,000 or less, B 5 for 75,000 to 150,000, B 6 for 150,000 to 300,000 and B 7 for counties with more than 300,000 inhabitants.[21] These pay scales are not to be considered the norm but rather the maximum. They are also to be applied only when the government unit actually approaches the upper size limit. Some allowances are made for special responsibilities or requirements of the office, resulting, for example, from the different forms of local government (*innere Verfassung*). Thus if a mayor or *Landrat* also chairs the local council, presides over a university city or health spa, etc., he may be moved up one rank in the pay scale.[22] As we saw above, federal law also sets entry conditions and training requirements for the far more numerous nonelected career civil servants (*Laufbahnbeamte*). Local governments are not restricted by federal rules in the number of career civil servants they may wish to hire; however, their pay scales are set by federal law.

The Organization of Local Bureaucracies

In addition to *Personalhoheit* the local governments also have *Organisationshoheit*, that is, the right to determine on their own responsibility the organizational structure of the local administration. This organizational structure is based on two plans, one which divides all local responsibilities into functional areas (*Aufgabengliederungsplan*) and one which organizes the functions according to administrative units (*Verwaltungsgliederungsplan*). Depending on the size of the administration and the number of units, there are one or two leadership levels responsible for supervising the various units of administration.

Though each local government could, in theory, have a separate organizational structure, most in fact have adopted voluntarily the model recommended by the *Kommunale Gemeinschaftsstelle für Verwaltungsvereinfachung* (KGSt), located in Cologne. This is a local government association dedicated to the simplification and improvement of local administration. The adoption of the model by about 700 local governments has probably made local organizational structures more uniform in the Federal Republic than in most other Western countries.[23]

The functional organization plan of the KGSt model is based on the assumption that the local government unit has a large population. Thus all of the potential functions that a local government might have are listed. There are 45 functional categories for cities and 38 for counties. Each category serves as the basis for an office (*Amt*). Generally in cities above 25,000 the offices are not supervised directly by the chief of administration but by intermediate, second-level area chiefs (*Dezernatsleiter*), who, like the chief, are elected civil servants (*Wahlbeamte*).[24]

The administrative organization plan establishes the units of administration that are responsible for carrying out the local governments' functions. In the process it also sets the internal and external lines of responsibility. In every plan the highest level (*Chefebene*) is occupied by the chief of administration, who, depending on the *Land*, will be a mayor or town or city manager in the municipalities and a *Landrat* or county manager in the counties. If justified by population size, a second level of leadership (*Dezernate, Referate*) is created; however, the number and nature of the positions at this level are not the result of administrative principles alone. They may be based in part also on political relationships and the interests of the civil servants involved.[25]

Some of the administrative principles that are assumed in the model are that for each local government the number of offices should be as few as possible and as large as possible. When an office becomes unwieldy or difficult to control, it should be divided. In the model (table 8.3) the office (*Amt*) is the third level, but in practice an office may be further subdivided.

The model divides cities and counties by population size, for example, Class I

Table 8.3. Administrative organizational plan of the KGSt for municipalities

1 General administration	2 Financial administration	3 Law, security and public order administration	4 Schools and culture administration
10 Main office	20 Treasurer	30 Legal office	40 School administration office
11 Personnel office	21 Payments	31 (not occupied)	41 Cultural affairs office
12 Statistical office	22 Taxes	32 Public order office	42 Library
13 Press office	23 Real estate office	33 Resident registry office	43 Adult education
14 Accounting office	24 Office for defense burdens	34 Marriage office	44 Music school
		35 Insurance office	45 Museum
		36 (not occupied)	46 Theater
		37 Fire protection	47 Archives
		38 Civilian defense office	

Source: Hans Hack, "Die institutionelle Organisation/Aufbauorganisation," in *Handbuch der kommunalen Wissenschaft und Praxis,* vol. 3: *Kommunale Aufgaben und Instrumente der Aufgabenerfüllung,* 2d ed., ed. Günter Püttner (Berlin and Heidelberg: Springer-Verlag, 1983), 113.

cities have more than 400,000 residents, Class 6 cities have from 10,000 to 25,000. Class 1 counties are larger than 250,000, Class 4 counties 100,000 or less. The model recommends a certain number of offices for each class, for example, 44 for Class 1 and 2 cities, 11 offices for Class 6 cities. As a result German cities of similar size should have not only a similar administrative organization but also a similar number of leading officials, in spite of the four different forms of local government found in the German territorial *Länder* and described in chapter 5.

Conclusion

In sharp contrast to the United States, the German civil service is educated, trained, organized, and paid according to generally uniform standards. The higher-level civil servants, including those that work for *Land* and local governments, are subject to federal regulation, including pay scales, and they may not strike. Public servants of medium and lower grades are represented by strong national unions that negotiate their salaries, wages, and working conditions with representa-

Table 8.3 (continued)

5 Social, youth and health administration	6 Buildings and grounds administration	7 Administration of public enterprises	8 Administration for economic and transportation activities
50 Social welfare 51 Youth office 52 Sports office 53 Health office 54 Hospitals 55 Equalization of burdens office	60 Building administration office 61 City planning office 62 Survey and land registry office 63 Building codes office 64 Home construction promotion office 65 Building construction office 66 Civil engineering office 67 Park and garden office	70 Sanitation office 71 Slaughterhouse 72 Marketplace office	80 Office for the promotion of economic and transportation activities 81 City-owned enterprises 82 Forestry office

Note: The single-digit numbers indicate the areas of municipal administration; the double-digit numbers indicate the offices under each area.

tives of the three levels of government or with an association of local government representatives, respectively. Both of these public service grades are allowed to strike.

In spite of the federal role in regulating important aspects of the public service, local governments do retain the crucial rights of hiring and firing their employees, and the *Länder* have some flexibility in the development of training programs for the medium- and lower-level public employees.

The German civil service, like that of several other continental European countries, has long enjoyed a reputation for honest and efficient administration. Until the emergence of the Third Reich, it could even be said that there was a strong identity and even interchangeability among conservative social, political, and administrative elites at all levels of government. While key bureaucrats are still influential at the national, *Land*, and local levels, their powers have been eclipsed to a significant extent by the political parties, the focus of the next chapter. This change of status has been brought about by the fact that since the establishment of the Federal Republic, key bureaucrats assume and not infrequently lose their positions as a result of majority party or majority coalition decisions. Today top civil servants can hardly be associated with any one political party or philosophy or social group; rather, they are identified with and in some cases even dependent on the dominant party or parties in the particular jurisdiction in which they operate.

9

Local Councillors, Parties, and Elections

From the material presented in the previous chapters, it is clear that there are a significant number of differences between Germany and the United States in the history, theory, structures, financing, and personnel policies of local government. It might be argued that in spite of these numerous differences, one should expect to find similarities in the political process at the local level in Germany and the United States or Great Britain. After all, these are all Western democratic societies whose local governments share a number of common problems. While evidence can be found to support this thesis, this chapter will demonstrate that in many important respects local politics in Germany is very different from local politics both in the United States and Great Britain. It differs from these two countries especially in the system of party patronage politics for key local government administrators which has developed since the 1950s and in the comparatively complex and sophisticated electoral systems found in the various *Länder*. Local politics in Germany stands also in sharp contrast to the American model in terms of a significantly higher electoral participation and in the dominance that the political parties now enjoy in most German local governments. In some respects the local political process in the United States resembles more the German situation before World War I, which is particularly ironic, given the fact that German local governments have been eager to adopt American public management and data-processing techniques because of the view that American local government is a model of modern public administration.

Local Councils and Councillors

The councils and local decision-making. The system of representation at the local level in the various *Länder* is generally quite uniform, but there are a number of differences: in the electoral system used to select local councillors, in the forms of local government (see chapter 5), in the terminology used to describe the chief administrative officer, the council and key officials, and in the length of terms of office for local councillors. For example, Bremen, Hesse, and Schleswig-Holstein have four-year terms, Bavaria a six-year term, and all other *Länder* have five-year terms for municipal and county councillors.

One of the common features of local government law in the *Länder* is the distribution of council seats according to population size. In the *Land* of Hesse, for example, the councils of municipalities with up to 3,000 inhabitants have 15 seats, councils in the municipalities with between 3,001 and 5,000 have 23 seats, etc. (see table 9.1). Council seats in the counties are distributed also by population size. With the territorial reforms of the 1960s and 1970s, the number of local councillors was reduced by 39 percent from 237,304 to 145,646.[1] In spite of these reductions, the proportion of local councillors to population is still much higher in Germany than, for example, in the United States.

Except for the smaller villages, where a division of labor is not usually required by the workload, most councils are divided into committees. Most of the real work of the council is done in these committees and in the *Fraktionen*, the party groups. By the time the public council meeting is held, the important decisions have been made before the council ratifies them. As a result visits to a local council meeting may provide a very incomplete picture of the local political process.

As at the *Land* and national levels in Germany and in other Western democracies, the local representative body, the council, is not a major source of legislative or administrative initiatives. The administration, and more specifically, the key elected professional administrators (*Wahlbeamte*), are largely responsible for initiating actions of various kinds. The next most important source of initiatives is the *Fraktion*, the party group. Even if a councillor is an independent, he and others like him will probably have to form a nonparty *Fraktion*, and he will normally have to persuade his *Fraktion* colleagues to go along with him if he wants to introduce a proposal of any kind. Without *Fraktion* approval, a measure usually has little if any chance of being taken seriously. But even when a *Fraktion* introduces a proposal that requires action, the details will probably be prepared by the administration.[2]

Local government law in all of the *Länder* gives the chief of administration the responsibility for preparing the decisions of council in such a manner that alternatives are offered and a vote can be taken on the measure. While the chief is legally responsible for such preparations and for other administrative initiatives in general, other key elected officials (*Dezernenten*) may have done most of the actual work. Nonelected career officials below the *Dezernenten* may also have contributed to the administrative decision-making process, so that in fact it is not just the chief who deter-

Table 9.1. Proportion of council seats to population in the municipalities and counties of Hesse

Population	Council seats
Municipalities	
3,000 or less	15
3,001 to 5,000	23
5,001 to 10,000	31
10,001 to 25,000	37
25,001 to 50,000	45
50,001 to 100,000	59
100,001 to 250,000	71
250,001 to 500,000	81
500,001 to 1,000,000	93
More than 1,000,000	105
Counties	
100,000 or less	51
100,001 to 150,000	61
150,001 to 200,000	71
200,001 to 300,000	81
300,001 to 400,000	87
More than 400,000	93

Source: Paragraph 38, Hessische Gemeindeordnung (HGO), 1960, revised 4 July 1980; paragraph 25, Hessische Landkreisordnung (HKO), 1960, revised 4 July 1980.

mines in every detail the direction and quality of the administration's efforts.

Once the administrative decision-making process is completed, the proposal goes to a committee composed of councillors designated as committee members by their *Fraktionen*. Depending on its importance, the initiative may be discussed in the *Fraktion* even before it reaches the committee; it most certainly will be considered by the *Fraktion* before it reaches the council. Sometimes non-council members who are considered to be citizen experts are also brought into committee meetings. Independents who do not join any *Fraktion*, which even a nonparty "voter group" (*Wählergruppe*) may form, may find themselves excluded from the committees altogether. If there is conflict between or even within the *Fraktionen*, a compromise is usually reached before the regular council meeting. Serious conflict in committees appears to be rare, however, because in most *Länder* the committee meetings are not open to the public and compromise is relatively easy to achieve, and in part also because of the advantages of information and expertise enjoyed by the administration, which probably introduced the initiative. In smaller villages, where there is less committee activity—and therefore less expertise—and perhaps more discussion in council, the administration enjoys even more advantages over the councillors.[3]

Not only is the position of the chief of administration strong vis-à-vis the council because of the fact that he introduces most initiatives, prepares council decisions, enjoys advantages of information and expertise, and implements council decisions. He also serves for a term of office longer than and not synchronized with the term of office of the councillors. In most local government *Land*-wide charter laws, the chief of administration may be removed from office only by a two-thirds vote if at all, with the recalled official receiving his salary until his term expires. Even if he is not reelected when his regular term expires, he receives a pension, the size of which depends on the years of service. In Baden-Württemberg, where the mayor is elected by popular vote, he even chairs the municipal council. Everywhere the chief of administration is seen as the municipality's or county's link to outside forces, whether higher-level authorities or private and public enterprises. The model of legislative direction by the council is, then, less realistic than the model of executive dominance.

This does not mean, however, that the executive has a monopoly of influence. The interest of key councillors, especially in the majority *Fraktion*, in obtaining information and exercising some power leads to cooperation, or collusion, between such councillors and the leading administrators. This cooperation is strongest, of course, where the key administrators were elected by the council majority. This may result in a considerable amount of decision-making taking place behind the scenes even before committee, *Fraktion*, and council meetings. Thus the part-time professional councillors, together with professionals and specialists inside and outside the administration, form an efficient transmission belt between the bureaucratic planning and preparation machinery and the political decision-making body. This "oligarchy" of decision-making may be defended on the grounds that it serves to iron out bugs in bureaucratic plans, anticipate potential difficulties, and reduce the time it would otherwise take to get proposals through the local administrative-political process.[4] On the other hand it works to the disadvantage of the minority *Fraktionen*, which may be effectively eliminated from the decision-making process. And the more critical they are of majority administrative practices, the more they may be kept uninformed.[5]

While there is generally much cooperation between the majority *Fraktion* and the administration, and while most decisions in the council are not controversial —which is true also of most national and regional legislative bodies in other Western democracies, this is not to say that there is never any competition, criticism or conflict. There is strong pressure on the minority party or parties to criticize at least some of the initiatives from the administration and majority *Fraktion* or to offer certain alternatives, and even the majority *Fraktion* may at times wish to demonstrate some degree of independence from the administration, especially in South Germany where the mayor is elected directly and may be more independent of the council.[6] Criticism and conflict are most likely to occur, however, when a new majority *Fraktion* is formed after an election and the key administrative officials are considered to be tied closely to the old majority.

The councillors. Until World War I in Germany, and to a very considerable extent still in the United States today, local councillors were mostly *Honoratioren,* that is, local notables such as large farmers in the villages and well-known families, large property owners, successful business and professional people in the towns and cities. While notables have not disappeared from German local politics, they are no longer dominant elements even in the villages. Today most councillors are recruited and nominated by political parties, while in the past the notables preferred to run as independents or on the slate of a nonpartisan "voter group." To the extent that they must now accept nomination by a party, most of the remaining notables become identified with and members of the "bourgeois" CDU/CSU (Christian Democratic Union/Christian Social Union) or the FDP (Free Democratic Party). The nonparty voter groups which are still a factor in the villages of some of the *Länder*—though a declining one—are also the province of local notables. The SPD (Social Democratic Party of Germany) has relatively few notables as members and candidates.

Studies of local candidate recruitment suggest that a number of generalizations can be made today about candidate recruitment at the village, town and city levels. Common criteria for nomination at all levels are a demonstrated willingness and ability to assume responsibility, for example, by occupying one or more offices in local clubs and organizations, including parties, a friendly, open personality, a good family life, being well known and respected in the community, and having some expertise and ability to express personal opinions. At the village level these qualities may be more important than party membership or activity; indeed, parties in the villages and small towns frequently seek out such persons to run for them, since their own pool of members may not contain a sufficient number of such persons. Once nominated, however, the candidate will be expected to join the party if he or she is not already a member.[7] The SPD is less likely to turn to a potential candidate outside the party than are the CDU and FDP.[8] In the villages election may be a test of social acceptance, and few who fail the test are willing to try again. The CDU and FDP tend to have an advantage in promoting village or small-town natives, while the SPD is more inclined to nominate newcomers.[9]

Workers are generally underrepresented (in the United States, they are hardly represented at all) in the councils, as are women. The self-employed—in the villages often farmers—tend to be overrepresented in some villages and small towns, but this group is declining in representation. The middle class, understood in the broader American sense, and especially the salaried middle-class elements, now dominate most councils.[10] Among these persons teachers and interest-group representatives are especially numerous.

In the larger cities recruitment efforts are complicated by the tremendous expenditure of time which councillors must or should spend on matters relating to council membership. Not only do they have council meetings, committee meetings, *Fraktion* meetings, personal discussions and extensive reading materials to absorb or at least review; they are also expected to attend and participate actively in local party meetings, often to hold important party offices, and to be active in one or more other social groups or unions. Given these time commitments, the question is being raised today whether the city councillor can still be considered to be a "lay" part-time politician who, in Max Weber's terms, lives "for" politics, or whether he has not in fact become a "part-time professional" who, through his compensation from the city for the many meetings he attends (*Sitzungsgelder*) and his expense money (*Aufwandsentschädigung*), is coming close to living "from" politics.[11] Indeed, some observers express the fear that the professionalization of large cities' councillors threatens the very concept of a "citizen" representative body.[12] It is not a little paradoxical that in spite of executive dominance, the workload of city councillors seems to become ever more burdensome. This is the result, of course, of the large and increasing number of local government responsibilities.

The demands made upon city councillors obviously have an effect on the kinds of candidates selected. Those most favored are persons with no occupation, for example, retirees and, to a lesser extent, older housewives. Self-employed persons who are "expendable" may become candidates, but salaried employees in certain occupations are the most likely prospects; those who no longer expect promotion, public servants (in sharp contrast to the United States and Great Britain) and teachers are prominent examples. Former skilled workers who have assumed union positions are obvious candidates, especially for the SPD. In some cases an employer may have an interest in having an employee serve on the council. Examples would include larger firms as well as unions and political parties (it is not uncommon for professional party agents, who serve as local party organizers or managers, to become members of the city council). Professionals are more likely to include architects than lawyers, unlike the United States.[13]

As indicated above, not all councillors are party members. Until the 1970s, and especially before the territorial reforms of that decade, a majority of village councillors in several *Länder* ran on the slates of non-party voter groups. These were more likely to include the traditional "notables" as candidates, in any case people who did not want to be identified with a party. Even though voter groups have declined sharply and most candidate recruitment now is done by parties, many party councillors retain considerable personal independence at the village level.[14]

Politics and Parties

Politics at the local level. In most Western democracies it has been commonplace to argue that there is no real "politics" at the local level. In the United States the conventional wisdom that "there is no Democratic or Republican way to pave a street," together with a middle-class reaction against corrupt party machines in a number of large cities, led to the practice early in this century of outlawing partisan elections in about two-thirds of American towns and cities. As a result most local elections in the United States today have a strongly independent flavor, although many candidates who run as independents or as part of a nonparty ticket can be identified with a party in one way or another.

In Germany the consensus that local government is nonpolitical no longer prevails. Until World War I middle- and upper-middle-class Liberals and the traditional conservative elements dominated local governments, and for them it was an article of faith that there was no politics in local government. With general, secret, direct and equal elections, proportional representation, and strong socialist and communist working-class movements and later the Nazis, it became very difficult in the Weimar Republic to argue that politics did not exist at the local level in larger cities and industrial towns. The polarization of many city councils between left, center, and right, and the perception of many observers, accurate or not, that politicized local government was government incapable of action, led to the replacement of local councillors and mayors by state commissars in hundreds of cities and towns. Polarized conditions in the cities also gave the Nazis an additional excuse to "synchronize" or "coordinate" (*gleichschalten*) local and higher levels of government in a totalitarian system directed from above.

After 1945 the view that local government was—or at least should be—nonpolitical was still strong, and it continues to exist today. This view found its best reflection in the nonparty local voter groups that formed, usually on an ad hoc basis, after 1945. These voter groups enjoyed widely varying degrees of success in the German *Länder*. By the late 1960s, for example, the local candidates of the national parties obtained 95 percent of the vote in local elections in North-Rhine Westphalia, 90 percent in the Saarland, 76 percent in Lower Saxony and 74 percent in Hesse. But they received generally no more than 60 percent of the vote in the local elections in Bavaria, Baden-Württemberg and the Rhineland-Palatinate. In terms of seats won, the candidates of the national parties rarely received more than one-third of the total in the three South German *Länder*, while they could expect between 40 and 55 percent of the seats in Hesse, Schleswig-Holstein and Lower Saxony. The disparity between votes and seats won resulted from the disproportionate strength of the voter groups in the small villages, where the ratio of councillors to residents is far more favorable than in the cities (see table 9.1). The voter groups were hardly represented in the cities, only weakly in the county councils, and often but not always weakly in the larger towns belonging to the counties.[15]

Aided by the territorial reforms of the late 1960s and 1970s, which led to the consolidation of thousands of small villages into larger units, the national parties have been receiving increasingly larger proportions of the votes in local elections. Local voter groups are in a period of decline, though they still held a majority of the seats in small towns and villages in Bavaria, the Rhineland-Palatinate, and Schleswig-Holstein at the end of the 1970s.[16] It is doubtful that they will disappear altogether, even though their influence will probably continue to decline.

Even during the 1950s and 1960s, however, there seemed to be a growing consensus among scholars, journalists, politicians at the higher levels and practitioners that politics was very much a part of local government. There was and is general agreement that politics can be seen in alternative plans, conflict over goals, procedures, priorities, and values at the local level, that what is in the interest of one group may not be in the interest of another. Such differences can be reflected to some extent in the candidate recruitment patterns of the parties and voter groups. Thus the SPD is more likely to recruit nonpracticing Protestants; workers, especially union officials; public service employees, especially teachers; and salaried white-collar workers. The CDU/CSU tends to recruit Catholics and practicing Protestants, the self-employed, including farmers, middle-class salaried employees, professionals, and also a good many teachers. The FDP is most likely to recruit from Protestants, the self-employed, and professionals. These recruitment patterns alone can lead to differences in the council with respect to the religious versus sectarian focus of schools and hospitals, to the degree of debt financing considered tolerable for various capital investments, to certain preferences for the public or private sector, and to the admission prices for public facilities or ticket prices for public transportation services.[17]

The recognition that politics exists at the local level can be seen also in numerous laws and practices. While the role of personality is not ignored in some of the local elections laws of the *Länder*, proportional representation features are stronger, and these are very much to the benefit of parties. North-Rhine Westphalia and the Saarland require a minimum level of permanent organization for voter groups, which hinders their activities and accounts in part for their traditional weakness in these two *Länder*.[18] Local government law in the *Länder* permits and encourages councils to divide into *Fraktionen* (party groups), and they specify that committees may be formed on the basis of the strength of the *Fraktionen* in the council. Contributions to local parties, but *not* to individuals and voter groups, can be deducted from income taxes, and local parties receive funds from higher-level party organizations for meeting some of their local election campaign costs. Councillors who attend *Fraktion* meetings are compensated just as they are for committee and council meetings. As organs of the local councils, *Fraktionen* also receive funds from the local treasury to provide for administrative expenses.

In spite of these and other examples of numerous practices and laws that favor political parties, and in spite of the ubiquitous activities of parties described only briefly in the section above, some German political scientists and others insist that there is still a strong anti-party and even anti-politics bias in Germany. But the real issue today is not whether there is politics at the local level, or even whether parties should play an important role, but rather how far the argument for party politics should and can be carried. The moderates in this dispute argue that it is one thing for the parties to recruit from somewhat different groups of the population, thus probably broadening considerably the participation in the political process of citizens who might not participate otherwise (witness the United States), to recognize that there may be differences on occasion between these groups or the *Fraktionen* over certain issues, to have local councils and committees organized by party *Fraktionen*, and to regret that local party organizations do not provide the virtually independent *Fraktionen* with more policy direction or ideas.[19] But most questions at the local level, even if they may be controversial, are not necessarily *partisan* in nature. Local government activities, according to this view, are more *project* than *program* oriented.[20] Given local financial constraints and higher-level laws and regulations affecting the sphere of local activities, there is not a great deal of room for maneuver at the local level in any case.

It is quite another matter, on the other hand, for the parties (with about 5 percent of the population as members and fewer than 25 percent of these as active members) to dominate completely the local recruitment process, so that those citizens who do not wish to become involved in intra- and inter-party conflicts have no choice but to withdraw from participation;[21] for the parties to form *Fraktionen* that exercise such a degree of party discipline that each *Fraktion* confronts the other as a cohesive, almost monolithic bloc that leaves little room for individual initiative; for the *Fraktionen* to permit party members who are not members of the council to join in *Fraktion* deliberations and even insist that the *Fraktion* do what the "party" (that is, the party activists) has decided should be done (imperative mandate); for the party or the *Fraktion* to exercise strong discipline when, especially in the small towns and villages, personality may be more important than party; for the trend toward party professionalization to alter the common and traditional understanding of local self-government; and, especially, for the parties and *Fraktionen* to insist on electing all key civil servants in the local administration on the basis of party membership. There are, then, those who believe that local politics should become far more partisan than it has been or in most cases is now, and they advocate the politicization of local government according to the model of national parliaments and cabinets.

Political parties and the constitution. During the 1950s and 1960s, there was considerable controversy among both academic and practicing circles over the role of political parties in the German political system. One school of thought said that since parties had come to dominate all levels, and since they were "responsible" parties with a fairly strong ideological foundation, dues-paying members, programs, and the disciplined *Fraktionen* to carry out most if not all of their promises, Germany had become a *Parteienstaat*, a party state, a condition common to all modern democracies (the advocates of this thesis appear to have had little knowledge of politics in the United States). It was even argued that this dominance of the state was sanctioned by article 21 of the Basic Law, which recognized officially the role of political parties in the German political system. In having done so, the Basic Law recognized a form of "plebiscitarian democracy."

This modern form of democracy was said to stand in sharp contrast to the nineteenth century concept of "representative democracy," which focuses on the right of the individual representatives to act for the common good on the basis of their own best judgment without a mandate from any person or group. Unfortunately, from the perspective of legal consistency, the Basic Law also recognized this older principle in article 38, which was a practice in German constitution-making for at least a hundred years. In giving official recognition to both party-plebiscitarian and representative democracy, the founders of the Federal Republic had placed two opposing principles in the constitution, and there could hardly be any compromise between the two.[22]

An important consequence of this controversy was the dispute which developed over the question of the "imperative mandate" versus the "free mandate," that is, over the issue of whether an elected politician is bound to the instructions of his *Fraktion* or party, or whether he is free to decide on his own best judgment. While this dispute has never been resolved to the satisfaction of all and continues on occasion to be a focus of attention, there seems to be a general consensus today that in practice the two principles as reflected in article 21 and article 38 are to some extent complementary. Thus *Fraktion* discipline is permitted, but not *Fraktion* dictation (*Fraktionszwang*). A politician who acts against party wishes may be removed from the *Fraktion*, but he does not lose his seat. The French Communist party practice of submitting a pre-signed letter of resignation or of turning over the parliamentary salary to the party for a much lower salary in return would not be allowed under article 38. Article 38 does, then, place certain important limits on the extent to which parties may discipline their elected "representatives."[23]

This controversy applies to the local level as well. Parties are the dominant force in the larger cities and counties, and they have been growing in strength in the towns and villages. At the same time all of the local government laws in the *Länder* include the traditional provisions which protect the free mandate of the local representatives.[24] Article 28 of the Basic Law, which guarantees the right of local self-government, that is, some degree of autonomy from the state, serves to complicate this issue even further. A party state brings centralizing pressures to bear on the local level, and party delegates in the local councils become agents of centralizing institutions that can and do undermine local autonomy.[25] Whether or not the centralizing influences of the parties are really that great—some doubt that they are[26]—there is some evidence that in the large cities, at least, the pressures to coordinate party policies with higher levels may be strong.

The national parties and local government. National parties do have a natural interest in local party organizations, if for no other reason than that these are important links in the recruitment process and in the provision of workers for the campaigns for all elections. Indeed, some observers suggest that the parties at the local level are primarily campaign organizations and recruitment agencies for local councils,[27] and that they have little to do with party goals or programs.

For the SPD the basic unit of the party is the *Bezirk*, the large district. All *Bezirke* are divided into *Unterbezirke*, or sub-districts, and these, in turn, are subdivided into *Ortsvereine*, or local organizations. In some cases the *Ortsverein* may be subdivided. For the CDU and CSU the *Kreisverband*, the county or city organization, is the basic unit. But most county organizations are subdivided into *Ortsverbände*, or local organizations. The FDP is usually organized at the county or city-county level only.[28] All of these organizations within each party may vary widely in size.[29] For many years after 1945 the SPD had stronger local organizations and far more members than the CDU/CSU; however, in the 1970s CDU/CSU membership grew dramatically, and today the SPD has only a slight membership advantage over the "bourgeois" parties.

All of the major parties have made references to local government in their party programs, and sometimes party conventions spend a considerable amount of time on local government matters. Special party conventions that deal exclusively with local government are also called on occasion. From these meetings, the pronouncements made in them, and the party programs, certain differences between the parties can be detected. In 1975 the SPD spoke of local politics of the larger society, in which the democratic socialist goals of freedom, justice and solidarity should be sought and achieved by changing existing society and introducing "democracy in all aspects of life." The result would be a higher quality of life, more equal opportunity and more citizen participation. In 1975 the CDU talked also of freedom, solidarity and equality, but in addition mentioned pluralism and effective government for improving the conditions of the individual. It opposed collectivism and state controls. The FDP in the same year focused on individual freedom together with a maximum of social justice.[30]

While these pronouncements are formulated in general and abstract terms, certain consequences do derive from them. The SPD focus on equality of opportunity has led to school reforms introduced by SPD *Land* governments which have polarized councils and citizens in many local communities. The focus on a higher quality of life and more equality has been at least partly responsible for increased deficit financing of capital investments and, for a while, for demands by the SPD left wing for free public services of various kinds. The demand for a higher quality of life has had some impact on the controversy over nuclear power plants, air, water and noise pollution, land-use policies, etc., while the resistance by the CDU/CSU to bureaucracy and increased public spending has encouraged the privatization of some public services and the raising of fees for others.

In spite of party programs that focus on the local level, one can hardly speak of centralized party influence unless there are party institutions designed to coordinate central-level activities or to provide some form of direction. Such institutions exist in the parties, at least on paper; however, the sheer number of local governments, the differences in size and location, the small professional staffs that are overwhelmed by the number of local responsibilities, and, above all perhaps, the lack of time for effective coordination, lead one to conclude that central direction is very weak at best.[31] On the other hand, the leading officials of the influential local government associations are selected in part on the basis of partisan background, which may have some impact on the nature of the advice and counsel that these associations provide. The national parties also have party-sponsored local government publications in the form of newsletters and magazines. Probably the best known of these is the CDU/CSU magazine, the *Kommunalpolitische Blätter*, published by the *Kommunalpolitische Vereinigung*, a party organization that deals specifically with the local level. The SPD publishes the magazine, *Die demokratische Gemeinde*, and the FDP the magazine, *Das Rathaus*.

While the influence of the national parties at the local level can be easily exaggerated, one of the criticisms that we have already noted is that the centralizing influence of the parties tends to undermine local autonomy. In spite of some evidence one can cite to support this view, there is another perspective that is frequently overlooked. A number of observers have suggested that precisely because of intergovernmental relations, the financial squeeze on local governments, and various pressures from higher levels which affect local autonomy and decision-making, it is important for the local governments to have partisan contacts with higher *Land* and federal levels, or, for towns and villages, with the county. These contacts make it possible for local governments to coordinate their efforts with higher authorities and to represent local concerns to these authorities. Thus strong party connections between levels of government may actually serve to promote local government interests and autonomy.[32] One of the problems with this argument, of course, is that it can be turned around. It is just as plausible to suggest that inter-level party linkages open local governments to even more state influences.[33] To what extent either view is empirically accurate has not been determined; however, in a study conducted several years ago in one medium-sized city, it was found that the numerous contacts between local party personalities and *Land* and federal politicians at local party meetings appeared to serve the primary function of keeping the local party members informed of political developments at the higher levels. It is doubtful that these particular links had any relevance either to securing local autonomy or to increasing state interference.[34] As we saw above, other observers have also suggested that the actual influence from above is not very strong.[35]

The controversy over party patronage and the "parliamentarization" of local government. In Germany as in many other countries there are two models of the proper role of political parties and their relationship to the local administration. The older, "classical" or nineteenth century Liberal model is that politics, or at least party politics, has no place in the municipal *Rathaus* or in the county administration building. Local bureaucrats are concerned above all with routine administrative matters and with problems essentially technical in nature, the solutions for which can be solved best by competent, experienced, well-educated key professionals. Party politics has nothing to do with such management responsibilities. Because of the important role these personnel (*Wahlbeamte*), especially the chief administrative officers, have in local government administration, proposing initiatives and working with the council and the public, they must be held accountable for the quality of their performance. That is why they are elected by the councils or, in South Germany in case of mayors, by the people.

But the election is for a set term of office, ranging from six to twelve years (depending on the *Land*), which in any case is longer than the term of office for the councillors. This is to give the chief administrative officer and his deputies some degree of freedom from the council, whose interference in administrative affairs or whose pressure on the key administrators to act in ways they consider inappropriate or even illegal must also be checked. In case of gross incompetence or misbehavior, key personnel may be removed in some *Länder* by a two-thirds vote of council. But normally a council must wait until the end of the regular term before it can vote to confirm or reject key administrative personnel. Even if it rejects the civil servant for another term, it must be prepared to pay a generous pension based on the number of years of service. This feature is designed to make such positions attractive in spite of the risk of not being reelected.

The opposing, newer, "democratic," — especially, but not only, social democratic — model is that not only politics, but partisan politics, is very much a part of local government, and this fact is and must be reflected both in the council and in the *Rathaus*. Local government is a part of the larger society, and if one wishes to change that society, to push through measures for more equality, more public services, more investments in public facilities and other initiatives that will probably be resisted by the older conservative or Liberal ruling classes, then not only is a disciplined majority *Fraktion* required but also a local administration that is sympathetic to the goals of the council majority. Since local governments today are responsible directly or indirectly for so many activities and services, administrative initiatives and even routine administration are bound to reflect personal philosophical values, and the council majority has the right to ensure that its values are shared by the administration. Key administrative personnel are not just objective technicians. In the past they were recruited from socially privileged groups, when a "bourgeois" majority controlled the council, and administrators from this background are not likely to act in conformity with the philosophy of a new, progressive majority.[36]

The consequences of this model ("democratic government is *party* government") are, first, that it is both necessary and proper for a council majority to view partisan political orientation in the form of party membership as an important if not key criterion among the other qualifications expected of a prospective chief administrator or his deputies. A second consequence is that pressure is now being placed on some *Land* parliaments to change local government laws so that the terms of office of councillors and key elected administrators will be synchronized, thus allowing a newly elected majority in the council to "clean house" and replace the old key officials with new ones.[37] Otherwise, say the proponents of this model, "self-government" will be no more than "self-government of the bureaucracy."[38] So far, however, only Hesse has passed such legislation, ironically in large part because of the controversy surrounding the efforts in 1977 of the new CDU majority in Frankfurt to increase the number of the local key administrators so that the new CDU mayor would not have to deal only with SPD officials. Again ironically, the CDU mayor later changed his mind and pushed through the council the reelection of an SPD deputy.[39]

From the perspective of the proponents of this second model, local government should be "parliamentarized" through increased "politicization."[40] As at higher levels, the dualism between the administration and the council should be replaced by—many would argue that in the large cities it has already been replaced by—a dualism between the administration and the council majority on the one hand versus the council minority on the other. As a general rule, but with numerous exceptions, it can be said that this model of "parliamentarized" local government is the one supported by the left in ideological terms and, in terms of academic discipline, by many German political scientists. The first model tends to find more support on the ideological right and, throughout the 1960s and to a lesser extent today, among legal scholars, including those specializing in public administration. Today the latter are more likely to support a model with elements from both of the two opposing models, in effect rejecting both of them.[41]

The critics of parliamentarized or policitized local government point not only to legal[42] and theoretical but also to certain practical issues which make this model less feasible or desirable than it appears to be to its advocates. It may be true, for example, that parties are "the essential elements of the political-democratic process"[43] at regional and national levels, but they are not seen to be so everywhere in the Western world (for example, in the United States), or at the local level in numerous democratic countries (again, especially in the United States).[44] Anyone who has talked to the residents or even councillors of a village or small town learns quickly that "party politics" is not entirely welcome in such communities.[45] It is true that "party politics" is understood frequently as "high politics,"[46] but even if a broader definition is granted, serious objections remain. Candidates selected by parties in such communities are not recruited because of their strong party orientations but because they are known and respected as individuals. The voter does not need the party for orientation purposes, since one knows the candidates. The party is just another organization among others. This serves to limit partisan conflict among inhabitants, which is important where the population is fairly homogeneous. On the other hand, where there are strong social or religious differences, party conflict may emerge.[47] Local parties may be necessary for carrying on election campaigns for the local as well as for higher levels, but they should not bring ideological conflict into the community. Thus the local parties have a "Janus head," with one face in the direction of local politics, where the party role is to be downplayed, and the other face in the direction of "high politics," where a partisan connection is crucial.[48]

The argument that those who object to more partisanship in local government are merely trying to protect their old privileges as *Honoratioren*, or traditional notables, and that the centralizing influence of parties is necessary in an age of intergovernmental relations,[49] is too simplistic. Relatively few persons are members of parties, and in some villages there are no members at all. If the parties insist on dominating the recruitment process, this will actually become a barrier to more participation, a new form of discrimination no less obnoxious than older forms. After all, many people do not wish to reveal their personal political philosophy, or they may wish to avoid intraparty and interparty quarrels.[50] Shop owners and proprietors of restaurants may be reluctant to become involved in partisan politics for business reasons, since they want to remain on good terms with everyone.[51] Especially in villages and small towns, citizens have little patience with attempts to introduce party politics into the local administration.[52] Even the elected mayor in South Germany is not seen as a politician, but as the local ambassador to higher levels and "outsiders."[53] The injection of too much partisan politics into the village and small town can have, and, in some areas has had, an anti-party effect which may contribute to the formation of nonpartisan citizen initiatives as well as to the older voter groups.[54] The "party state" is not only not an accepted fact in all other democratic countries, it is not even an accepted fact in most German villages and towns.

One might counter that these arguments apply mostly to medium and small municipalities, not to the larger cities or even to the counties. That a parliamentarization of local government is desirable is an argument that has been made primarily in the context of the politics of larger local units. But here, too, many observers remain skeptical of the model. The view that the local level should be politicized implies a mobilization of the local party organization to move beyond the traditional representative function and to assume new functions such as proposing initiatives for societal change and spending large amounts of time reviewing candidates for key administrative posts. This would not only overtax the capabilities of the local party organizations; it also assumes that voters can be mobilized along such lines of action. What is more likely to occur with increased politicization is that the focus of power will be located in the party organization, not the elected *Fraktion* or council. With the "imperative mandate" in effect, this would mean that the voters would become the mere subjects of a very small, activist partisan minority.[55] Even in the cities, voters are not inclined to favor excessive partisanship, and some observers have noted that too much party patronage can lead to citizen distrust of public authorities.[56] Indeed, the loss of the SPD's traditional majority or of directly elected mayors in a large number of cities in the 1970s may be interpreted in part as a voter reaction against the party's "pro-politicization" left wing in many city party organizations.

If one accepts without question the view that all key local administrators should be of the same party as the council majority (which is not the case in many cities where a kind of proportional representation in the bureaucracy is required by law), how is the council in fact to exercise effective control over the administration?[57] That is, what is to prevent the administrators from controlling the council majority, and what is to prevent the majority from introducing patronage at middle and even lower levels of the bureaucracy? Even those who strongly favor parliamentarization have voiced concern about the potential for such abuse on the grounds that nonelected career officials are not decision-makers. To include them in the patronage package is nothing more than a "service patronage" that has nothing to do with political control over the bureaucracy. Rather, there is a serious danger of a hopeless degree of mutual advantage-taking between the long-standing majority and the local public service which can lead to a degeneration of local politics to little more than a struggle for personal positions.[58] Some observers note that a broadened party patronage already exists in some local governments.[59]

A different line of argument is that a parliamentarization of local government would undermine seriously the role of the council as a deliberative body, since the majority *Fraktion* leaders and the key administrators would practically ignore the minority and decide important issues outside of council and its committees.[60] This would, among other things, eliminate or severely limit the opportunity for the minority opposition to participate in the planning process and to suggest alternatives to the administration-majority concept for the future.[61] Even if one concedes that this has already happened to a large extent in those cities with a long-standing council majority and a sympathetic local administration, there are still many cities in which council majorities change and key administrators remain in office. To synchronize the terms of office of councillors and administrators would lead to a new set of problems. For example, what should be done if an administrator is to be elected between council elections? If the next election result were uncertain, how would one find a qualified candidate willing to take the position? Even a term of office the same as the local council (usually five years) is hardly long enough to attract capable officials, given the risk of not being reelected. The value of continuity in the key positions of the local administration seems to have been completely ignored by the advocates of synchronization. Nor has much thought been given to the costs in party and council time and effort in finding capable replacements or to the probability that as newly elected administrators were taking up their positions the influence of the nonelected career officials would increase. More conflict would be introduced into the council as a result of a partisan-inspired personnel turnover, with the danger of a partisan corruption of the local bureaucracy. Finally, little thought seems to have been given to the financial costs of hiring and firing highly paid key personnel whose early pension rights would have to be retained if qualified candidates were to be recruited for local administrative posts.[62]

The problem of personnel costs is already a serious one for local governments, as was noted in chapter 7. Some argue that the placement of party loyalists in career positions has become a factor in explaining the rising number of local government personnel during the past twenty years,[63] while others point to the difficulty of reducing personnel costs when local council majorities seem committed to extending their patronage at every opportunity and to electing "their own" to key positions when the old terms have expired. The costs to the public of early retirement of leading civil servants are substantial.[64]

It is probably fair to say at this point that the nonpartisan model represents largely the "good old days" and the second party government model represents hopes yet to be achieved. In some villages and small towns the first model may still prevail, and in several of the larger cities the second model comes close to realization. In most municipalities and counties, however, actual practice lies somewhere in between.

Citizen initiatives and "the Greens": the new challenge. As the voter groups began their decline in the late 1960s and 1970s, and the parties began to dominate local elections in increasing numbers of villages and small towns, a new phenomenon, the citizen initiatives (*Bürgerinitiativen*), began to appear on the local scene. By 1977 it was estimated that there were 50,000 citizen initiatives in the Federal Republic with almost as many members as the total for all political parties.[65] The citizen initiatives, which have declined in number since the late 1970s, are forms of spontaneous, direct, collective political participation with a focus on decision-making or concrete problems.[66]

Supporters praise them for bringing a grass-roots, direct democratic element into an otherwise purely representative local government system (except for some public participation in the local planning process[67] and certain plebiscitarian features of local law in Baden-Württemberg) and for countering local apathy and submissiveness. But critics complain, among other things, that they are spontaneous and temporary organizations that dissolve quickly after success or failure (thus "membership" represents no long-term commitment), that they represent mostly narrow interests of largely middle-class citizens, and that they react to problems rather than initiate new proposals.[68]

There is no agreement on the causes of the growth of citizen initiatives. One view seems to be that most participants in such initiatives are middle-class people who have discovered yet another means of representing their interests in addition to the parties in which they are also well represented.[69] Most other observers would probably disagree with this explanation. Some would argue that an important factor which helps explain the rise of citizen initiatives was the overly pragmatic orientation of the parties and their lack of ideology, which meant that they ceased offering sufficiently clear alternatives.[70] A related, but quite different, perspective is that the growing monopoly of the parties over candidate recruitment, together with the preoccupation of the local parties with internal party matters rather than with policy alternatives or initiatives, has encouraged extra-party activities by disaffected citizens.[71] Others suggest that it was precisely the politicization of local governments since the 1960s that made many citizens recognize that local government also had something to do with setting political priorities and not merely with ratifying objectively necessary decisions of the local bureaucracy.[72] Still others see the citizen initiatives as reactions to the welfare-service state. Citizens receive numerous benefits in such a state, but they are also subject to much bureaucratic regulation as a result. These regulations can be affected only by organizing. It is not so much service deficits that bother the people in the citizen initiatives (these are issues more appropriate for the parties), but rather service excesses and service breakdowns.[73] Obvious examples would be large construction and urban renewal projects, air, water and noise pollution, chemical "poisons" in food and waste dumps; lack of low-rent housing in the cities, and, above all, nuclear power plants and, in the 1980s, nuclear weapons.[74] Another hypothesis, which I have not found in the literature but which seems plausible, is that citizen initiatives can be understood in part as reactions to a new set of issues that transcend to a considerable extent the traditional issues and divisions that still separate the established political parties. It is frequently difficult at best to place the new issues on a traditional left-right continuum or to argue that there are "progressive" and "conservative" stands on such issues. This explains in part the problems the parties have had in adjusting to these new challenges, and their hesitation has been an encouragement to those who demand clear responses.

Nuclear power is a good example of a new issue that has created new, crosscutting divisions. Serious opposition to nuclear power plants occurred first in the mid-1970s, and it grew rapidly thereafter. A number of books were published at this time also which drew a connection between the problems of nuclear waste and other problems of the environment. Many young people, in particular students, were drawn into an environmental protest movement in the 1970s which later emerged as the Green movement and then the Green party in the 1980s. The first local election in which the Greens participated was for the county councils of Hameln-Pyrmont and Hildesheim in Lower Saxony in October 1977. The *Wählergemeinschaft Atomkraft—Nein, danke*, received 2.3 percent of the vote in Hameln-Pyrmont, the county in which the village of Grohnde—where a nuclear power plant was being constructed—was located. The *Grüne Liste Umweltschutz* in the county of Hildesheim received 1.2 percent. Since Lower Saxony, unlike most of the other *Länder*, has no 5 percent barrier which a party or group must pass in order to obtain seats, one seat was won in each county council. In March 1978 the Greens received 6.6 percent and 6.0 percent in two counties in Schleswig-Holstein near Brokdorf, the site of another nuclear power plant.[75] In that same year the Greens received several percentage points in the *Land* elections of Hamburg and Lower Saxony, though not enough to pass the 5 percent barrier; however, they did enter the parliaments of Bremen and Baden-Württemberg that year. Since then they have been successful in gaining seats in large numbers of local governments, in several *Land* parliaments, in the federal parliament in 1983, and in the European parliament in 1984.

It is somewhat ironic that the politicization of local governments through the parties that was the subject of so much controversy in the 1960s and 1970s now seems to be much less of a problem than the kind of politicization which the citizen initiatives and, in particular, the Greens, have brought into local government councils. It is also ironic that the increased politicization, especially in the cities, that was demanded by the left-wing youth group of the SPD, largely in the name of party democracy, was achieved with much greater success first by nonpartisan citizen initiatives and then by the youthful but anti-party Greens. The Greens, unlike the citizen initiatives, began to put up candidates for election and, as a result, introduced into many local councils the kind of conflict over goals, priorities and procedures that the young SPD left had itself hoped to initiate. It is perhaps not surprising that many of the younger members of the SPD have gone over to the Greens.

Local Election Law

According to article 28, paragraph 1, sentence 2 of the Basic Law, all of the *Länder* must provide for local elections that are general, direct, free, equal and secret. Within these guidelines, *Land* laws can and do call for procedures and conditions that differ in numerous important respects.

All German citizens who have reached the age of 18 and have been residents of a municipality for three, six or twelve months, depending on the *Land*, are eligible to vote. Voting participation in local elections ranges from about 50 to 85 percent (in any case more than double the normal rate in the United States), depending on the *Land* and the particular election. To be a candidate, one must be twenty one in Lower Saxony, twenty-three in the Saarland, and of voting age in the other *Länder*.[76]

A major controversy in recent years has surrounded the issue of local voting rights for foreign workers, many of whom have lived in Germany for a decade or longer. If they become German citizens, there is, of course, no problem with the right to vote; however, most claim that they intend to return home someday, and so far the *Länder* have refused to grant foreigners the right to vote.[77]

As a general rule local governments, like governments at the *Land* and federal levels, operate on the principle of representative democracy. Affected citizens have some rights of direct participation in local planning decisions, but until recently Baden-Württemberg was the only *Land* that provided for a petitioning process for local referenda, public assemblies and proposals from citizens at large to be placed before council (*Bürgerantrag*).[78] In large part as a reaction to the activities of citizen initiatives in the 1970s, other *Länder* have begun to provide for these and other features of public participation, such as public committee hearings.[79]

In spite of certain features providing for single-member districts and simple majorities in federal and *Land* election laws, candidates at these levels are elected essentially by proportional representation. Various forms of proportional representation have been adopted by the *Länder* for the local level as well. Only in North-Rhine Westphalia are large numbers of candidates elected in single-member districts (about one-half in the municipalities, two-thirds in the counties). In Schleswig-Holstein two to four direct candidates may be elected in villages which serve as a multimember district. In both *Länder*, however, the details of the system work in such a manner as to promote virtual proportionality.[80]

All of the other *Land* local election laws provide for a slate or ticket system

(*Blockwahlsystem*). Each party or voter group provides a list of candidates (*Wahlvorschlag*), which may contain as many names as the local council has members. Hesse, the Rhineland-Palatinate and the Saarland have—or, until recently, had—"pure" proportional representation, in which the voter casts one vote for the list of his choice. The number of seats won by each party or voter group depends on the proportion of votes received for the list. Once that number is determined, candidates enter the council according to their order on the slate. Thus, if there are thirty seats on the council and the party list contains thirty candidates, and if the party receives eight seats based on its proportion of the vote, the first eight candidates on the list are elected. The next and ninth candidate would be the first to enter the council from that list if and when a vacancy should occur before the next election. In case only one list or even no list is submitted—which would happen normally only in small villages—election is by majority vote as in a multimember district. In North-Rhine Westphalia and Schleswig-Holstein, the voter selects a party or voter group candidate by majority vote, but at the same time he is voting for a list.[81]

The system of pure proportional representation described above is also called a strict list (*starre Liste*). Other *Länder* have a loosely tied (*lose gebundene*) list or a free list (*freie Liste*).[82] The loosely tied list is or was found in Lower Saxony and Berlin. Until 1977 in Lower Saxony the voter had one vote which he could give either to a list or to a particular candidate on the list. Once it was determined how many seats the list had won, the candidates on the list with the most votes became the elected councillors. Lower Saxony is the only *Land* that permits individual, independent candidates to run. In this case the candidate was and is treated still today as a one-person list.

The most interesting and complicated are the "free list" systems of Baden-Württemberg and Bavaria and, since 1977 and 1984, Lower Saxony and the Rhineland-Palatinate. In the first two Länder the voter has as many votes as there are council seats, which means that in the largest cities he could have up to 60 (Baden-Württemberg) or 80 (Bavaria) votes. If the voter wants all of his votes to go to the party or voter group list with the candidates in the order presented, he merely tears that particular list from the rest of the perforated ballot and places it in the ballot box. This has the effect of giving each candidate on the list one vote (whether or not the list contains as many names as there are council members), but the list as such receives the total allowed to each voter. If, on the other hand, the voter wishes to make a selection among the candidates on the list, he may give from one to three votes to any one candidate, a process called *Kumulieren*. Furthermore, in a process called *Panaschieren*, the voter may select candidates from different lists. Thus, if he had forty votes, the voter could give one vote each to forty candidates spread among the different lists or give up to three votes each to any combination of candidates.

176 Local Government in the German Federal System

Table 9.2. Application of the d'Hondt and Hare-Niemeyer methods of calculation

Total seats to be distributed: 15
Total votes cast: 9000

a. Distribution of votes by slate and candidate

Party A		Party B		Party C		Voter group	
1. Weber	580	1. Schneider	990	1. Evers	120	1. Becker	210
2. Albers	830	2. Wagner	110	2. Feldkamp	30	2. Fröhlich	70
3. Engler	190	3. Eilers	260	3. Lindner	80	3. Teigeler	50
4. Sievert	80	4. Hartmann	180	4. Wesemann	130	4. Heimann	130
5. Wieling	440	5. Schuster	30	5. Bauer	200	5. Förster	200
6. Kramer	90	6. Koch	410	6. Trautmann	70	6. Nolte	110
7. Büchner	30	7. Hilgers	170	7. Werner	90	7. Busch	180
8. Schulte	670	8. Müller	40	8. Jensen	50	8. Grau	40
9. Meyer	220	9. Weiss	70	9. Einhaus	40	9. Moser	10
10. Schmidt	60	10. Hölting	60	10. Liesen	60	10. Reiners	100
11. Baumann	130	11. Forbach	50	11. Elsing	10		
12. Schwarz	340	12. Krüger	310	12. Bramer	20		
13. Brinkert	10	13. Bachmann	220				
14. Jäger	270	14. Alfkötter	80				
15. Teichert	40	15. Rosskamp	20				
Total	4000	Total	3000	Total	900	Total	1100

b. D'Hondt method of calculation

		Party A		Party B		Party C		Voter group	
		Votes	Sequence of seats won	Votes	Sequence of seats won	Votes	Sequence of seats won	Votes	Sequence of seats won
Divide total vote received by	1	4000	(1)	3000	(2)	900	(9)	1100	(6)
	2	2000	(3)	1500	(4)	450		550	(15)
	3	1333	(5)	1000	(8)	300		367	
	4	1000	(7)	750	(11)	225		275	
	5	800	(10)	600	(13)	180		220	
	6	667	(12)	500		150		183	
	7	571	(14)	429		129		157	
Total seats		7		5		1		2	

The councillors are selected in a two-step process. First the list votes are calculated and the proportion which the list received to the total vote is determined, then the candidates within each list are selected based on their individual vote totals.[83] In Lower Saxony the voter has a total of three

Table 9.2 (continued)

c. Hare-Niemeyer method of calculation

	Party A	Party B	Party C	Voter group
Computation of proportional numbers	$\frac{15 \times 4000}{9000} = 6.66$	$\frac{15 \times 3000}{9000} = 5.00$	$\frac{15 \times 900}{9000} = 1.50$	$\frac{15 \times 1100}{9000} = 1.83$
Seats by whole numbers (13)	6	5	1	1
Seats by remainders (2)	1	—	—	1
Total seats (15)	7	5	1	2

d. Distribution of seats by slate (either method)

Party A		Party B		Party C		Voter group	
(7 seats)		(5 seats)		(1 seat)		(2 seats)	
1. Albers	(830)	1. Schneider	(990)	1. Bauer	(200)	1. Becker	(210)
2. Schulte	(670)	2. Koch	(410)			2. Förster	(200)
3. Weber	(580)	3. Krüger	(310)				
4. Wieling	(440)	4. Eilers	(260)				
5. Schwarz	(340)	5. Bachmann	(220)				
6. Jäger	(270)						
7. Meyer	(220)						

Note: Based on the data provided in example b, Party A wins the first of the 15 seats, Party B the second, Party A the third, and so forth until the Voter Group wins the fifteenth and last seat. Using either method of calculation, the candidate Albers takes the first seat for Party A since he is the top vote-getter on the list. He is followed by Schulte. Though placed at the top of the list, Weber takes the third of 7 seats won by Party A. For Party C, the only candidate who receives a seat is Bauer, the top vote-getter for that party.
Source: See "Berechnungsbeispiel nach dem geänderten NKWG," *Die niedersächsische Gemeinde* 8 (1977):237, and Werner Sixt, *Kommunalwahlrecht in Baden-Württemberg* (Stuttgart: Richard Boorberg Verlag, 1980), *80.*

votes which he may use for *Panaschieren* or *Kumulieren*. In the Rhineland-Palatinate, on the other hand, the voter now has six votes which he may use for *Kumulieren* only. In Bavaria, the party or voter group may list any one *candidate* up to three times. This ensures the election of major candidates, since a ballot cast for the list as such gives such candidates three votes.[84]

In Baden-Württemberg about four-fifths of the ballots are actually changed by voters to reflect *Panaschieren*, but this occurs more in the smaller municipalities than in the cities, where straight-slate voting is more common. The large parties, that is, CDU and SPD, benefit more from straight-slate voting. It is not always easy to determine the effect of *Kumulieren*. One study suggested that particular occupational groups benefit to the disadvantage of others (occupations are provided on the ballots following the names of the candidates). Academicians, skilled workers and craftsmen, and especially social workers, union officials, and factory worker committee (*Betriebsrat*) members tended to receive more votes than average, while self-employed merchants, factory owners, businessmen, and white collar workers received fewer votes than average.[85]

In Baden-Württemberg as in several other *Länder*, a multimember district majority election is permitted when no list or only one list is submitted. This occurred quite frequently in the past, but normally only in small villages. With the increase in the size of municipalities brought about by the territorial reforms of the 1960s and 1970s, there are few such cases any more.[86] Baden-Württemberg provides for special consideration being given to small villages joined together with larger, core villages or towns. In part as a result of the territorial reforms, these small villages were promised representation in the general council in spite of their size. Until a *Land* court decision in 1979 forced some changes in the law to provide for a more proportional effect in the election results for the remainder of the municipal unit, these *Teilortswahlen* were controversial due to inevitable inequities in representation on the council.[87]

Established parties and voter groups, that is, those groups with sitting members of council, are qualified automatically to submit lists in local elections. New parties or groups must collect signatures on petitions. The number of signatures required is not a serious obstacle, since in Baden-Württemberg, for example, only ten signatures are required for villages up to 3,000 inhabitants and 250 for cities with more than 200,000 residents.[88] All of the *Länder* except Baden-Württemberg, Bavaria, and Lower Saxony have a 5 percent clause. This barrier has no effect on direct seats won in North-Rhine Westphalia or Schleswig-Holstein. Designed for the federal and *Land* levels to discourage small splinter parties from fragmenting the parliament along the lines of the Weimar Republic, thus promoting democratic stability in spite of proportional representation, the application of the 5 percent clause at the local level has not been without controversy.[89]

For the computation of seats won, all of the *Länder* except Hesse and Lower Saxony use the d'Hondt method of proportional allocation. This is the method of calculation used traditionally since 1945 at the *Land* and federal levels to determine the proportions of seats won by the various parties. Hesse, the Saarland, and

Lower Saxony, and for one election only, North-Rhine Westphalia, have abandoned the d'Hondt method for *Land* and local elections. Lower Saxony, which, like North-Rhine Westphalia, adopted the Hare-Niemeyer system in the 1970s, returned to the d'Hondt method in 1985.[90] A comparison of the methods is presented in table 9.2.

In the example used in table 9.2, either method produces the same results. Experience in Lower Saxony and North-Rhine Westphalia, however, suggests that the Hare-Niemeyer system favors the small parties, whereas the d'Hondt method favors the larger parties. Since Lower Saxony has no 5 percent clause, splinter groups have been able to enter local councils and make it more difficult to form majorities. Needless to say, the relatively small Free Democrats (FDP) and the Greens opposed a return to d'Hondt.[91]

Conclusion

Some of the most striking differences between local government in the Federal Republic and the United States can be found in the methods of election for the councils and in the political processes involving the relationships among local parties, party groups, and the administrative leadership. The ubiquitous role of the parties, especially in recruiting candidates, conducting election campaigns, and forming party groups in the councils, stands in sharp contrast to the tendency in the United States toward nonpartisan local elections. While a politicization of the council and administration is not unknown in the United States, where racial, ethnic, or group conflict may be more relevant than party, a relatively nonpartisan—if not nonpolitical—local political process is still common. Even in Britain, where parties are more relevant in local elections than in the United States, the model of a strictly neutral town clerk still predominates. In Germany, on the other hand, politicization of council-administrative relationships has become widespread through party patronage regarding key administrative positions, program, and, to a lesser extent, ideology. The pre-World War I model of nonpolitical local government has long been replaced in Germany, but the struggle between the model of limited partisanship and a thoroughly parliamentarized partisan local political process continues.

An even more apparent difference to the outside observer between the German and the Anglo-American local political processes can be found in the local electoral schemes of the various *Länder*. In contrast to the simple single-ballot, single-member ward or multimember ("at large") district system, the Germans have designed a variety of elaborate proportional representation schemes designed to provide representation in the local councils for every meaningful current of opinion. The large number of councillors in proportion to the voting population can therefore reflect a diversity of interests in the community that would be difficult for the much smaller American councils to match. Whether such a diversity of views is actually reflected, given the degree of party discipline and *Fraktion* unity that tends to prevail, is another question. The rise in the 1970s of citizen initiatives and the Greens suggests that the potential for a broad representation of views offered by the various electoral systems has not always been met.

10

Local Government

and Intergovernmental Relations

In the preceding pages and chapters the Federal Republic has been described and analyzed as a "spatial" federal system. With some notable exceptions such as defense, foreign affairs, the postal and telecommunications services, and the rail system, the federal government is not responsible for the administration of national policies and laws. Instead, these are generally turned over to the subnational governments for implementation within national guidelines. At each subnational level the chief executive officer is legally responsible for the administration of almost all laws and public activities within his jurisdiction. General-purpose local government units not only administer most of the laws of higher levels; they are also self-governing bodies responsible for local concerns.[1] With recent trends toward a system of intergovernmental relations in the Federal Republic, as described in the section below, questions have been raised about the continued viability of the traditional system of spatial federalism in Germany.[2]

Questions concerning the viability of the American functional model of "dual federalism" have, in contrast, been raised since the New Deal of President Franklin D. Roosevelt. The American system of federalism changed to a system of "cooperative federalism" from the 1930s to the 1960s. By the 1970s it had developed further into a highly complex and confusing mixture of shared responsibility with little transparency for either the citizen or the politician. What to do about the American system, or "nonsystem," as some would describe it, became an important political and to some extent even partisan issue by the end of the 1970s.

Intergovernmental Relations and the Undermining of German Spatial Federalism

The Development of *Politikverflechtung*

During the 1950s the relatively strict separation between lawmaking at the national level and administration at the local level was breached by a number of grant-in-aid programs which the federal government made available to the *Länder* along with numerous and detailed regulations. In spite of the lack of constitutional authorization and the invasion of *Land* autonomy which it represented, federal assistance was deemed necessary in order to deal effectively with problems distributed unevenly among the *Länder*; to provide the *Länder* with incentives for acting in certain areas; and to allocate scarce resources according to need. Federal grants were welcomed especially by the financially weaker *Länder*.[3] In 1969 federal aid programs were rationalized and given a constitutional foundation, and the finance reform of that year (described in chapter 7) provided *Land* and local governments with important shares of major taxes. A new era of "cooperative federalism" was ushered in, and optimism about its positive effects prevailed for a number of years among scholars and practitioners.

In the meantime "cooperative federalism" has led to what many believe is a "unitary federal state" or a system of intergovernmental relations (*Politikverflechtung*) with serious implications for German federalism. This is a condition in which the "federal and *Land* governments (and also local governments) operate together—and/or against one another—in a complex manner at many levels and in numerous functional areas and in the process have developed forms of political decision-making and/or non-decision-making that are not or are only partially provided for by the constitution and laws."[4] Today for a whole series of functional areas, neither the federal government, the *Land* nor the local governments have the power to make decisions alone. "All public levels cooperate, plan together, negotiate, agree or fail to agree; and finally: the constitution, laws, and regulations provide no certainty as to who is responsible for and capable of making decisions and who is to accept responsibility for them."[5] This system of "mature federalism" represents a significant departure from traditional federalism, which focused on providing a larger economic base and defense for the constituent states or regions while simultaneously protecting some degree of their autonomy. It is different in important respects from the more modern view of federalism, the legitimacy for which rests on such elements as administrative decentralization, the protection of minority rights, the securing of a role for an opposition, or the integration of diverse opinions. Whether it is possible to continue justifying federalism in the context of intergovernmental relations seems to be an open question.[6]

According to Fritz W. Scharpf, one of the leading experts on intergovernmental relations and the first to popularize the term *Politikverflechtung*, there are three forms of intergovernmental relations: horizontal, hierarchic and joint action.[7] The horizontal form is the least problematic, since it emanates from the subnational units and involves cooperation within one level of administration. It includes coordination among the *Länder* in formal and informal meetings of various kinds, such as the Minister-President (governors') conferences; conferences of individual cabinet members, the best example of which is probably the conference of ministers of education; and the meetings of top officials in the offices of the *Land* heads of government. Committees and commissions of various kinds as well as formal agreements are additional examples of cooperation among the *Länder*.

The hierarchic form involves decision-making by central authorities that affects the subnational and subregional units. As we have seen in previous chapters, a traditional characteristic of German administration has been the delegation of the administration of federal laws to the *Länder* and the further delegation of these laws and of *Land* laws to the regional and local governments (*Auftragsverwaltung*). The *Land* governments can also mandate functions of a wide variety to local governments to carry out on the basis of often detailed regulations (*Pflichtaufgaben*). Since the 1960s in particular, complaints have multiplied that the number of laws and regulations (*Gesetzesflut*) affecting local governments has narrowed increasingly the scope of local responsibility and initiative. Thus it is charged that "there are hardly any functions left that the municipalities and counties can actually administer and develop on their own on the basis of their discretionary powers [*Allzuständigkeit*]."[8] By 1976 the federal government and the *Land* of North-Rhine Westphalia together had passed 3,352 measures relevant to local government, including 881 laws and 2,471 regulations. Most of the laws were passed by the federal parliament, whereas the regulations derived mostly from the *Land*. Thus the tendency has been to narrow the scope of local government over time.[9]

The *Länder* have contributed to the increased burdens placed on local governments not only by issuing numerous regulations and passing laws but also by participating in the federal law-making process via the *Bundesrat* (see chapter 3). The proportion of federal laws requiring *Bundesrat* approval has increased over the decades, which is reflected to some extent by the fact that during the first twenty-five years of its existence only two of twenty-one amendments to the Basic Law did not affect federal-*Land* relations.[10] More indirectly the *Bundesrat* has been involved in the increasing number of Common Market regulations that affect the *Länder*, but there is rarely discussion of them in the *Bundesrat* itself.[11]

Of the three forms of *Politikverflechtung*, the joint actions (*Verbundsystem*) of the federal and *Land* governments are the most common focus of attention. These joint actions can be divided into two kinds: bilateral actions involving *Land* grants to the local governments and multilateral actions where all subnational units work with the federal government. These multilateral actions are the so-called "joint tasks" (*Gemeinschaftsaufgaben*).

The multilateral joint tasks. In 1969 a new section of the Basic Law, section VIIIa, with two new articles, 91a and 91b, ushered in the era of "cooperative federalism." Article 91a authorized the federal government to assist the *Länder* in several areas that had traditionally been *Land* responsibilities. Thus the construction of university facilities, including hospital clinics, regional economic development assistance, and agricultural structure and coastal protection measures became responsibilities to be shared by the federal and *Land* governments. Planning for these activities is accomplished in joint planning committees. The federal funding share is set at 50 percent for university construction and regional economic development aid and at least 50 percent for agricultural assistance and coastal protection. Article 91b authorizes the federal and *Land* governments to enter agreements for the purpose of educational planning and the improvement of facilities for and the promotion of scientific research.

Until the latter half of the 1960s, there had been relatively little interest in planning in West Germany, but a change of attitude was reflected around the middle of the decade in the local government reform movement which began then. With the recession of 1966–67, theories of economic fine-tuning with coordinated anticyclical policies became popular at the federal and *Land* levels of government. Optimism concerning economic planning and regional economic development also reached an all-time high in the late 1960s. The constitutional reforms of 1969 were a reflection of the new enthusiasm for an integrated and coordinated system of planning and financing.[12]

Thus joint planning committees were formed as coordinating organs for the various joint tasks, as called for by articles 91a and 91b. The *Länder* were given one vote each, while the federal government received eleven votes; therefore, neither the *Länder* together nor the federal government alone can outvote the other side. Decisions in the planning committees are made to cover four years, with adjustments in these plans made annually. These plans set the goals, indicate the kinds of activities or programs to be promoted, determine the geographical location, set the relevant criteria and project the costs. Implementation remains a responsibility of the *Länder*, in accordance with the German federal tradition.[13] The problem, according to some critics, is that in the process of planning, the federal government frequently becomes involved directly or indirectly in making decisions formerly reserved for the *Länder*, decisions such as how the money is to be spent, where it is to go, and how the project is to be administered. On the other hand, it has been argued that the federal government and the *Länder* operate in a framework of consensus and that conflict avoidance strategies in effect deny the federal government any capacity to manage or direct developments.[14]

While the *Land* governments participate actively in this process, their participation involves mostly ministers and bureaucrats. The federal and *Land* parliaments are left with little more than a theoretical possibility of control through budget review procedures. This has led Gerhard Lehmbruch to suggest that "cooperative federalism" in Germany should be called "executive federalism." It is not practical for parliamentary bodies or even their committees to become involved in negotiations that affect all of the *Länder*. This is, he asserts, an "executive privilege" analogous to that for international affairs. He argues that this is a delayed victory for Bismarck, who created the first *Bundesrat* as a body for cooperation among *Land* government ministers and as a device to avoid parliamentary interference.[15]

The impotence of *Land* parliaments is underscored by the reluctance of *Land* ministers to involve them and thus to invite interference, by the commitment of time and expertise that would be required on the part of *Land* deputies for serious and effective participation, and by considerations of the political costs of undermining the authority or credibility of the majority's own government or of having to accept responsibility for certain actions. When *Land* parliaments have attempted to participate in the planning for joint tasks, they have generally failed because they attempted to add new areas or more funding in opposition to the agreements made between the *Länder* and the federal government.[16] Ratification of the agreements made by the *Land* governments and acceptance of their budget projections for joint tasks appears to be the only realistic alternative for the *Land* parliaments. This, in turn, raises questions about the proper functions and future of the *Land* legislative bodies.[17]

Bilateral "investment aid." An important element of the finance reform of 1969 was article 104a, paragraph 4, which authorizes the federal government to provide the *Länder* with grants for their own and for local government investments that have the purpose of countering a disturbance of the overall economic balance, of equalizing differences in economic potential, or of promoting economic growth. Given the broad sweep of language in the paragraph, investment grants can cover a large number and variety of projects. So far the focus has been on public housing (funds for which were cut back even before the change in government in 1982), home modernization, urban development, traffic and transportation, and hospital construction.

Since federal funds are involved on a matching basis, federal regulations limit the scope of *Land* and local governments in their investment plans. The federal government is charged with distorting the priorities of the *Länder* and these with distorting the priorities of their local governments, since both levels find it difficult to resist matching funds even where the need is perhaps less great than in other areas. Some local governments may find it impossible to participate due to a lack of administrative capacity for preparing the paper work, although the territorial reforms were supposed to have corrected such problems; some local governments may lack the financial capacity to prepare potentially useful applications at the right time; and some local governments may simply lack the funds to pay their share of the matching grant,[18] while other, more affluent localities, may accept grant aid simply in order to benefit from the matching features. In its eagerness to direct investment plans, the federal government even provides grants for which there is questionable legal authority on the grounds that they conform to "the nature of the situation" (grounds that seem somewhat comparable to the "necessary and proper" clause of the American Constitution). Even if it is true that federal control in fact is mitigated by *Land* actions in the *Bundesrat*,[19] investment grants tend to weaken the traditional distinction between *Land* and local government spheres (*eigener Wirkungskreis*) and delegated spheres of activities (*übertragener Wirkungskreis*).[20]

Other examples of intergovernmental relations. Other examples of hierarchic and joint action forms of intergovernmental relations include various aspects of planning and federal-*Land* voluntary cooperation. Planning has already been mentioned in regard to the "joint tasks," but other kinds of federal and *Land* plans also contribute to the problems created by intergovernmental relations. At the federal level "persuasive planning" of the kind represented by the "concerted action" of the Karl Schiller era involving the federal government, business, and labor interests and by actions of the planning staff of the Chancellor's Office can be cited. A more ominous example, however, is the "imperialistic planning" of the functional ministries, the effects of which—for example, highways or railways —may place burdens on other levels for some period of time. Most ominous of all planning, however, in terms of intergovernmental relations, is the vertical joint planning by functional experts at the federal, *Land*, and local levels respectively. According to Frido Wagener, these experts, including civil servants, politicians, and interest group representatives, have entered a "functional brotherhood" in the manner of an American "iron triangle" and have conspired to promote the interests, through increased funding of grant programs, of particular functional areas regardless of the impact of such grants on *Land* and local government autonomy or on traditional patterns of relations in the German federal system. Thus a "*Ressortkumpanei*," a kind of functional "buddy system" similar to American "picket federalism" involving executive officials (mostly civil servants), has major consequences for the functioning of the federal and *Land* parliaments that in effect are left out of the decision-making process. The *Länder* are also guilty on numerous occasions of establishing *Land*-wide and regional plans that are far too detailed from the perspective of autonomous local governments.[21]

Thus the opening up of a new industrial area, for example, may no longer be a matter for local governments, interested groups, county and district authorities to negotiate, but also an issue which involves the *Land* officials concerned with functional matters such as highways and streets, the environment, agriculture, and, of course, with *Land* and regional area planning. The final decision may well be made by the *Land* Ministry of Interior.[22] The overall result is a development toward a vertical system of intergovernmental relations characterized by joint planning, joint decision-making and joint financing by the federal, *Land*, and local governments.[23]

Finally, an aspect of intergovernmental relations that is not mentioned so frequently as the above examples is the informal and formal cooperation and coordination that exists between federal and *Land* levels. Institutionalized forms would include discussions between the Chancellor and the *Land* minister-presidents, the meetings of functional ministers of both levels, and the meetings of cabinet office officials of both levels. Additional examples would be the science council (*Wissenschaftsrat*) for planning and coordinating scientific research and hundreds of federal-*Land* committees that deal with the promotion of uniform laws and regulations, model legislation, etc. "For all practical purposes federal and *Land* ministries are intermingled in some form, informally or institutionally, in every area of executive activity."[24] As indicated before, the *Länder* have reacted to the transfer of power to the federal level by strengthening their participation in federal decision-making via the *Bundesrat*. As a consequence the *Bundesrat* has been strengthened, but at the expense of the *Land* parliaments.[25]

Causes and Consequences of *Politikverflechtung*

While the changes in German federalism are the result of multifarious causes, some of which are probably not understood fully, the major factors which account for intergovernmental relations appear to be a mixture of constitutional development and interpretation as well as social, economic and value changes since 1949.

The constitutional elements have been alluded to in previous chapters and sections, but they bear repeating here. Article 20, paragraph 1, establishes the Federal Republic as "a democratic and socially just [*sozialer*] federal state." Another translation might be "a democratic federal welfare state." In any case this provision, together with article 72, paragraph 2, sentence 3, which authorizes federal actions to "maintain the uniformity of living conditions" in the *Länder*; article 91a, paragraph 1, which provides for federal support for "improving living conditions"; and article 104a, paragraph 4, which authorizes grants for investments by the *Land* and local governments that serve to "equalize the different economic potential" of regions in the country, offers powerful legal support to those who favor various economic and social measures that promote equality.

Against the constitutional support for a more egalitarian welfare state, however, one can find other constitutional provisions that encourage decentralized decision-making. The same provision that was quoted above from article 20, paragraph 1, says, after all, that the Federal Republic is a *federal* state, which suggests that the Basic Law recognizes that differences in social and economic policy may exist among the *Länder*. Also, article 28, paragraph 2, guarantees the local governments discretionary powers over local concerns and the right of self-government, and paragraph 3 commits the federation to protect these rights. It can be argued, therefore, that the guarantee of decentralized decision-making in these provisions is no less important than the egalitarian features of the welfare state, and that one cannot be interpreted to supersede the other. Rather, the Basic Law requires that a balance or compromise be maintained among contradictory constitutional principles.[26]

Some observers remain doubtful that the guarantees of decentralized decision-making can in fact be upheld. The interdependence of virtually all activities of importance, now including even the measures of the European Common Market, the public pressures for the equal provision of public services[27] (which in practice usually means provision at the highest existing level), the necessity of central direction in economic affairs, limited resources which must be shared, and the increased pressure to cooperate and coordinate policies among different levels of government are among the reasons for this doubt. The "dualism," the contrast between the state and local self-government that was a characteristic of German administration in the nineteenth century, appears to have reemerged in a new form with the establishment of a democratic welfare state. Indeed, "the democratic welfare state may well be an 'enemy' of local self-government."[28] In any case as long as there are local governments with the authority to govern themselves, there will be tension between the autonomy of local governments and state efforts to achieve greater equality.[29]

The pressures toward uniformity of services and standards through the process of intergovernmental relations are strengthened perhaps by the Federal Republic's relatively small size, although the Swiss appear to be more tolerant of economic and social diversity in their even smaller federation. And the French and English, even with their unitary states, seem to accept, for whatever reasons, considerably greater differences among the regions of their countries. However, in spite of shared revenues and financial equalization devices that bring about a comparatively high degree of fiscal equality among the German *Länder* and local governments, in spite of a relatively broader and more even dispersion of industrial and commercial activity in the Federal Republic in comparison to her European neighbors, and in spite of a generally high standard of living in all parts of the country, the pressure remains strong to fine-tune the constitutional and legal order so as to ensure that as much equality exists as is possible. Indeed, many complaints can be heard that there is still too little equality in the provision of public services in the individual *Länder* and local governments, and that such inequality surely violates articles 20, 72, 91a, and 104a of the Basic Law. Pressures for greater equalization are probably due as much as anything else to an ineradicable penchant in the German culture for perfectionist solutions.

In any case it has been suggested that multilevel problems cannot be resolved optimally by single-level decision-making structures, and that a single-dimension decentralization-centralization scheme is not an appropriate analytical instrument for determining effective problem-solving institutions.[30] In this view article 28 and the guarantee of local self-government are no longer consistent with current realities. Thus the provisions of article 28 should be changed to secure local participation in the overlapping decision-making processes. Local self-government should be understood as complementing state administration, as a part of a functional division of labor which does not preclude and is even dependent on central direction. A wide range of uncoordinated activities by different levels of government is no longer adequate to meet modern conditions.[31]

Thus one consequence of *Politikverflechtung* has been the encouragement of an interpretation of local government and a demand for constitutional changes that are very different from traditional German concepts. The new interpretation was not accepted by a kind of "royal commission" (*Enquete-Kommission*) on federal-*Land* relations that reported in 1976, even though it did express some sympathy for such ideas.[32] Indeed, there were some expectations that due to growing criticisms of the effects of the 1969 reforms, steps would be recommended for disentangling some of the shared responsibilities that were deemed by many to be a real or potential threat to the subnational government units. In spite of its consideration of various problems in the relationships between federal, *Land* and local governments, the Commission recommended little change.[33]

Yet a number of problems persist that many observers believe are serious enough to require more attention and corrective measures. In addition to the discussion in the previous section, one could point to the effects of German intergovernmental relations on efficiency; bureaucratization tendencies, including a more expensive administration of relevant laws; greater complexity of administration; perfectionist regulations; a tendency toward higher expenditures, since no one level is responsible for all of the costs; too little concern for maintenance costs of investment projects; and distribution of grant funds based on equality of the *Länder* rather than actual needs of the *Länder*.

Other effects, noted before, include the dominant role played by the functional ministries in intergovernmental relations, the limitations placed on the scope of *Land* and local government activities and the distortion of local and *Land* priorities, the limited transparency and lack of accountability of the participants in the decision-making process, and the exclusion of parliaments from that process.[34] More fundamentally, some critics suggest that some of the areas in which the federal government has intervened could be handled more than adequately by the *Länder* themselves if they were merely given a slightly larger share of the taxes.[35]

Given these and other criticisms, why have the federal and *Land* governments failed to reform the system of intergovernmental relations in such a manner as to eliminate some of its most apparent weaknesses? Conferences of *Land* officials and *Land*-federal conferences have met to discuss problems of intergovernmental relations. It appears to be difficult, however, to find suitable alternatives. Since intergovernmental relations make the establishment of new programs easier through cost-sharing, the vertical alliance of functional specialists at all three levels resists change that would threaten its advantage. The lack of transparency makes it difficult to blame any particular set of participants for negative decisions, which makes it easier for each level to reject individual proposals or demands. Intergovernmental relations also give individual programs more stability, since it is more difficult to eliminate programs in which all levels share in some manner. For all of these reasons, the "generalists," such as chiefs of administration, finance ministers and city treasurers, deputies and councillors, are likely to perceive intergovernmental relations as dangerous.[36] But the pressures to promote uniform living conditions, the fear of the financially weaker *Länder* that they would not benefit from possible alternatives, and a general immobilism on the intergovernmental relations front have conspired to promote resistance to changes and adjustments.

A different and less critical perspective suggests that intergovernmental relations are merely an expression of centralizing tendencies found in all or most modern federations. Demands for a return to dual federalism, at least in Anglo-Saxon terms, may be unrealistic. A kind of balance of power between government levels may be the most one can expect, and such a balance may be "more favourable and stable in West Germany than in other federations like, for instance, Australia."[37] In spite of the criticism that can be made of intergovernmental relations in Germany, cooperation and shared decision-making persist because they are mutually beneficial, thus enlarging, in the view of some observers, the scope of autonomy for subnational governments.[38]

Intergovernmental Relations and the Undermining of American Functional Federalism

The Development of Intergovernmental Relations

From its origin in 1789 until the Great Depression of the 1930s, the United States operated, with some exceptions, according to a concept of functional dual federalism. Governmental functions were very limited by present-day standards, and they were divided between the two "sovereign" and "equal" levels of administration. Thus the federal government had its limited set of functions, and the states had theirs. While it was challenged by nationalist and state-centered theories, the concept of dual federalism remained dominant through the decades. Even in the period following the Civil War up to the Depression, dual federalism prevailed. In the first decades of the twentieth century, several federal grants-in-aid to the states emerged. By 1930, fifteen grant programs, especially for highways, were in operation; however, in spite of the growth in federal functions during this period, for example, in the area of regulation, and given the modest amounts and the nature of the assistance involved, the concept of dual federalism was not seriously breached.[39]

Dual federalism began its decline in the 1930s, due to Roosevelt's New Deal response to the Depression and several crucial decisions by the Supreme Court favoring a larger federal role in domestic affairs. World War II led to an even greater growth in executive powers and responsibilities at the federal level. After the War federal government activity and expenditures increased dramatically, federal grants-in-aid grew rapidly, and there was a massive expansion of state aid to local governments. To the 15 separately authorized permanent federal grant programs existing in 1930, 15 were added between 1933 and 1940, another 41 between 1941 and 1952, and 61 more during the last years of the period between 1930 and 1960. In 1960 there were 132 separate grants authorized for fifty-eight basic programs.[40] Of these 132 grants, only 15 bypassed the states for a direct line of assistance between the federal and local governments.

A number of federal provisions "combined to fashion a nonarticulated theory of grants administration that addressed the vertical, functional, bureaucratic linkages and the protective strengthening of administrative counterparts at the recipient level. Under it, the administrative role of elected chief executives and the administrative shaping powers of legislative bodies were de-emphasized, if not ignored."[41] Bypassing the state and ignoring the administrative role of regional chief executives were and still are features of American cooperative federalism that contrast sharply with German practices; however, cultivating vertical, functional bureaucratic linkages and ignoring legislative bodies are now common to both federal systems.

In spite of the growth of federal grants, which created some "intergovernmentalized" services at the state and even a few at the local level,

> a significant portion of state services and the vast bulk of local governmental activities were not touched by this expansion of federal grants. The states were the prime recipients of what federal grant funds there were, and by 1960 nearly three-quarters of these monies assisted programs that had a lengthy history of federal-state collaboration behind them, ranging from forty-four years in the case of highways, to twenty-seven years with employment security, to twenty-five years with old-age assistance and aid to dependent children.
>
> The localities, on the other hand, were far more affected by the growth in state aid and in state mandating than by federal programs. School districts and counties generally were the most heavily affected, given the state focus on education, highways, health, and hospitals.[42]

Between 1960 and 1980 federal grant programs expanded even more dramatically than during the preceding three decades. The five years of President Johnson's Administration alone created 209 new grants, conforming to the theory of Creative Federalism, which reflected

> a belief that the system was chiefly characterized by a federal-state-local sharing of responsibilities for practically all governmental functions (which the earlier practice of cooperative federalism did not). It assumed implicitly that no division of functions between levels was either possible or desirable. It trumpeted the ideal that officials at all levels were allies, not adversaries, under the system. And it accepted the concept that the system was "first conceived as one government serving one people," hence the president's call for the Great Society.[43]

As a reaction to Creative Federalism, Richard Nixon's New Federalism attempted to decentralize the increasingly complex system of intergovernmental relations. One of the most important initiatives of the New Federalism was the introduction in 1972 of general revenue-sharing, which offered the states assistance for a range of purposes without most of the numerous conditions of the traditional categorical project and formula grants. Several block grants, with some conditions but for broader purposes than categorical grants, were also initiated. Nevertheless, in spite of efforts under the New Federalism to reverse the trend toward increasing intergovernmental relations, Congress passed more than sixty new categorical grant programs during the Nixon years and about thirty more during the Ford presidency. By 1976 there were 448 federal aid programs, and by the end of the Carter years there were more than 500.[44]

Causes and Consequences of Intergovernmental Relations

Congressional preference for categorical grants, a quadrupling of interest groups located in Washington, D.C., and the decline in the ability of Congress to resist special group demands all account in part for the continuing growth of federal grants even in periods of more conservative executive leadership. In the meantime Congress was treating the states and substate government units virtually as equals, with one unit as likely to receive aid as the next. "This greatly expanded concept of partnership produced a 'pinwheel pattern' of grant administration, with each of the governmental and quasi-governmental recipient groups constituting a separate spoke in the wheel and with Washington (and by implication, Congress) serving as its hub."[45]

By 1980 the variety of assisted activities had expanded greatly over the number of areas that traditionally had received federal aid. The result was that

> hardly any governmental activity at the subnational levels was ineligible for some form of federal assistance, albeit in many instances meager, and practically all of the most national of services were caught up in the grant-in-aid system as well as the plainly intergovernmental (like energy, the environment, and transportation) along with an array of presumably local, if not private, concerns. Among the last, there were programs for urban gardening, noise control, snow removal, police disability payments, aqua-culture, displaced homemakers, rat control, education of gifted children, residential repair services for the elderly, the development of bikeways, pothole repair, runaway youth, art education, rural fire protection, and school security. National purpose as defined through the national political process clearly had come to encompass just about everything.[46]

The number of government units receiving aid by 1980 had also expanded dramatically. Not only all of the states, but also all of the cities, counties and towns and almost all public and private school systems as well as one-third of all special districts, or about 80 percent of the 80,000 units of state and local government were receiving some federal aid. The larger units were likely to be participating in more than one grant program; by 1974 cities over 50,000 were receiving an average of about nine grants, counties above 100,000 about 18–19. Many of these grant programs bypassed the states. Indeed, 25–30 percent of federal grant money went directly to substate units by 1980.[47]

According to David Walker, Assistant Director of the Advisory Commission of Intergovernmental Relations (ACIR), these developments led to qualitative changes in the relationship between the federal, state, and substate units. These changes are reflected in the forms of federal assistance, with block grants and general revenue-sharing being added to the traditional and still-dominant categorical grants; in the kinds of programs supported by grants, with people-related and assistance programs receiving more attention; in the conditions attached to federal grants, with the congressional tendency to increase conditions in spite of the emergence of block grants and general revenue-sharing; in the increase in the federal share of financing for programs; and in the shifting of aid from nonurban to urban areas, with a number of cities in the Northeast and Midwest becoming dependent on federal aid.[48]

The increasing federal role since 1960 has resulted in what Walker has described as an "overloaded" and "dysfunctional" system of intergovernmental relations. He notes that in the regulatory realm alone the number of federal mandates on state and local government has risen from 10 in 1960 to 224 in 1978, with an increase in mandates imposed as conditions for federal aid from 4 to 1,034 during the same period. In the meantime state mandates for local governments increased dramatically as well, ranging in the 1970s from 1,479 in California to 259 in North Carolina.[49] New or revised regulations in the *Federal Register* grew from 14,479 pages in 1960 to 71,191 pages in 1979. While twelve new regulatory agencies were created in the period between 1930 and 1960, fourteen new agencies emerged between 1960 and 1980. In addition to the dramatic increase in federal regulations, federal promotional efforts and assistance programs have also had a significant impact on federal-state-local relations. In the meantime implementation of most of the growing number of national programs has been turned over to the fifty states and about 63,000 localities, but with federal guidelines and supervision by an overwhelmed federal bureaucracy. Thus in 1978 the states alone were responsible for implementing 38 percent of the 492 categorical grants, the localities 6 percent, and the states, localities, and nonprofit organizations together 43 percent.[50]

With the growth in the number of local services that are financed in part by federal funds, the old dual federal concept of linking services at one level to financing by the same level has been supplanted by intergovernmental fiscal transfers mixed with own-source revenues. Since most federal aid and 90 percent of state aid is conditional, authority for the performance of most services is divided between the levels of government involved. This makes it difficult to assign accountability for the services delivered. Intergovernmental relations, added to the already complicated delivery of services by five kinds of local governments (counties, municipalities, towns and townships, special districts, and school districts), make the American system of local government perhaps the most fragmented in the world.[51]

Walker argues that the American federal system is not only complicated but also dysfunctional. The expansion of the federal role vis-à-vis the states and of both of these levels vis-à-vis the local governments, the implementation of more and more national policies by the subnational governments, the growing financial dependency of local governments on the state and federal governments, the increasing number of federal and state regulations and conditions placed on various grants, the relatively small group of federal officials attempting to supervise and monitor over five hundred assistance programs in which tens of thousands of subnational governments are participating, twelve million state and local employees under differing administrative and personnel systems implementing their own as well as national programs, the "massive fragmentation of administrative responsibility among programs, agencies and governmental levels" that the vertical, diagonal, and horizontal linkages of the current system produce, the numerous financial inefficiencies in intergovernmental fiscal transfers, and the distortion of local budget priorities through the availability of categorical grants that often are pushed by special interest groups—these are the kinds of obstacles in the way of a more effective and efficient administration of domestic programs and among the causes of "a current confusion at all levels as to their respective functional role."[52]

The American federal system is also "overloaded," according to Walker. There is *judicial* overload, caused by a judicial activism that supports federal initiatives in areas previously left to the subnational units or to the private sector, a *fiscal* overload that results in an increased tax burden to cover the underestimated costs of federal programs, a *servicing* overload, in which clearly national and intergovernmental concerns have been joined by what were once state and local matters to thoroughly undermine any lingering concept of dual functional responsibilities, an *administrative* overload in the "supervision" by the federal government of about 63,000 subnational units and twelve million state and local employees in their administration of more than five hundred federal programs, a *regulatory* overload, with both the federal and state governments using grants as an instrument for mandating a wide range of actions and behavior, a *political* overload reflected in the weakening and fragmentation of the political parties by functional, social, moralistic and economic interest groups, an *intellectual* overload, due to the lack of understanding of the current federal system both by politicians and the citizenry, and a *philosophic* overload mirrored in the conflicting concepts and inconsistent assessments of American federalism.

The consequences of these examples of overload include a decline in subnational government autonomy and discretionary powers, a proliferation of functional agencies and an increase in agency autonomy, with a focus on vertical rather than horizontal linkages within program areas, and growing resentment of the interference by the federal government in local decision-making and the dependency of local governments on federal aid.

The New "New Federalism"
of the Reagan Administration

The inauguration of the Reagan administration in January 1981 marked the beginning of a new era in intergovernmental relations. The "New Federalism" of the Nixon-Ford years, which saw an effort to reduce the reliance on categorical grants with their numerous regulations and restrictions by initiating a new, more flexible program of general revenue-sharing, was replaced by President Reagan's *new* "New Federalism" which in some respects was reminiscent of the "old" dual federalism. To a remarkable extent, the President made federalism a major agenda item for his administration, and there has probably been more serious public discussion of federalism since 1981 than in the previous two or three decades combined.[53]

In his efforts to reduce federal expenditures, President Reagan cut back on a variety of federal grant programs. In addition, the Omnibus Reconciliation Act of 1981 consolidated 77 categorical programs into nine block grants, thus almost doubling the number of block grant programs in existence.[54] At the same time, a number of individual program funds were reduced. Because of these reductions, many who might have supported block grants as a principle were opposed to the Reagan package. And since 1981, in spite of 23 additional proposals to expand block grants, only one has been enacted. Unlike its Republican predecessors, the Reagan administration has not been willing to sacrifice the goal of budgetary reduction in return for block grant consolidation.[55]

In his 1982 State of the Union address, President Reagan proposed a swapping of functions between the federal and state governments. According to the initial proposal, Medicaid was to become a federal responsibility, while food stamps and the Aid to Families with Dependent Children (AFDC) program would become state responsibilities. About forty other grant programs were also to become state responsibilities by 1988. This "realignment" of functions would be financed by the proceeds of federal excise taxes that would be given to the state. It was assumed that in the end neither the federal government nor the states would suffer or benefit financially from the "swap" and "turnback" elements of the proposal, but such an assumption was based on the premise that Congress would accept a number of cuts in the affected programs. Unable to convince the states that they would not end up with increased costs, the "sorting out" process did not make much progress during the years of the first Reagan administration. When confronted with the choice between a "realignment" and cutting the federal domestic budget, the administration chose the latter.

A new focus on "economic deregulation" respecting the private sector was accompanied in the Reagan administration by a serious effort to effect "social deregulation" as well. The Office of Management and Budget (OMB) was given new, centralized powers to review agency regulations, and the result was a significant decline in regulatory activity in 1981.[56] A President's Task Force on Regulatory Relief was also created to review already-existing regulations and to identify and possibly eliminate rules that are duplicative, inconsistent, or overlapping.[57] On the other hand, it appears that as conflicts arose increasingly between deregulation in the private sector and public sector deregulation that would give more authority to the state and local governments, "the Administration . . . sided repeatedly with business interests" and, if it deemed it necessary, took regulatory powers away from the states.[58] Examples of the latter can be found in national product liability legislation, federal regulation of trucking and drinking age standards, energy policies, and social policy (workfare and medical care for handicapped infants).[59] Thus a recent study concludes that in spite of his rhetorical support for the values of federalism, "President Reagan resembles his more liberal predecessors—perhaps more than either would care to admit—by his willingness to sacrifice federalism whenever it conflicts with his other deeply held policy objectives."[60]

By the end of its first term, it was clear that the Reagan administration's proposals to swap certain functions between the federal and state governments in a modest but significant move toward a renewed dual federalism had failed to gain consensus. His proposal to consolidate thirty-four programs into four block grant programs also failed in 1983. On the other hand, federal grant spending, though increasing to about $100 billion by fiscal year 1984, was stabilized; with inflation factored in, this was actually less than the budget for grant programs in 1982. The only new program passed was the "Job Training Partnership Act of 1982" for $4.6 billion. While general revenue-sharing was renewed in 1983, it was done so without enthusiasm and with provisions leaving out the states altogether for a direct federal-local transfer of funds.[61] Thus in reviewing Reagan's New Federalism during its first three years, one observer suggested that "a rebalancing is occurring, but it is being done without any formal 'sorting out' of governmental roles and responsibilities. The national government's attention is increasingly riveted on matters that are indisputably national in scope. Meanwhile, state and local governments did what it took to service the recession and have sharpened their own priorities, in the process sometimes restoring federal grant reductions they deemed most hurtful."[62]

Intergovernmental Relations in the Federal Republic and the United States: Some Differences

While there are a number of obvious parallels between the German and American experience in the development of their respective federal systems toward cooperative federalism and, then, toward an even more complex system of intergovernmental relations, there are also some interesting and notable differences. For example, Walker views the separation of national policy *making* from actual policy *execution* at subnational levels to be one of the causes of "dysfunctional federalism" in the United States,[63] while such a separation is one of the cornerstones of German federalism. Indeed, it is the undermining of this division of labor in the current practice of mixed financing, joint planning, and shared administration that is the focus of concern in Germany.

Another major difference appears to lie in the most important direct source of pressures for an increased sharing of responsibilities. In Germany it is the national and *Land* executive branches that have initiated and pushed through joint programs on grounds of equity, more rational and effective use of scarce resources, and the need for more comprehensive planning. In the United States, it has frequently been congressional responses to multifarious interest-group demands even more than an executive eagerness to use grants as an instrument of national policy that explain the sharp growth of federal grants and regulations in virtually all areas of expanding government activity.[64] While Congress may have a larger role than the *Bundestag* in shaping the system of intergovernmental relations, American state and German *Land* legislatures are both left with little, if any, real influence. In neither country do the legislative bodies at *any* level exercise much *control* over programs once they are authorized.[65] On the other hand, *Land* executives, through their representation in the *Bundesrat*, can and do exercise an influence that American state executives can only approach much more indirectly through the use of state congressional delegations and lobbyists in Washington.[66]

The role of Congress in promoting even modestly funded federal grant programs as a means for achieving some national goal is also one of the explanations for the much larger number of grant-in-aid programs in the United States than in Germany. In the German federal tradition it is not necessary to initiate a grant program for this purpose, since the federal government possesses the legal power to make general policy for all but a few areas without having to resort to grants (through the device of *Auftragsverwaltung*), and the majority party or parties supporting the government at the federal level are sufficiently disciplined to prevent the passage of framework laws or grant programs that the government does not want. On the other hand, it should be noted that in the United States too, federal and state mandates and regulations without grants have become more common in recent years.

Another important factor in the promotion of intergovernmental relations in Germany has been the perceived need for more joint planning and coordination between and among various levels of government. Thus a fairly comprehensive and coordinated system of national, *Land*, regional, and local planning exists, at least in theory, if less in practice—a system which in any case has made governments more conscious of their actions on other units, the environment and the economy. In the United States a number of laws enacted during the Johnson administration and the so-called A-95 review process led to the formation of hundreds of regional councils that were given area planning and coordination responsibilities; however, the planning that was encouraged never became as comprehensive or systematic as was and is the case in the Federal Republic. And the even greater weakness of the roots of the American planning institutions is evidenced by the replacement of the A-95 review process by the Reagan administration in favour of much less restrictive procedures.

Still another difference is found in the common standards and the uniformity of the German administrative and personnel systems in the various *Länder* as opposed to the differences among these systems in the American states. This may have an influence on the degree of administrative flexibility allowed the subnational units by respective executive and legislative bodies in carrying out national and state goals. Thus one might assume that in a system such as the German, where personnel at all levels are virtually indistinguishable in terms of recruitment, qualifications, and salary scales, there would be a greater tendency to leave administrative details to local governments and to make federal and state regulations somewhat less onerous.

Of course, other, more fundamental cultural and institutional differences also exist, such as the more homogeneous German population, which perhaps explains to some extent, along with different historical developments, the greater focus in Germany on equality of living conditions. The German system of shared taxes, the close ties between the federal and *Land* governments promoted by the *Bundesrat*, the German spatial federal administrative tradition and the relatively disciplined and cohesive political parties that discourage interest group lobbying of individual legislators are all institutional factors that make German federalism different in certain respects from the American and other federal models.[67]

These examples of differences between the German and American systems of intergovernmental relations suggest that in spite of numerous, often striking, similarities, the German system is neither so complex nor as confusing as the current American system. In both countries, however, there is a serious gap between theory (of functional [dual] federalism in the United States and spatial federalism in Germany) and the reality of intergovernmental relations. And while the theory of cooperative federalism more or less officially replaced each of the respective theories, first in the United States, then in Germany, there appears to be a growing dissatisfaction in each country with the continued development toward an ever more complex and problematic system of intergovernmental relations and a widespread concern that any remaining substance in the traditional understanding of federalism has been lost.

11

Intergovernmental Relations and the Undermining of Traditional Administrative Systems

In the literature of American political science one finds frequent references to the unitary versus federal or even confederal organization of state territory and to the competing principles underlying each of these forms. These principles are usually defined in terms of "centralized" versus "decentralized" administration, or as a centralization of powers at the national level versus a division of powers between one national and several regional governments. Only within the subfield of public administration is one likely to encounter an occasional discussion of the principles of territorial, areal or "spatial" organization as opposed to functional or special-purpose organization. By ignoring these latter perspectives, one may fail to understand that both unitary and federal systems may be organized according to the principles of spatial or functional administration, or that what exists in any system may be some peculiar combination of these two principles in addition to a unitary or federal structure.

Models of Administration

The Functional Model

In the functional model of administration the focus is on an organization of government by special tasks or related sets of activities. If a service is to be provided, a particular revenue to be raised, or a certain behavior to be regulated, a central ministry or agency with responsibility for the activity can organize a bureaucracy with a more or less hierarchic chain of command from the center to regional and local field agencies. The regional field agencies' area of responsibility may not necessarily conform to the territorial boundaries of subnational political divisions, and the areas of responsibility of central ministry local field agencies may not conform to the boundaries of local government units. There may be varying degrees of coordination and cooperation between central government field agencies and subnational political units. In any case the central field agencies are organizationally separate from the regional or local government units with which they may or may not have close contacts.

As an alternative to assuming direct responsibility for the administration of its programs, the central government may also turn these over to regional or local governments for implementation without necessarily worrying about the coordination of the numerous central government services or regulations, let alone coordination among central, regional, and local services and regulations. The nature, number, and variety of special-purpose authorities organized at the regional and local levels either by the central government or by regional and local governments in order to carry out central government policies would depend on the constitutional-legal framework—such as implied powers, supremacy clauses, and residual powers—and on the extent to which government is expected to deal with social and economic problems.

The functional model is sometimes referred to as "vertical administration." Frido Wagener uses this term to describe special-purpose administration, that is, administration by function or task, irrespective of the level of administration within the political system.[1] In the United States "picket fence federalism," involving two or even all three levels of government, is an example of vertical functional administration in Wagener's sense of the term. "Iron triangle" relationships are another example. Unfortunately, "vertical" has been given different definitions by other scholars. Arnold Brecht[2] described the American system of dual federalism as a "vertical" division of powers between nation and states. For Brecht, then, "vertical" meant specifically a functional division of labor between the national and state levels of government (dual federalism), not functional administration in general. More recent writers also sometimes use "vertical" to describe the American system of dual federalism.[3] For K. C. Wheare, who wrote a classic study of federalism, *only* dual federalism is real federalism. That is, only when the nation is responsible for one set of activities and the states or provinces for another, does federalism exist.[4] To add to the confusion, "vertical" is used in a wholly atheoretical way by some American textbook writers as a mere description of relations between local, state and national levels of government.[5] Because of the confusion resulting from these various usages, "vertical administration" is not as satisfactory a term as "functional administration" for describing the administrative organization of either a unitary or a federal state. "Functional administration" also seems preferable to the apparently identical concept of "dual administration" developed by Gordon Smith, since the latter term, though used by Smith for a *general* concept, could be confused with "dual federalism."[6]

The Spatial Model

In the preceding chapters we have seen that German administration is based on a model of spatial, or territorial, administration. According to this model, the central authorities are responsible for most lawmaking, while subnational units administer on their own responsibility the laws of the higher authorities. At the same time, however, these same units maintain a degree of autonomy over areas of their own concern in what Gordon Smith calls a "fused" system of administration.[7] Each level of administration is legally responsible for all of the public services and activities, whether delegated, mandated or self-generated, within its territory (*Einheit der Verwaltung*). If some of these are delegated further to lower levels, this responsibility consists of a right to supervise the lower levels in their administration of the laws. Supervision involves above all assuring that the actions of the lower level are legal; in some cases supervision may also include technical matters.

The German model of spatial administration is not, however, that of a highly centralized state characterized by a strong degree of uniformity. Even the Prussian unitary state contained numerous features of decentralized administration, the most important examples of which were the limited autonomy granted the eight provinces and their local governments and the relatively strong position of the Prussian cities. Strong local discretionary powers were the result of the legal principle of *Allzuständigkeit*, or the right of local governments to regulate on their own responsibility all matters of local concern within the framework of the law. This is similar to the "devolution of powers approach" in the United States, which only three states have adopted.[8]

German federalism in the Bismarck Reich of 1871 added a new dimension to the German principles of spatial administration. In some respects, federalism merely added one new administrative or governmental level. This level was, of course, the new central government in Berlin. After 1871, the most important laws affecting the people of the new nation would be made in Berlin, but they would continue to be administered by the twenty-five constituent states. Unlike dual federalism in the United States, where the national government was to have one set of powers and the states and their local governments another, with each of the levels administering its own laws with its own officials, the German federal tradition is based on a dualism of rule-making at the central level versus rule application at the *Land* and local levels. Thus the division of powers in American federalism has been functional (national problems to the federal government, regional and local problems to the states), whereas it has been territorial or spatial in Germany (each level of administration is responsible to the next higher level for the administration of all state laws within its territory; however, each level of general-purpose administration is also self-governing).

The spatial model in Germany has been described both as "executive-legislative federalism" and "administrative federalism"[9]; however, it is described more frequently as "horizontal administration." Frido Wagener uses this term in contrast to "vertical administration," and he, Arnold Brecht, Nevil Johnson, P. Bernd Spahn and others characterize German federalism as "horizontal."[10] While this term may be less problematic than "vertical," it, too, is used atheoretically by some American writers as a description of relationships among administrative structures within one level of government.[11] Because "horizontal administration" has been used with different meanings, "spatial administration" has been the term used in this study.

The Mixed Reality

In practice each model allows for numerous exceptions in the direction of the competing model. With the functional model one will find regional and/or local units of government or administration that are organized on the basis of territory. All general-purpose local governments, for example, have a territorial dimension and are responsible for the administration of a variety of activities within that territory, including some regional or national programs and policies. Nevertheless, a major characteristic of administration under the functional model at the level of local government will be its fragmentation into separate areas of responsibility for schools, water services, public power, waste disposal, fire protection, parks, etc. Government by special districts in the United States is, of course, the perfect example of functional administration at the local level. The special functional local field agencies of the central government will also be separate to some extent from the local general-purpose government. There is, then, only a limited unity of administration at this and at any regional level.

The spatial model exists also as an ideal type only, even though it is frequently referred to as the "classical model" of bureaucracy. In practice the central state retains a limited number of activities for administration according to the principles of the functional model. Common examples would be military forces and the diplomatic corps as well as postal, telecommunication and rail services. Such activities are not delegated normally to subnational units, and their regional and local branches are responsible directly to central state authorities. The subnational units, especially those at the local level, may find it convenient and even necessary to make arrangements with other units for the provision of certain services which any single unit does not have the financial or administrative capacity to operate on its own. Common examples of cooperative associations between or among local administrative units would include electricity, gas and water works, transportation facilities, special schools, and hospitals. In the spatial model there may be many examples of cooperative special-purpose functional organization;

however, they remain an exception to the general rule of organization of administrative activities within a single territory under the general responsibility of a single chief administrative officer. Indeed, many special-purpose organizations at one level will fall under the administrative responsibility of a higher level, thus preserving the principle of unity of administration for the next higher level.

Unitary and Federal Variations of the Functional and Spatial Models

Each of these basic models of administration can be further subdivided into two other types of territorial organization: unitary or federal. Both France and Germany serve as classic examples of the spatial model of organization. Yet since Napoleon, France has been considered to be an example of a highly centralized, unitary state, while Prussia was far more decentralized, and the Bismarck Reich created in 1871 was a federal state organized according to the spatial model.

Just as the territories of France and Germany, in large part spatially administered, were organized as unitary and federal states, respectively, so also were the British and American systems, in general functionally administered, organized differently as unitary and federal states. Since the nineteenth century, and especially during the twentieth century, the British have created numerous ad hoc special-purpose authorities, including the so-called "quangos," for the autonomous administration of economic activities, planning, health care, water services, and river authorities, etc. And though local governments are, of course, responsible for the administration of many delegated state functions in the areas within their boundaries, there are numerous functional links between the local and central governments in the form of direct contacts between the professional administrators at the central and local levels.[12]

American federalism, especially in the original form of dual federalism which persisted until about the 1930s, assigns a wide variety of powers, expressed and implied, to the national government, which also enjoys certain inherent powers. All powers not granted to the national government and not prohibited by the Constitution are reserved to the states or the people. Powers which are not assigned exclusively to the national government may be exercised concurrently by both levels unless there is a conflict, in which case the national power is supreme. According to the principle of dual federalism, each level of government should administer its own laws with its own administrative personnel, but with the growth of cooperative federalism and especially in the current system of intergovernmental relations, many federal programs are administered by state and local officials together with federal officials or under the supervision of federal officials. This administration is still organized largely along functional lines, however, with federal, state, and local government officials in one program

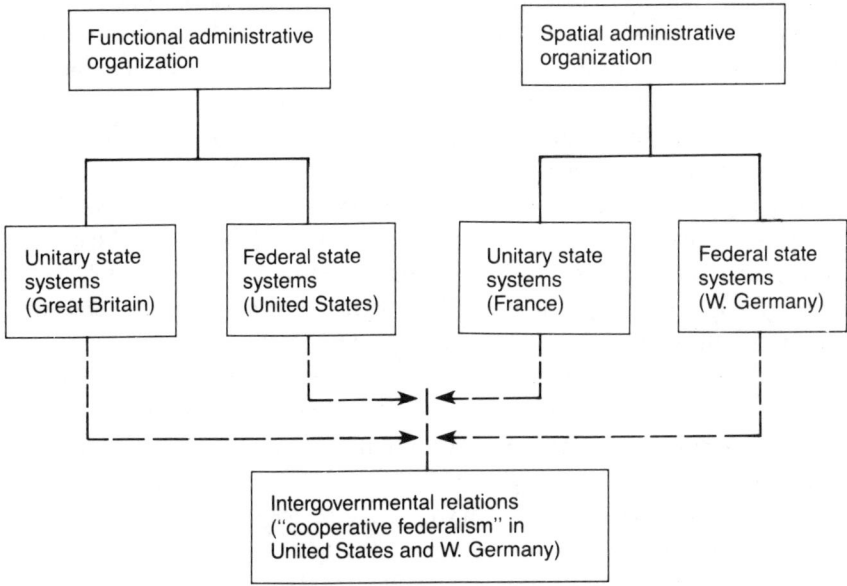

Figure 11.1. Two basic models of administrative organization and the division of state powers

frequently maintaining little if any contact with their counterparts in other programs.

Intergovernmental Relations as a New Model

Figure 11.1 presents a simplified picture of the interrelationships that may exist between the functional and spatial models of administration on the one hand and the division of powers according to unitary and federal forms on the other hand. The broken lines indicate recent trends, which appear to exist to a greater or lesser extent in advanced Western industrial states in the direction of more *shared*, functional patterns of administrative organization.

In the United States, for example, the fifty years since the election in 1932 of Franklin D. Roosevelt brought the growth of various stages of "cooperative federalism," which is now generally referred to as "intergovernmental relations."[13] Intergovernmental relations, in contrast to traditional dual federalism, suggests a system of federal, state and local government cooperation and sharing of responsibility in the performance of public functions or tasks which affect all levels of government. With the federal government taking the initiative in many areas of the enlarged public sector, setting goals, outlining the requirements and standards to be met, and providing substantial proportions of the funding for projects and programs to be completed or administered at the regional or local levels, many administrative structures are now organized according to shared rather than "dual" functional and hierarchical patterns of federal, state, and local relationships. State governments, and especially large cities, have become dependent to varying degrees on the federal government for administrative and, in particular, financial support. To the extent that state and local governments feel that they must participate in federal grant programs in order to benefit from the federal funds that are offered, they also have delegated to the federal government significant responsibilities for policy-making and goal-setting. Even significant proportions of state and local government employees now are involved directly or indirectly in implementing or administering a wide variety of federal grant programs in a manner somewhat in accordance with the spatial model of administration.

Dual federalism in the United States has been replaced by intergovernmental relations for a number of reasons, among which are a traditional reluctance on the part of many states to tap their own revenue sources—which may also be inadequate in any case—to provide for certain public services or facilities or to do so without federal assistance. Congress, on the other hand, has often been eager to see such services and facilities provided. Some groups, especially racial minorities and the underprivileged, might question also the willingness of many state legislatures to assume on their own responsibility certain social and economic activities which Congress has encouraged through numerous grant programs. Nevertheless, criticism of intergovernmental relations in the United States has become widespread, and the Reagan Administration's "New Federalism" initiatives, especially those proposing a "swapping" or a sorting out of federal and state/local responsibilities, are a reflection of dissatisfaction with current conditions and trends.

The complex system of intergovernmental relations which is characteristic of contemporary American federalism appears to be an increasingly common feature in other countries as well. Whether in the German spatial-federal model or in the French spatial-unitary model, functional forms of administration involving national and subnational units in a wide range of cooperative ventures are now common. The blurring of territorial boundaries of responsibility between administrative levels in Germany, which is called *Politikverflechtung*—although the more descriptive term would be *Verwaltungsverflechtung*—and the increasing functional separation of tasks in both Germany and France have been subjected to severe criticism in both countries, and numerous reform proposals have been made which would reorganize and strengthen spatial relationships.

In both functionally and spatially administered systems, then, there is resistance to the new pattern of intergovernmental relations which is characterized by functional administration and shared powers among levels of government, together with a blurring of lines of accountability and a resulting loss of administrative control. Many Americans fear that the sharing of so many functions today has undermined traditional federal principles to the extent that states and local governments have been reduced to the status of mere junior partners. German criticisms of "cooperative federalism" rest on the argument that too many important functions have been removed from the political-administrative responsibility of the *Länder* and the general-purpose local governments, which, according to spatial administrative principles, should administer on their own responsibility virtually all functions within their respective territories. Because of the resistance to the continuing growth of shared powers, the lower lines of figure 11.1 are broken rather than solid. Thus the trend toward the intergovernmental relations pattern could be slowed, halted or perhaps even reversed, even though each of these possibilities is progressively unlikely. In any case the reactions of different countries with contrasting models of administration and different forms of division of powers to the apparently common and irresistible trend toward shared functional relationships will be a major focus of scholarly and political attention in the years to come.

12

German and American Local Government: Some Comparisons and Conclusions

In chapter 10 we traced the development of the German and American federal systems toward cooperative federalism or, as it is called more frequently today, intergovernmental relations. Chapter 11 suggested that the administrative systems of Germany and the United States as well as Britain and France might be characterized at the present time as somewhat different versions of what appears to be an increasingly common model of intergovernmental relations.

Understanding the current role of local government in these and other Western political systems is one of the keys to understanding this development. But local government is only a part of a larger tradition of administration, and some familiarity with the relevance of this tradition is also helpful in the effort to gain a better understanding of recent governmental-administrative trends in a variety of different settings. The purpose of this final chapter is to review briefly some of the findings concerning German local government and to make a number of comparisons between German and American local governments.

Germans and Americans share a common tradition of strong local government, in spite of the discontinuities in German history during the past 100–150 years, and both peoples take considerable pride in the historical exercise of self-government at the local level. Local self-government stood in such sharp contrast to the bureaucratic tutelage and autocracy of "the state," whether Prussia or one of several other smaller German territorial units, that a kind of dualism between the state and local municipal government arose. German cities grew rapidly during the nineteenth century, and in addition to retaining their reputation for honest and effective administration, they demonstrated considerable initiative in meeting the challenges of the industrial revolution and rapid population growth. Indeed, "municipal socialism" became a characteristic of German local government even without significant working-class participation or influence.

Americans take pride in their long tradition of grass-roots democracy and in the strong local governments that have always been a part of the American political system. The Jeffersonian and Jacksonian democratic traditions focused on the local level and helped to create a body of myths concerning local democracy that is probably unmatched anywhere in the world.

While the pride expressed in traditions of local self-government in both countries may be justified to a considerable extent, one should be wary of an uncritical acceptance of the popular version of the history of local governments. German local self-government in the nineteenth century was limited largely to the cities and larger towns, and, as in England, it was "democratic" only for the middle and upper classes until shortly before or after World War I.

In the United States local self-government was more democratic in theory, but in practice local middle-class "notables" also controlled the local councils and, in order to keep taxes low, offered as few public services as possible; or one ethnic group or combination of groups dominated the local government at the real or perceived expense of other groups. Corruption, especially in the larger cities, was all too common, and "reforms" designed as correctives frequently served to return local government to the control of middle- and upper-middle-class groups. In spite of the views of Jefferson and Jackson, most local governments were given little discretionary power by the states, and as a result local governments in the United States hardly have a general reputation for innovation and initiative in meeting social and economic challenges.

One of the sharpest contrasts between German and American local government since World War I concerns the role of political parties and the methods of election to local councils. The introduction after 1918 of proportional representation at all levels of government in Germany made possible a degree of participation in local elections unknown before, and it also made it easier for radical elements of all persuasions to disrupt and polarize the local councils along ideological lines. The Nazis, of course, put an end to this, through their policy of coordination and synchronization. After World War II, local governments in the three Western occupation zones emerged as the foundation of the new democratic order that was established later at the *Land* and, in 1949, at the "national" level in West Germany. The reintroduction of various forms of proportional representation at the local, *Land* and federal levels did not lead to the kind of polarization characteristic of the Weimar Republic. The number of major parties declined to two or three in most localities, although local nonpartisan voter groups continued to play a major role in many smaller towns and villages until recent years. With the growth in the 1970s of a socialist youth organization in the SPD interested in seeing a parliamentarization of local government, and with the emergence of the radical democratic Greens since the late 1970s, a new potential for ideological polarization in local affairs has emerged in some local councils.

The relevance of political parties at the local level in the United States is significantly less than in pre- and post-World War II Germany, which is sometimes referred to as a classic "party state." Even today, nonpartisan elections are held in about two-thirds of American local governments, although parties do run candidates in most larger cities. This has not, of course, eliminated "politics," as some reformers had hoped; it has merely made local councillors less accountable to the voters in any sense of a majority or minority "team." And it has served to some extent to insulate local bureaucratic leadership from the control of a consistent council majority. Where minority groups are large enough to have a determining influence on local government, tension and even polarization may be found in the councils, but more because of racial and ethnic conflict than because of partisan ideology. Where racial or ethnic divisions are not so relevant to local politics, middle- and upper-middle-class elements continue to win majorities in elections in which—by the much higher participatory standards in Germany—only a small proportion of the electorate participates.

Another obvious contrast between German and American local governments is the number of local council members elected to serve on the council. Many Germans complain that the number of councillors, especially in small towns and villages, has declined dramatically since the territorial reforms of the late 1960s and 1970s. While this is true, it is also interesting to note the continuing contrast to a far more limited representativeness of American local councils. The number of councillors in proportion to population in Germany is several times that found in most American local governments. Together with the single-member ward or even the multimember ("at large") district election systems, this makes American local governments potentially far less representative of relatively small but important groups than they might otherwise be. Whether party discipline and the expectation of some degree of uniformity within the *Fraktion*, or party group, serve to place limits on the actual degree of representativeness at the local level in Germany is a question that can be answered only through empirical studies.

The financing of local governments is also very different in the two countries. Local property taxes exist in Germany, as in the United States and Great Britain, but in contrast to these two countries this tax is not the main source of own revenue for German local governments. For most German municipalities, this is the business tax, which, of course, varies widely from one municipality to another. Far more important than these and other local taxes, however, are the taxes that are shared by specific constitutional direction with the *Land* and federal governments. These include the personal income tax, and, more indirectly, the corporation tax and the value-added tax. In addition there is an elaborate system of fiscal equalization that brings about a remarkable degree of fiscal uniformity for all *Länder* and most local governments. As in the United States, some fiscal equalization among states and localities is achieved through various grants-in-aid as well, but the remaining differences in fiscal strength among American states and local governments is extreme by German standards.

A significant difference between German and American local government can be found regarding personnel. As in the United States, local government personnel are hired and fired by local authorities, but German federal law regulates the educational background and training requirements, salary scales and benefits of middle- and higher-level civil servants. As a result, differences among local governments of comparable size in salaries and working conditions are insignificant in comparison to the United States. There may be less federal intrusion in matters of personnel by the federal government in the United States, but federal antidiscrimination legislation has placed certain limits on conditions of employment in local governments. Affirmative action, age discrimination, overtime pay, and other issues are now subject to federal regulation in the United States. German pension and early retirement provisions for local administrators—for example, city managers and governing mayors, even in cases of nonrenewal of contracts or firing by the local councils—are very generous by American standards, and they can make all but the most ideologically polarized council in Germany pause before deciding to remove a leading official from office.

While both German and American local governments operate within the framework of a federal system, local governments in Germany are not creatures of the states in the same sense as they are in the United States. German local governments are protected as institutions by the constitution, and local discretionary authority is a constitutional right in theory if less so in practice. There is no nationwide uniformity in local government forms and procedures in either country, yet it is easier to speak of a "system" of local government in Germany than in the United States. In part this is due to the fact that there are eleven states in one country—only eight of which are "territorial" states—and fifty in the other. But it is also due to the tradition of statewide charters for municipalities and counties in Germany, to the influence of Baron vom Stein and Prussia on the other German states, and to the greater insistence in Germany on uniform legal procedures and living conditions.

Another striking contrast, in spite of the federal organization of both countries, is the ability and willingness of German states to carry out widespread local government territorial reforms. During the 1960s and 1970s, county and municipal boundary changes, which involved a large number of consolidations of local government, took place regardless of the party make-up of the *Land* governments. While differences among the *Land* governments were reflected in part in the extent and nature of the reforms, what is remarkable in the American context is that it is possible in a federal system for all of the states to carry out more or less simultaneously comprehensive local government reforms. In the United States it is usually very difficult to bring about a boundary change even for one limited area within a state; a statewide or even regional reform of significance would hardly be possible.

Some of the differences that we have noted thus far are the result of special historical traditions and conditions. Some are the result of different conceptions of the purposes of local government and general attitudes about government and society. Some may also be the result of the different administrative traditions noted in previous chapters, that is, the spatial tradition in Germany and the functional tradition in the United States. In spite of these differences, there are trends operating in both countries that seem to be making German and American federalism, and of necessity their local governments, more similar in certain respects than they have been in the past. Such trends include the development of intergovernmental relations.

While it is recognized in both countries that certain centralizing pressures, including demands for more services and facilities delivered on a more equitable basis in the various regions, are powerful causes of the growth of intergovernmental relationships, there is also considerable dissatisfaction shared by many Germans and Americans concerning the trends and developments associated with their respective federal systems. But as in the examples cited above, there are some differences between Germany and the United States with respect to the phenomena of intergovernmental relations. First, it appears that intergovernmental relations are more executive-centered in Germany than in the United States. The initiatives for the changes in German law that have encouraged intergovernmental relations have come generally from the national, *Land*, and local executives, both elected officials and civil servants. The participation of the *Bundesrat* in the national policy-making process that involves federal-*Land* relations gives the German *Länder* a far more direct legislative role than is enjoyed by the American Senate; however, it is the *Land* cabinets that are represented in the *Bundesrat*, not the *Land* parliaments. The "iron triangle" relationships in the German context appear to involve federal, *Land* and local elected *executive* officials, federal, *Land* and local bureaucracies, and certain interest groups. In the United States, they appear to involve to a greater extent *elected* members of Senate and House committees, federal bureaucracies, and, even more than in Germany, a plethora of interest groups, including regional interests promoting the Sun Belt, the Northeast, the tobacco industry, etc. Therefore, it seems justified to suggest that intergovernmental relations in Germany are more executive-centered, while in the United States national legislators play a more significant role. One of the many consequences of this difference may be the special regional focus in much of the American legislation, in contrast to the more national orientation of German law. Related to this suggestion is the view which can be heard in Germany that intergovernmental relations serve to help *Land* executives resist demands from their legislatures and to minimize conflict between and among the *Länder*.

It could be argued, in contrast, that intergovernmental relations in the United States have had an opposite effect. They have provided national lawmakers with the means to respond to increased demands and, to the extent that the continued financing of hundreds of intergovernmental programs is now in doubt, they have become more controversial than ever before. The result is that today the Reagan Administration would like to reduce sharply federal domestic spending in general and the federal involvement in intergovernmental programs in particular. In Germany, on the other hand, it appears to be mostly local and *Land* officials and scholars that are critical of intergovernmental relations and are demanding a sorting out of federal, *Land* and local responsibilities.

In spite of these and other differences, there are important common threads running through the German and American federal systems that have drawn these two countries more closely together in a general framework of intergovernmental relations. Some studies suggest that the unitary states of Britain and France can also be described today as systems in which intergovernmental relations are of crucial importance. Whether a general model of intergovernmental relations is developing that applies to these four countries and, perhaps, to all or most industrialized democracies is an intriguing and still open question.

Notes

1. Introduction

1. F. F. Ridley, ed., *Government and Administration in Western Europe* (Oxford: Martin Robertson & Co., 1979), 1.

2. Herbert Jacob, *German Administration Since Bismarck: Central Authority versus Local Autonomy* (New Haven and London: Yale University Press, 1963), 8–9, 26–66.

3. As Daniel Elazar appears to do in his essay, "American Federalism and Prefectorial Administration," *Publius* 11 (Spring 1981): 9, 17–18.

4. Robert C. Fried, "Prefectorialism in America?" ibid., 23, 27.

5. Nevil Johnson, "Some Effects of Decentralization in the Federal Republic of Germany," in *Decentralist Trends in Western Democracies*, ed. L. J. Sharpe (London and Beverly Hills: Sage Publications, 1979), 240–56.

6. Elazar, "American Federalism," 14. Gordon Smith suggests that West Germany combines "decentralization," i.e., some measure of self-government, and "deconcentration," the "simple delegation of authority from one level of the administrative hierarchy to a lower one." See his *Politics in Western Europe*, 4th ed. (New York: Holmes and Meier Publishers, 1984), 218, 234.

7. Ridley, *Government and Administration*, 3.

8. Max Weber, *Wirtschaft und Gesellschaft*, 5th ed. (Tübingen: J. C. B. Mohr, 1972), 126.

9. Ridley, *Government and Administration*, 3.

2. The Development of Local Government in Germany, 1808–1949

1. Heinrich Mitteis and Heinz Lieberich, *Deutsche Rechtsgeschichte: Ein Studienbuch*, 15th ed. (Munich: C. H. Beck'sche Verlagsbuchhandlung, 1978), 227; for a review of the early history of German cities, see Hugo Preuss, *Die Entwicklung des Deutschen Städtewesens* (Leipzig: B. G. Teubner, 1906), chaps. 1 and 2.

2. Mitteis and Lieberich, *Deutsche Rechtsgeschichte*, 298–99, and Preuss, *Entwicklung*,

chap. 3.

3. Waldemar von Grumbkow, *Die Geschichte der Kommunalaufsicht in Preussen* (Berlin: Carl Heymanns Verlag, 1921), 13–15.

4. Franz-Ludwig Knemeyer, *Regierungs- und Verwaltungsreformen in Deutschland zu Beginn des 19. Jahrhunderts* (Cologne: Grote'sche Buchhandlung, 1970), 21.

5. Ernst Rudolf Huber, *Deutsche Verfassungsgeschichte seit 1789*. Band *I, Reform und Restauration, 1789 bis 1830*, 2d ed. (Stuttgart: W. Kohlhammer Verlag, 1967), 41–46.

6. Ibid., 41–42, 60.

7. Ibid., 112–21.

8. Gerhard Ritter, *Stein: Eine politische Biographie* (Stuttgart: Deutsche Verlagsanstalt, 1958), 189–90, and Huber, *Deutsche Verfassungsgeschichte* 1:173.

9. Ernst Maste, "Freiherr vom Stein: Zur 150. Wiederkehr seines Todestages," *Aus Politik und Zeitgeschichte* 24 (13 June 1981):8.

10. Franz Herre, *Freiherr vom Stein: Ein Leben, Seine Zeit* (Cologne: Kiepenheuer & Witsch, 1973), 152.

11. Ritter, *Stein*, 201.

12. Heinrich Heffter, *Die Deutsche Selbstverwaltung im 19. Jahrhundert: Geschichte der Ideen und Institutionen*, 2d ed. (Stuttgart: K. F. Koehler Verlag, 1969), 91.

13. Herre, *Stein*, 153.

14. The full text can be found in Walter Hubatsch, ed., *Freiherr vom Stein: Das Reformministerium (1807–1808)*, vol. 2, pt. 2 (Stuttgart: W. Kohlhammer Verlag, 1960), 947–79.

15. Ritter, *Stein*, 190.

16. For summaries of the Charter Law of 1808, see, for example, Heffter, *Selbstverwaltung*, 94–95; Huber, *Verfassungsgeschichte*, 1:175–76; Ritter, *Stein*, 263; and Erich Becker, "Entwicklung der deutschen Gemeinden und Gemeindeverbände im Hinblick auf die Gegenwart," in *Handbuch der Kommunalen Wissenschaft und Praxis*, vol. 1: *Kommunalverfassung*, ed. Hans Peters (Heidelberg: Springer-Verlag, 1956), 80.

17. von Grumbkow, *Kommunalaufsicht*, 36, and Heffter, *Selbstverwaltung*, 95.

18. *Preussische Städteordnung vom 19. November 1808*, paragraphs 1 and 152.

19. von Grumbkow, *Kommunalaufsicht*, 44.

20. Heffter, *Selbstverwaltung*, 96.

21. Ritter, *Stein*, 260–62; see also Preuss, *Entwicklung*, 281–82.

22. von Grumbkow, *Kommunalaufsicht*, 45.

23. Huber, *Verfassungsgeschichte*, 1:174.

24. Ritter, *Stein*, 266–68.

25. von Grumbkow, *Kommunalaufsicht*, 56–66; Heffter, *Selbstverwaltung*, 214–15; and Preuss, *Entwicklung*, 318–19.

26. von Grumbkow, *Kommunalaufsicht*, 67.

27. Heffter, *Selbstverwaltung*, 104–6, 119; Knemeyer, *Regierungs- und Verwaltungsreform*, 28–44.

28. Heffter, *Selbstverwaltung*, 228.

29. Knemeyer, *Regierungs- und Verwaltungsreform*, 118–50.

30. Ibid., 261.

31. Ibid., 132, and Heffter, *Selbstverwaltung*, 126, 183–84.

32. Georg-Christoph von Unruh, *Der Kreis: Ursprung und Ordnung einer kommunalen Körperschaft* (Cologne and Berlin: Grote'sche Verlagsbuchhandlung, 1964), 91–92.

33. Ibid., 96, 104; see also Heffter, *Selbstverwaltung*, 111.

34. Heffter, *Selbstverwaltung*, 221–23; and Huber, *Verfassungsgeschichte*, 1:179–80.

35. Heffter, *Selbstverwaltung*, 132.

36. Ibid., 131; von Unruh, *Der Landkreis*, 113; Frido Wagener, *Die Städte im Landkreis* (Göttingen: Verlag Otto Schwartz & Co., 1955), 32.

37. For an excellent description in English of the Prussian levels of administration in the nineteenth century, see Herbert Jacob, *German Administration since Bismarck: Central Authority versus Local Autonomy* (New Haven: Yale University Press, 1963), chap. 2.

38. Huber, *Verfassungsgeschichte*, 1:163–64; and Heffter, *Selbstverwaltung*, 120–21.

39. *Verfassung des Deutschen Reiches vom 28. März 1849*, sec. 6, art. 11.

40. Heffter, *Selbstverwaltung*, 295–304.

41. Ibid., 312–14.

42. Ibid., 315, and von Unruh, *Der Kreis*, 119–20.

43. *Verfassungsurkunde für den Preussischen Staat vom 31. Januar 1850*, art. 105; this article and other important parts of the Prussian Constitution of 1850 can be found in Horst Hildebrandt, ed., *Die deutschen Verfassungen des 19. und 20. Jahrhunderts*, 10th ed. (Paderborn: Ferdinand Schöningh, 1977).

44. Ludwig von Könne, ed., *Die Gemeindeordnung und die Kreis-, Bezirks- und Provinzialordnung für den Preussischen Staat, nebst dem Gesetze über die Polizeiverwaltung, vom 11. März 1850* (Brandenburg: Adolph Müller Druck und Verlag, 1850). This book provides not only an excellent introduction which outlines briefly the arguments in the Prussian parliament for and against the new statewide municipal charter, but also a highly detailed commentary on each provision of the law for the municipalities, counties, districts, provinces and police administration.

45. Heffter, *Selbstverwaltung*, 316–19; von Unruh, *Der Kreis*, 121; Huber, *Verfassungsgeschichte*, 3:126–27; von Grumbkow, *Kommunaluufsicht*, 70–79; Preuss, *Entwicklung*, 342–45.

46. For a legal commentary with introduction, see H. Gräff, *Die Städteordnung für die sechs östlichen Provinzen des Preussischen Staates* (Breslau: Georg Philipp Aderholz, 1853).

47. *Städteordnung für die Rheinprovinz und Gesetz betreffend die Gemeindeverfassung in der Rheinprovinz vom 15. Mai 1856*. The City Charter Laws for the Rhine province and Westphalia can be found in Otto Kotze, *Die Preussischen Städteverfassungen* (Berlin: Verlag von Gustav Hempel, 1879).

48. Heffter, *Selbstverwaltung*, 331.

49. Ibid., 330.

50. Ibid., 334–35.

51. Ibid., 345–49.

52. Ibid., 408–14.

53. Ibid., 415–24.

54. Ibid., 480.

55. Ibid., 335.

56. For a book that contains this and other local and regional Prussian laws, see Gustav Dullo, *Die Preussischen Verwaltungsgesetze* (Berlin: J. J. Heines Verlag, 1890).

57. von Unruh, *Der Kreis*, 145. For descriptions of this law, see ibid., 170–75, and Heffter, *Selbstverwaltung*, 549–56.

58. von Unruh, *Der Kreis*, 170.

59. Ibid., 173–75; Wolfgang Hofmann suggests that the proportion of nobility was as high as 59 percent in 1904. See his "Die Entwicklung der kommunalen Selbstverwaltung von 1848 bis 1918," in *Handbuch der kommunalen Wissenschaft und Praxis*, vol. 1: *Grundlagen*, 2d ed., ed. Günter Püttner (Berlin and Heidelberg: Springer-Verlag, 1981), 78.

60. Heffter, *Selbstverwaltung*, 554–55.

61. Dullo, *Die Preussischen Verwaltungsgesetze*, 211ff.

62. Heffter, *Selbstverwaltung*, 603.

63. Ibid., 351.

64. Ibid., 608.

65. Frido Wagener, *Die Städte im Landkreis*, p. 186; Koppel S. Pinson, *Modern Germany: Its History and Civilization*, 2d ed. (New York and London: Macmillan Company, 1966), 238–39.

66. Heffter, *Selbstverwaltung*, 610–11.

67. Ibid., 697–704; 715–16.

68. Ibid., 719.

69. Ibid., 707.

70. Ibid., 615; data for the city of Bielefeld in 1834, 1871 and 1911 can be found in Hofmann, *Handbuch* (1981), 1:82.

71. Ibid., 616.

72. Ludwig von Mises suggests that Liberals in the East also confronted the dilemma of choosing authoritarian rule by the nobility and Berlin or more democratic rule that would lead to participation by Polish and Lithuanian populations and an undermining of German control. See his *Nation, State, and Economy*, trans. Leland B. Yeager (New York and London: New York University Press, 1983), 104–5.

73. Heffter, *Selbstverwaltung*, 761–62.

74. Preuss, *Entwicklung*, pp. 276–79; Hans Herzfeld, *Demokratie und Selbstverwaltung in der Weimarer Epoche* (Stuttgart: W. Kohlhammer, 1957), 14–16.

75. Herzfeld, *Demokratie und Selbstverwaltung*, 19.

76. Roger H. Wells, *German Cities: A Study of Contemporary Municipal Politics and Administration* (Princeton: Princeton University Press, 1932), 6–14.

77. For an assessment of the effect of PR in the cities of the Weimar Republic, see ibid., 93.

78. As suggested by Heffter, *Selbstverwaltung*, 776–77.

79. This is the argument made by Dieter Rebentisch, "Die Selbstverwaltung in der Weimarer Zeit," in *Handbuch* (1981), 1:88.

80. Becker, "Entwicklung," in *Handbuch* (1956), 1:101.

81. Pinson, *Modern Germany*, 399–401.

82. Heffter, *Selbstverwaltung*, 769–71; Wells suggests that there may have been more state supervision after World War I than before, especially in matters of finance. See Wells, *German Cities*, 143.

83. Wells, *German Cities*, chap. 5.

84. Herzfeld, *Demokratie und Selbstverwaltung*, 20–22.

85. Heffter, *Selbstverwaltung*, 778–80.

86. von Unruh, *Der Kreis*, 186.

87. Heffter, *Selbstverwaltung*, 781–82.

88. Ibid., 782.

89. See, for example, Becker, "Entwicklung," in *Handbuch* (1956), 1:91; also Rebentisch, "Selbstverwaltung," in *Handbuch* (1981), 1:97.

90. For a list of examples of such responsibilities, see von Unruh, *Der Kreis*, 178.

91. Herzfeld, *Demokratie und Selbstverwaltung*, 30.

92. Becker, "Entwicklung," in *Handbuch* (1956), 1:103.

93. Horst Matzerath, "Die Zeit des Nationalsozialismus," in *Handbuch* (1981), 1:104.

94. Ibid., 106, 111–12; also Heffter, *Selbstverwaltung*, 788.

95. von Unruh, *Der Kreis*, 193–94.

96. For a description of the extent of destruction, see Michael Balfour and John Mair, *Four-Power Control in Germany and Austria, 1945–1946* (New York: Oxford University Press, 1956), 7–14.

97. Ibid., 65.

98. James R. Newman, former U. S. Land Commissioner for Hesse, quoted in J. F. J. Gillen, *State and Local Government in West Germany, 1945–1953* (Office of the U.S. High Commissioner for Germany, 1953), 3–4, and in ibid., 65–66.

99. Gillen, *State and Local Government*, 4.

100. For brief reviews of local government after 1945, see Theo Stammen, "Die Erneuerung der kommunalen Selbstverwaltung in Deutschland nach 1945," in *Aspekte und Probleme der Kommunalpolitik*, ed. Heinz Rausch and Theo Stammen, 3d ed. (Munich: Verlag Ernst Vögel, 1973), 10–32; and Christian Engeli, "Neuanfänge der Selbstverwaltung nach 1945," in *Handbuch* (1981), 1:114–32.

101. Potsdam Agreement, sec. 2, paragraph 9.

102. Wolfgang Rudzio, *Die Neuordnung des Kommunalwesens in der Britischen Zone* (Stuttgart: Deutsche Verlag-Anstalt, 1968), 43.

103. Ibid., 43–45.

104. Ibid., 46, and Balfour and Mair, *Four-Power Control*, 188.

105. Ibid., 29.

106. Ibid., 209–11.

107. Ibid., 203–7.

108. Ibid., 213–14.

109. Ibid., 21.

3. The German Administrative Tradition, the Federal Framework, and Local Government Institutional Structure

1. Howard Machin, *The Prefect in French Public Administration* (London: Croom Helm, 1977), 18.
2. Brian Chapman, *Introduction to French Local Government* (London: George Allen and Unwin, 1953), 19–20.
3. For a brief outline in English of German administrative structure with a focus on the local level, see Raymond C. McDermott, "The Functions of Local Levels of Government in West Germany and Their Internal Organization," in *Local Government Reform and Reorganization: An International Perspective*, ed. Arthur B. Gunlicks (Port Washington: Kennikat Press, 1981), 182–201; see also David Southern, "Germany," in *Government and Administration in Western Europe*, ed. F. F. Ridley (Oxford: Martin Robertson, 1979), 107–55.
4. Frido Wagener, "Aeusserer Aufbau von Staat und Verwaltung," in *Öffentliche Verwaltung in der Bundesrepublik Deutschland*, ed. Klaus König, H. J. von Oertzen, and Frido Wagener (Baden-Baden: Nomos Verlagsgesellschaft, 1981), 81–82.
5. For a brief description of *Land*-level structures and functions, see Ulrich Becker, "Länderorganisation," in *Handwörterbuch der Organisation*, 2d ed., ed. Erwin Grochla (Stuttgart: C. E. Poeschel Verlag, 1980), cols. 1183–92.
6. Ibid., col. 1187.
7. Eberhard Laux, "Verwaltung des ländlichen Raumes," in *Öffentliche Verwaltung*, 169.
8. Werner Thieme, "Die Gliederung der deutschen Verwaltung," in *Handbuch der kommunalen Wissenschaft und Praxis*, vol. 1: *Grundlagen*, 2d ed., ed. Günter Püttner (Berlin, Heidelberg, and New York: Springer-Verlag, 1981), 145.
9. For a discussion of local decentralization, see Rolf Wiese, "Systeme der Ortschaftsverfassung und der Bezirksgliederung," in ibid., vol. 2: *Kommunalverfassung* (1982), 328–42.
10. A detailed discussion of regional associations in Northern Germany can be found in Klaus Meyer-Schickerath, "Die höheren Gemeindeverbände in Norddeutschland," in ibid., 452–73.
11. For regional associations in Southern Germany, see Joseph Witti, "Die höheren Gemeindeverbände in Süddeutschland," in ibid., 432–51.
12. For a discussion of metropolitan associations, see Frido Wagener, "Stadt-Umland-Verbände," in ibid., 413–30.
13. See Hans-Werner Rengeling, "Formen interkommunaler Zusammenarbeit," in ibid., 385–412.
14. Janbernd Oebbecke, "Zweckverbände und kommunale Gebietsreform in Nordrhein-Westfalen," *Die öffentliche Verwaltung* 3 (February 1983):99–105.
15. For briefer treatments of the general subject of intergovernmental cooperation, see Werner Thieme, "Gliederung," in *Handbuch* (1981), 1:147, and Rüdiger Robert Beer and Eberhard Laux, *Die Gemeinde: Einführung in die Kommunalpolitik*, 3d ed. (Munich: Günter Olzog Verlag, 1981), 161–70.

4. Territorial and Administrative Reforms at the Local Level

1. There is a vast literature from the 1960s and early 1970s on the need for reform of local governments in Germany. For two references in English, see my "Restructuring Service Delivery Systems in West Germany," in *Comparing Urban Service Delivery Systems*, ed. Vincent Ostrom and Frances P. Bish, vol. 12 of Urban Affairs Annual Reviews (Beverly Hills: Sage Publications, 1977), 173–79, and "The Reorganization of Local Governments in the Federal Republic of Germany," in *Local Government Reform and Reorganization: An International Perspective*, ed. Arthur B. Gunlicks (Port Washington: Kennikat Press, 1981), 169–74.

2. For recent reviews of the territorial reforms and their rationale, see Werner Thieme and Günther Prillwitz, *Durchführung und Ergebnisse der kommunalen Gebietsreform*, vol. 1, pt. 2: *Die kommunale Gebietsreform*, ed. H. J. von Oertzen and Werner Thieme (Baden-Baden: Nomos Verlagsgesellschaft, 1981), 31–42, and Herbert-Fritz Mattenklodt, "Territoriale Gliederung—Gemeinden und Kreise vor und nach der Gebietsreform," in *Handbuch der kommunalen Wissenschaft und Praxis*, vol. 1: *Grundlagen*, 2d ed., ed. Günter Püttner, (Berlin and Heidelberg: Springer-Verlag, 1981), 154–82.

3. Staatskanzlei des Landes Rheinland-Pfalz, *Verwaltungsvereinfachung in Rheinland-Pfalz: Eine Dokumentatioin* (Mainz: Deutscher Gemeindeverlag, 1966), 1:1.

4. See Werner Weber, "Entspricht die gegenwärtige kommunale Struktur den Anforderungen der Raumordnung?" in *Verhandlungen des 45. Deutschen Juristentages*, (Munich and Berlin: C. H. Beck'sche Verlagsbuchhandlung, 1964), vol. 1.

5. For a contrasting view that these provisions were meant originally to be authorizations for federal action, not constitutional rights that politicians and citizens could demand, see Frido Wagener et. al., *Staat und Gemeinden* (Cologne: Deutscher Gemeindeverlag, 1980), 28–29.

6. Thieme and Prillwitz, *Durchführung und Ergebnisse*, 45–49.

7. Mattenklodt, "Territoriale Gliederung," in *Handbuch* (1981), 1:166.

8. The most comprehensive and influential of these was probably the work of Frido Wagener, *Neubau der Verwaltung* (Berlin: Duncker & Humblot, 1969). A brief review in English of parts of this book can be found in Gunlicks, "Restructuring," in *Urban Affairs*, 12:179–81.

9. For example, Niedersächsischer Minister des Innern, *Verwaltungs- und Gebietsreform in Niedersachsen (Weber-Kommission): Gutachten der Sachverständigenkommission für die Verwaltungs- und Gebietsreform* (Hannover, 1969).

10. For a review of considerations of municipal size and for the discussion that follows, see Thieme and Prillwitz, *Durchführung und Ergebnisse*, 51–61; see also Mattenklodt, "Territoriale Gliederung," in *Handbuch* (1981), 1:166–71.

11. See, for example, Arthur B. Gunlicks, "Die parteipolitischen Präferenzen beim niedersächsischen Entscheidungsprozess für eine Gebietsreform im Spannungsfeld von Effizienz, Gleichheit und Freiheit," *Zeitschrift für Parlamentsfragen* 7, no. 4 (December 1976):475–78.

12. Cf. Mattenklodt, "Territoriale Gliederung," in *Handbuch* (1981), 1:179.

13. Cf. Thieme and Prillwitz, *Durchführung und Ergebnisse*, 61–65.

14. Gunlicks, "The United States in Cross-National Comparison," in *Local Government*, 205–12.
15. Thieme and Prillwitz, *Durchführung und Ergebnisse*, 69–72.
16. Gunlicks, "Die parteipolitischen Präferenzen," 472–88.
17. Mattenklodt, "Territoriale Gliederung," in *Handbuch* (1981), 1:156–57.
18. See also Thieme and Prillwitz, *Durchführung und Ergebnisse*, 78.
19. Ibid., 77.
20. Arthur B. Gunlicks, "Coalition Collapse in Lower Saxony: Political and Constitutional Implications," *Parliamentary Affairs* 29 (Autumn 1976): 437–49.
21. Thieme and Prillwitz, *Durchführung und Ergebnisse*, 74, 239.
22. Ibid., 88–94.
23. Peter Schäfer, "Die preussisch klare Dreiteilung: Die Bedeutung der Funktionalreform in Nordrhein-Westfalen für die Flexibilität der Verwaltungsorganisation," *Archiv für Kommunalwissenschaften* 20 (1981):270–71.
24. Ibid., 270.
25. Frido Wagener, ed., *Zukunftsaspekte der Verwaltung*, vol. 81 of Schriftenreihe der Hochschule Speyer (Berlin: Duncker & Humblot, 1980), 42–43.
26. Thieme and Prillwitz, *Durchführung und Ergebnisse*, 95–96.
27. Ibid., 96–100.
28. Ibid., 104–6.
29. A detailed analysis of the role of the courts and a listing by *Land* of relevant cases to 1976 can be found in Wolfgang H. Bott, "Rechtssprechung und Gebietsreform: Eine Analyse der Verfassungsgerichtlichen Entscheidungen" (Dissertation der Hochschule für Verwaltungswissenschaften Speyer, 1977).
30. Cf. Thieme and Prillwitz, *Durchführung und Ergebnisse*, 233–39.
31. For a brief review, see Dieter Schimanke, "Folgen und Folgeprobleme der kommunalen Gebietsreform: Literaturbericht," *Archiv für Kommunalwissenschaften* 21 (1982): 307–19.
32. Thieme and Prillwitz, *Durchführung und Ergebnisse*, 82–83.
33. Ibid., 82.
34. Ibid., 84–88.
35. In fact there has been a significant reduction in the number of *Zweckverbände* since the reforms were implemented. On the other hand new kinds of joint authorities have emerged in the place of older authorities, though in smaller total numbers. See Janbernd Oebbecke, "Zweckverbände und kommunale Gebietsreform in Nordrhein-Westfalen," *Die Öffentliche Verwaltung* 3 (February 1983):101.
36. Arthur B. Gunlicks, "Heutige Einstellung der Abgeordneten des Niedersächsischen Landtages zu der Verwaltungs- und Gebietsreform der 70er Jahre auf Gemeinde- und Kreisebene," *Zeitschrift für Parlamentsfragen* 13 (April 1982):33–52.
37. Gunlicks, "Die parteipolitischen Präferenzen," pp. 481–85.
38. For a criticism of these expectations, see Mattenklodt, "Territoriale Gliederung," in *Handbuch* (1981), 1:181.

5. The Legal Framework of German Local Government

1. See Philip M. Blair, *Federalism and Judicial Review in West Germany* (Oxford: Clarendon Press, 1981), viii.

2. See Willi Blümel, "Die Rechtsgrundlagen der Tätigkeit der kommunalen Selbstverwaltungskörperschaften," in *Handbuch der kommunalen Wissenschaft und Praxis*, vol. 1: *Grundlagen*, 2d ed., ed. Günter Püttner (Berlin and New York: Springer-Verlag, 1981), 231.

3. For an exhaustive commentary on article 28, paragraph 2, see *Kommentar zum Bonner Grundgesetz (Bonner Kommentar)* (Zweitbearbeitung Art. 28/December 1964), 27–82. It should be noted that there is disagreement among legal scholars regarding the extent to which counties enjoy *Allzuständigkeit*.

4. See Klaus Stern, "Die Verfassungsgarantie der kommunalen Selbstverwaltung," in *Handbuch* (1981), 1:205, 219–23.

5. Ibid., 207–8.

6. Ibid., 206.

7. Cf. Blümel, "Rechtsgrundlagen," in ibid., 243–46.

8. Ibid., 247–49; the complete texts of the city and county charter laws for all German *Länder* can be found in Gerd Schmidt-Eichenstaedt, Isabell Stade, and Michael Borchmann, *Die Gemeindeordnungen und die Kreisordnungen in der Bundesrepublik Deutschland*, Stand 1982, Schriften des Deutschen Instituts für Urbanistik, vol. 47 (Stuttgart: Verlag W. Kohlhammer/Deutscher Gemeindeverlag).

9. For a detailed discussion, see Ernst Pappermann, "Status der Gemeinden und Kreise als Gebietskörperschaften," in *Handbuch* (1981), 1:299–300.

10. Ibid., 304.

11. Ibid., 305–6. Cf. the now somewhat dated discussion concerning county law in Georg-Christoph von Unruh, *Der Kreis: Ursprung und Ordnung einer kommunalen Körperschaft* (Cologne and Berlin: Grote'sche Verlagsbuchhandlung, 1964), 218–36.

12. Hinrich Lehman-Grube, "Verwaltung der grossen Städte," in *Öffentliche Verwaltung in der Bundesrepublik Deutschland*, ed. Klaus König, H. J. von Oertzen, and Frido Wagener (Baden-Baden: Nomos Verlagsgesellschaft, 1981), 152.

13. Eberhard Schmidt-Assmann, "Die kommunale Rechtssetzungsbefugnis," in *Handbuch*, vol. 3: *Kommunale Aufgaben und Instrumente der Aufgabenerfüllung* (1983), 182–200.

14. Werner Thieme, "Die Gliederung der deutschen Verwaltung," in *Handbuch* (1981), 1:138–42.

15. Ibid., 143.

16. Gerhard Schneider, "Die Magistratsverfassung in Hessen und Schleswig-Holstein," in ibid., vol. 2: *Kommunalverfassung* (1982), 209–21.

17. Heinz Dreibus, "Die Bürgermeisterverfassung in Rheinland-Pfalz, im Saarland und in Schleswig-Holstein," in ibid., 241–63.

18. Hans-Georg Wehling, "Die Süddeutsche Ratsverfassung in Baden-Württemberg and Bayern," in ibid., 230–40.

19. See Wilfried Berg, "Die Direktorialverfassung in Nordrhein-Westfalen und

Niedersachsen," in ibid., 222–40.

20. For a discussion of county charters, see Günter Seele, "Die Kreisverfassungssysteme," in ibid., 343–82. A now-dated commentary can be found also in Unruh, *Der Kreis*, 223–25.

6. Local Government and the Distribution of Administrative Responsibilities

1. A. H. Marshall, *Local Government Administration Abroad*, vol. 4: *Management of Local Government* (London: Her Majesty's Stationery Office, 1967), 141–42.

2. For a review of federal administrative activities and responsibilities, see Werner Thieme, "Aufgaben der öffentlichen Verwaltung," in *Öffentliche Verwaltung in der Bundesrepublik Deutschland*, ed. Klaus König, H. J. von Oertzen, and Frido Wagener (Baden-Baden: Nomos Verlagsgesellschaft, 1981), 193–99.

3. Ibid., 182–89.

4. Cf. Marshall, *Local Government*, 159.

5. For a detailed discussion of local government supervision, see Franz-Ludwig Knemeyer, "Die Staatsaufsicht über die Gemeinden und Kreise," in *Handbuch der kommunalen Wissenschaft und Praxis*, vol. 1: *Grundlagen*, 2d ed., ed. Günter Püttner (Berlin and New York: Springer-Verlag: 1981), 265–87.

6. Ibid., 266–68, and Rüdiger Robert Beer and Eberhard Laux, *Die Gemeinde: Einführung in die Kommunalpolitik*, 3d ed. (Munich: Olzog Verlag, 1981), 156.

7. Ibid., 268–70.

8. For a complete list of activities, see Klaus Meyer-Schickerath, "Die höheren Gemeindeverbände in Norddeutschland," in *Handbuch*, vol. 2: *Kommunalverfassung* (1982), 468–71.

9. Ibid., 472–73.

10. Ibid., 465–68.

11. Joseph Witti, "Die höheren Gemeindeverbände in Süddeutschland," in ibid., pp. 443, 450.

12. Ibid., 450–51.

13. Ibid., 436–40.

14. Cf. Heinz Köstering, "Das Verhältnis zwischen Gemeinde- und Kreisaufgaben einschliesslich der Funktionalreform," in *Handbuch*, vol. 3: *Kommunale Aufgaben und Instrumente der Aufgabenerfüllung* (1983), 40–41.

15. Waldemar von Grumbkow, *Die Geschichte der Kommunalaufsicht in Preussen* (Berlin: Carl Heymanns Verlag, 1921), 20–22.

16. F. W. Schildheuer, "Die Entwicklung des eigenen und des übertragenen Wirkungskreises zu den Selbstverwaltungs- und Auftragsangelegenheiten der Gemeinden" (Dissertation, Universität Göttingen, 1930), 19.

17. For three descriptions of increasing detail and complexity, see Werner Thieme, "Die Gliederung der deutschen Verwaltung," in *Handbuch* (1981), 1:149–50; Erwin Schleberger, "Kommunale Verfassungssysteme im Überblick," in ibid. (1982), 2:202; and Gerd Schmidt-Eichstaedt, "Die Rechtsqualität der Kommunalaufgaben," in ibid. (1983), 3:20–21. The simplest description of local government tasks of which the author

is aware is Frido Wagener's. Placed in order of increased state direction or control, his categorization consists of five stages: (1) Voluntary tasks (*freiwillige Selbstverwaltungsaufgaben*). These are activities or services assumed voluntarily by the local government. The only role of the state supervisory authority in this area is to ensure the legality of the function. (2) Obligatory self-government tasks (*Pflicht-Selbstverwaltungsaufgaben*). These are tasks which the local governments must carry out; however, the local governments are free to decide how and by whom they are to be accomplished, which gives the local governments considerable flexibility. Again, the only role of the state supervisory authority in this area is to ensure legality. (3) Obligatory task with limited instructions (*Pflichtaufgabe mit eingeschränktem Weisungsrecht*). Tasks which the local governments must carry out according to certain instructions which they may receive from the supervisory authority. These functional instructions are not comprehensive regarding the entire activity or service. The state supervisory authority continues to ensure legality. (4) Delegated matter (*Auftragsangelegenheit*). Tasks which the local government carries out on behalf of the state. The supervisory authority exercises both functional and legal supervision. (5) "Organ borrowing" (*Organleihe*). The *Land* "borrows" the chief administrative officer or another organ of administration and has this organ carry out certain state tasks as an agent of the state. (Source: Communication to the author.)

18. Schmidt-Eichstaedt, "Die Rechtsqualität," in *Handbuch* (1983), 3:20–21.
19. Cf. Knemeyer, "Die Staatsaufsicht," in ibid. (1981), 1:271–80.
20. Ibid., 275–76; see also Beer and Laux, *Die Gemeinde*, 154–58.
21. Ibid., 278 and 280.
22. Ibid., 285–86.
23. Cf. Thieme, "Die Gliederung," in *Handbuch* (1981), 1:144–45.
24. For a detailed discussion, see Günter Seele, "Die allgemeine untere Verwaltungsbehörde in der Kreisstufe," in ibid. (1983), 3:69–70, 76–82.
25. Ibid., 82–83.
26. Ibid., 84–87.
27. Ibid., 87–92.
28. Köstering, "Das Verhältnis," in *Handbuch* (1983), 3:40–41.
29. Ibid., 41–42.
30. Ibid., 42–44.
31. Ibid., 45.
32. Ibid., 47–48.
33. Ibid., 49–50; see also Frido Wagener, "Landkreise und Kreisfinanzen," in Frido Wagener, ed., *Kreisfinanzen*, vol. 1 of Schriften des Niedersächsischen Landkreistages (Göttingen: Verlag Otto Schwartz & Co., 1982), 18–20.
34. Ibid., 50–55.
35. Ibid., 59.
36. Ibid., 60.
37. Ibid., 60–61.
38. Frido Wagener, "Zur zukünftigen Aufgabenstellung und Bedeutung der Kreise," *Die Öffentliche Verwaltung* 8 (April 1976):258.
39. Hinrich Lehman-Grube, "Verwaltung der grossen Städte," in *Öffentliche*

Verwaltung, 133.

40. Ibid., 134–43.

41. For a general overview in English of German planning, see K. R. Kunzmann, "The Federal Republic of Germany," in *Planning in Europe: Urban and Regional Planning in the EEC*, ed. R. H. Williams (London and Boston: George Allen and Unwin, 1984), 8–25.

42. Ibid., p. 13, and Günter Püttner, "Überblick über die Planungsarbeit der Kommunen," in *Handbuch* (1983), 3:321.

43. For a detailed discussion of reasons why state, regional, and even local planning in Germany is not likely to be very successful, especially during times of economic stagnation or decline, see Fritz W. Scharpf and Fritz Schnabel, "Steuerungsprobleme der Raumplanung" (Berlin: International Institute of Management, Wissenschaftszentrum, 1977).

44. Heinz Köstering, "Kommunale Selbstverwaltung und staatliche Planung," *Die Öffentliche Verwaltung* 18 (September 1981):691.

45. Joachim Jens Hesse, "Räumliche Planung," in *Öffentliche Verwaltung*, 225.

46. Ibid., 226.

47. Ibid., 227–29.

48. Jochen Schulz zur Wiesch, "Regionaplanung ohne Wirkung? Überlegungen zur Situation der übergemeindlichen Planung," *Archiv für Kommunalwissenschaften* 17 (1978): 36–37.

49. Gundolf Bork, "Das Verhältnis der kommunalen Planung zur staatlichen Planung," in *Handbuch* (1983), 3:324.

50. Günter Gaentzsch, "Das geltende Planungsrecht," in ibid., 368–69.

51. Hanno Adrian, "Stadtplanung Heute," in ibid., 360.

52. Frido Wagener et al., *Staat und Gemeinden* (Cologne: Deutscher Gemeindeverlag, 1980), 28–29 and 35–36.

53. Köstering, "Kommunale Selbstverwaltung," 693.

54. Ibid., 694.

55. Ibid., 696.

56. Gaentzsch, "Das geltende Planungsrecht," in *Handbuch* (1983), 3:370–73.

7. Local Government Finance

1. Rüdiger Voigt, *Die Auswirkungen des Finanzausgleichs zwischen Staat und Gemeinden auf die kommunale Selbstverwaltung von 1919 bis zur Gegenwart*, vol. 259 of Schriften zum öffentlichen Recht (Berlin: Duncker & Humblot, 1975), 61–62.

2. Ibid., 63.

3. George F. Break, *Financing Government in a Federal System* (Washington, D.C.: The Brookings Institution, 1980), 45.

4. Voigt, *Auswirkungen*, 70.

5. A number of German commentaries on the Basic Law contain highly detailed discussions of the separate provisions of section X. See, for example, Ingo von Münch, ed., *Grundgesetz-Kommentar* (Munich: C. H. Beck'sche Verlagsbuchhandlung, 1978),

3:615–832; for three recent books on the subject of local government finance, see Hermann Elsner, *Das Gemeindefinanzsystem* (Cologne: Verlag W. Kohlhammer, 1979); Jürgen E. Rosenschon, *Gemeindefinanzsystem und Selbstverwaltungsgarantie* (Cologne: Verlag W. Kohlhammer und Deutscher Gemeindeverlag, 1980); and Rüdiger Voigt, *Das System des kommunalen Ausgleichs in der Bundesrepublik Deutschland*, no. 5/6: *Kommunalforschung für die Praxis* (Stuttgart: Richard Boorberg Verlag, 1980).

6. Rosenschon, *Gemeindefinanzsystem*, 26.

7. von Münch, ed., *Grundgesetz-Kommentar*, 3:683–84.

8. Ibid., 690.

9. Ibid., 415–25.

10. Ibid., 637–39; see also Willi Blümel, "Die Rechtsgrundlagen der Tätigkeit der kommunalen Selbstverwaltungskörperschaften," in *Handbuch für kommunale Wissenschaft und Praxis*, vol. 1: *Grundlagen*, 2d ed., ed. Günter Püttner (Berlin and Heidelberg: Springer-Verlag, 1981), 229–64.

11. Ibid., 642.

12. Ibid., 644 and 651; for a discussion in English of federal grant policies and developments to the mid-seventies, see Bernd Reissert, "Federal and State Transfers to Local Government in the Federal Republic of Germany: A Case of Political Immobility," in *Financing Urban Government in the Welfare State*, ed. Douglas E. Ashford (London: Croom Helm, 1980), 158–78.

13. H. Zimmermann, *Studies in Comparative Federalism: West Germany* (Washington, D.C.: Advisory Commission on Intergovernmental Relations, 1981), 38–39.

14. Ibid., 16.

15. For a discussion in English of the methods used to calculate tax potential and tax needs, see ibid., 35–38.

16. Ibid., 38.

17. Voigt, *Das System des kommunalen Finanzausgleichs*, 13–14.

18. Ibid., 19–20.

19. Ibid., 9.

20. Ibid., 85.

21. Ibid., 88.

22. Ibid., 65–66; for a different categorization scheme, see Elsner, *Das Gemeindefinanzsystem*, 170.

23. Voigt, *System des kommunalen Finanzausgleichs*, 72–78, and Elsner, *Gemeindefinanzsystem*, 161.

24. Voigt, *System*, 67–68.

25. Ibid., 69.

26. Rolf Wandhoff, "Staat und Finanzen," in *Kreisfinanzen*, vol. 1 of Schriften des Niedersächsischen Landkreistages, ed. Frido Wagener (Göttingen: Otto Schwartz & Co., 1982), 75.

27. Ibid.

28. Erhard Meichsner, "Kreis und Gemeindefinanzen 1983," *Der Landkreis* (February 1983):70.

29. Frido Wagener, "Landkreise und Kreisfinanzen," in *Kreisfinanzen*, 1:27–30.

30. Ibid., 37–38.
31. Ibid., 40–42.
32. Herbert Droste, "Gemeinden und Kreisfinanzen," in ibid., 67–68.
33. Wagener, "Landkreise und Kreisfinanzen," in ibid., 33–34.
34. Unfortunately, different standard sources give different statistics. These data are from the Bundesfinanzministerium, *Finanzbericht 1984*, 129, and Elsner, *Das Gemeindefinanzsystem*, 97. For somewhat different figures but the same trends, see Hanns Karrenberg and Engelbert Münstermann, "Gemeindefinanzbericht 1984," *Der Städtetag* (February 1984):86, and Rosenschon, *Gemeindefinanzsystem*, 139. For a review of local finances in English, see Günther F. Schäfer, "Trends in Local Government Finance in the Federal Republic of Germany since 1950," in *The Local Fiscal Crisis in Western Europe*, ed. L. T. Sharpe (Beverly Hills and London: Sage Publications, 1981), 229–69.
35. Karrenberg and Münstermann, "Gemeindefinanzbericht 1984," 86.
36. Ibid., 87–88.
37. Ibid., 89–90.
38. Ibid., 90–92.
39. BMF, *Finanzbericht 1984*, 135.
40. Gunner Schwarting, "Die Verschuldung der Städte und Gemeinden in der Bundesrepublik Deutschland," *Aus Politik und Zeitgeschichte* 5B 5 (31 January 1981):23–30.
41. BMF, *Finanzbericht 1984*, p. 134.
42. Karrenberg and Münstermann, "Gemeindefinanzbericht 1984," 105.
43. For detailed discussions of various proposals for reforming the local tax system, see Konrad Littmann, "Ergebnisse und Empfehlungen des Gutachtens des Wissenschaftlichen Beirats beim BMF zur Reform der Gemeindesteuern—Sollte die Gewerbesteuer durch eine Wertschöpfungssteuer ersetzt werden?" *Der Gemeindehaushalt* 8 (1983):178–84, and Bruno Weinberger, "Neuordnung des Gemeindesteuersystems statt schrittweiser Gewerbesteuerbeseitigung," *Kommunale Steuer-Zeitschrift* 33 (March 1983):41–46.
44. BMF, *Finanzbericht 1984*, p. 128.
45. Hanns Karrenberg and Englebert Münstermann, "Gemeindefinanzbericht 1985," *Der Städtetag* (February 1985):73.
46. Hans Herbert v. Arnim, "Ansätze, Chancen und Hemmnisse einer Drosselung öffentlicher Personalausgaben," in *Finanzpolitik im Umbruch: Zur Konsolidierung öffentlicher Haushalte*, ed. Hans Herbert v. Arnim and Konrad Littmann, Schriftenreihe der Hochschule Speyer, vol. 92 (Berlin: Duncker & Humblot, 1984), 189–90, and Karrenberg and Münstermann, "Gemeindefinanzbericht 1984," 100–101.
47. Karrenberg and Münstermann, "Gemeindefinanzbericht 1984," 102–3.
48. Rolf Wandhoff, "Staat und Finanzen," in *Kreisfinanzen*, 71–74.
49. Ernst Pappermann, "Mischfinanzierung als Hemmnis der Haushaltskonsolidierung?" in *Finanzpolitik im Umbruch*, 247–48.
50. Ibid., 249–50.
51. Ibid., 251–53.
52. Ibid., 250.
53. Ibid., 254–60.

8. The Public Service and the Organization of Local Bureaucracies

1. All data are taken from Statistisches Bundesamt, *Wirtschaft und Statistik 12/1982* (Stuttgart: W. Kohlhammer Verlag, 1982), 918–21. See also Gerald Kreissig, "Personalstand und Personalentwicklung bei Bund, Ländern und Gemeinden," *Der Städtetag* (March 1982):188–94.
2. The term used by Renate Mayntz and Fritz W. Scharpf, *Policy-Making in the German Federal Bureaucracy* (New York: Elsevier, 1975), 50.
3. The term used by David Southern, "Germany," in *Government and Administration in Western Europe*, ed. F. F. Ridley (Oxford: Martin Robertson and Co., 1979), 134.
4. *Wirtschaft und Statistik 12/1982*, 921.
5. Southern, "Germany," 134.
6. Calculated from figures supplied by Johannes Hintzen, "Das kommunale Dienstrecht," in *Handbuch der kommunalen Wissenschaft und Praxis*, vol. 3: *Kommunale Aufgaben und Instrumente der Aufgabenerfüllung*, 2d ed., ed. Günter Püttner (Berlin and Heidelberg: Springer-Verlag, 1983), 217.
7. Ibid., and *Wirtschaft und Statistik 12/1982*, 921.
8. Helmut Kauther and Ernst Pappermann, "Aus- und Fortbildung für den kommunalen öffentlichen Dienst," in *Handbuch* (1983), 3:273–74.
9. Gerhard Brinkmann, Wolfgang Pippke und Wolfgang Rippe, *Die Tätigkeitsfelder des höheren Verwaltungsdienstes* (Opladen: Westdeutscher Verlag, 1971), 56, 60, 62, 64, and 65.
10. Ernst Pappermann, "Juristen in der Kommunalverwaltung," *Archiv für Kommunalwissenschaften* 21 (1982):4–8.
11. Ibid., 9–22.
12. Ibid., 22.
13. Kauther and Pappermann, "Aus- und Fortbildung," in *Handbuch* (1983), 3:266–73.
14. Ibid., 265–66.
15. Ibid., 276–78.
16. Ibid., 278–79.
17. For some of the difficulties experienced by local governments in absorbing these displaced personnel, see Klaus-Günter Dietel, "Personalpolitik aus Sicht der Landkreise," *Der Bayerische Bürgermeister* (May 1982):20–23. On the other hand a study of municipalities in Baden-Württemberg showed that personnel displaced by the territorial reforms did not account for increases in local personnel. See Hartmut Kübler and Klaus Fuchs, *Personalwesen und Gebietsreform: Untersuchung ausgewählter Gemeinden in Baden-Württemberg* (Baden-Baden: Nomos Verlagsgesellschaft, 1979), 45.
18. Eberhard Schmidt-Assmann, "Gemeinden und Staat im Recht des öffentlichen Dienstes—Aktuelle Fragen zur kommunalen Personalhoheit," in *Öffentlicher Dienst: Festschrift für Carl Hermann Ule*, ed. Klaus König et al., (Cologne: Carl Heymanns Verlag, 1977), 464–72, 477.
19. Ibid., 473–81.
20. Johannes Hintzen, "Das kommunale Dienstrecht," in *Handbuch* (1983), 3:228–29.
21. Ibid., 231.

22. Bruno Schwegmann and Thassilo Unverhau, "Auf dem Wege zur einheitlichen Kommunalbesoldung—Gedanken zur Kommunalbesoldungsverordnung des Bundes," *Zeitschrift für Beamtenrecht* 2 (1979):32.

23. Hans Hack, "Die institutionelle Organisation/Aufbauorganisation," in *Handbuch* (1983), 3:110, 113.

24. Ibid., 113–14.

25. Ibid., 116.

9. Local Councillors, Parties, and Elections

1. Werner Thieme and Günther Prillwitz, *Durchführung und Ergebnisse der kommunalen Gebietsreform* (Baden-Baden: Nomos Verlagsgesellschaft, 1981), 80. Other sources suggest that the reductions were from 276,000 to 153,000 or even to 180,000. See Arthur B. Gunlicks, "The Reorganization of Local Governments in the Federal Republic of Germany," in *Local Government Reform and Reorganization: An International Perspective*, ed. Arthur B. Gunlicks (Port Washington and London: Kennikat Press, 1981), p. 177 and n. 22.

2. For a discussion of the political process at the local level, see Wolfgang Holler and Karl-Heinz Nassmacher, "Rat und Verwaltung im Prozess kommunalpolitischer Willensbildung," *Aus Politik und Zeitgeschichte* B4/76 (24 January 1976):10–15; Hermann Schönfelder, *Rat und Verwaltung im kommunalen Spannungsfeld* (Cologne: Deutscher Gemeindeverlag, 1979); Konrad-Adenauer-Stiftung, *Politik und kommunale Selbstverwaltung* (Cologne: Deutscher Gemeindeverlag, 1984), 7–32; and Robert Hess, "Rat und Verwaltung in der gemeindlichen Willensbildung," in *Kommunalpolitik im Wandel der Gesellschaft*, ed. Oscar W. Gabriel (Mainz: Landeszentrale für politische Bildung Rheinland-Pfalz, 1979), 119–40.

3. Herbert Schneider, "Lokalpolitik in einer Landgemeinde," *Aus Politik und Zeitgeschichte* B3/77 (22 January 1977):24–25.

4. Holler and Nassmacher, "Rat und Verwaltung," 15–18.

5. Adenauer-Stiftung, *Politik*, 19–20.

6. Ibid., 25, and Schneider, "Lokalpolitik," 25.

7. Karl-Heinz Nassmacher and Wolfgang Rudzio, "Das lokale Parteiensystem auf dem Lande: Dargestellt am Beispiel der Rekrutierung von Gemeinderäten," in *Dorfpolitik*, ed. Hans-Georg Wehling (Opladen: Leske Verlag, 1978), 131–32; Gerhard Lehmbruch, "Der Januskopf der Ortsparteien," *Der Bürger im Staat* 25 (March 1975):4; Schneider, "Lokalpolitik," 27; and Armin Klein, "Parteien und Wahlen in der Kommunalpolitik," in *Kommunalpolitik im Wandel*, 105–10.

8. Arthur B. Gunlicks, "Gemeindevertreter und politische Parteien in Niedersachsen," *Archiv für Kommunalwissenschaften* 7 (1968):291.

9. Nassmacher and Rudzio, "Das lokale Parteiensystem," 134.

10. Ibid., 135–40.

11. Adenauer-Stiftung, *Politik*, 2, and Holler and Nassmacher, "Rat und Verwaltung," 5–6.

12. Adenauer-Stiftung, *Politik*, 7.

13. Ibid., 8; Holler and Nassmacher, "Rat und Verwaltung," 6–7.
14. Lehmbruch, "Der Januskopf," 5; Schneider, "Lokalpolitik," 26.
15. Heino Kaack, "Parteien und Wählergemeinschaften auf kommunaler Ebene," in *Aspekte und Probleme der Kommunalpolitik*, ed. Heinz Rausch and Theo Stammen (Munich: Verlag Ernst Vögel, 1973), 139–40; for a study in English of local voter groups and parties in the Rhineland-Palatinate before the territorial reforms had taken effect, see Linda Dolive, *Electoral Politics at the Local Level in the German Federal Republic* (Gainesville: University Presses of Florida, 1976).
16. Thomas Möller, *Die kommunalen Wählergemeinschaften in der Bundesrepublik Deutschland* (Munich: Minerva-Publikation, 1981), 166, 171.
17. Gunlicks, "Gemeindevertreter," 295.
18. Lehmbruch, "Der Januskopf," 3.
19. Adenauer-Stiftung, *Politik*, 26–27.
20. Ibid., 3.
21. Möller, *Die kommunalen Wählergemeinschaften*, 165.
22. For a brief discussion in English of this view and relevant citations, see Arthur B. Gunlicks, "Representative Role Perceptions Among Local Councillors in Western Germany," *Journal of Politics* 31 (May 1969):444–45.
23. There is a vast literature on this controversy. See the citations in Arthur B. Gunlicks, "Coalition Collapse in Lower Saxony: Political and Constitutional Implications," *Parliamentary Affairs* 29 (Autumn 1976):437. See also any of the several commentaries on the Basic Law for articles 21 and 38. Also Wilhelm Henke, *Das Recht der politischen Parteien*, 2d ed. (Göttingen: Verlag Otto Schwartz and Co., 1972).
24. Gerd Lintz, *Die politischen Parteien im Bereich der kommunalen Selbstverwaltung* (Baden-Baden: Nomos Verlagsgesellschaft, 1973), 54–71; Gunlicks, "Representative Role Perceptions," 445.
25. Lintz, *Die politischen Parteien*, 45–46, 53.
26. Otto Ziebill, *Politische Parteien und kommunale Selbstverwaltung*, 2d ed. (Stuttgart: Verlag W. Kohlhammer, 1972), 51.
27. Heino Kaack, *Geschichte und Struktur des deutschen Parteiensystems* (Opladen: Westdeutscher Verlag, 1971), 473–74.
28. See Heino Kaack and Reinhold Roth, eds., *Handbuch des deutschen Parteiensystems* (Opladen: Leske Verlag, 1980), 1:23–80.
29. Kaack, *Geschichte*, 470.
30. Lutz-Rainer Reuter, "Kommunalpolitik im Parteienvergleich," *Aus Politik und Zeitgeschichte* B34/76 (21 August 1976):3–37; Klein, "Parteien und Wahlen," 114–17.
31. For a discussion of federal-*Land*-local relationships within all three major parties, see Christoph Böckenförde, Roman Herzog, and Victor Kirst, "Die innerparteiliche Willensbildung im Verhältnis Bund, Länder und Gemeinden," in *Politikverflechtung zwischen Bund, Ländern und Gemeinden*, Schriftenreihe der Hochschule Speyer, vol. 55 (Berlin: Duncker & Humblot, 1975), 65–98.
32. Kaack, "Parteien und Wählergemeinschaften," 146; Franz M. Kreiter, "Kommunale Entwicklungsplanung und Politische Parteien," in *Strukturprobleme des lokalen Parteiensystems*, ed. Konrad-Adenauer-Stiftung (Bonn: Eichholz Verlag, 1975), 113;

Schneider, "Lokalpolitik," 24-25; Theo Trachternach, *Parteien in der kommunalen Selbstverwaltung* (Würzburg: Verlag Schmitt and Meyer, 1974), 109-10.

33. Heinz Zielinski, "Politik und Verwaltung in Kommunen," *Die Verwaltung* 15 (February 1982):160.

34. Arthur B. Gunlicks, "Intraparty Democracy in Western Germany: A Look at the Local Level," *Comparative Politics* 2 (January 1970):238.

35. Trachternach, *Parteien*, 110; see also Herzog, "Die innerparteiliche Willensbildung," 86.

36. For a detailed and sympathetic presentation of this view, see Trachternach, *Parteien*, 157-208.

37. Eckart Klein, "Zur Gleichgestimmtheit zwischen Gemeindevertretung und kommunalen Wahlbeamten," *Die Öffentliche Verwaltung* 33 (December 1980):853.

38. Trachternach, *Parteien*, 213-14.

39. Michael Borchmann, "Kommunale Selbstverwaltung und parlamentarische Organisation," *Die Öffentliche Verwaltung* 33 (December 1980):864-65.

40. For the most uncompromising version of this view, see Wolfgang Rudzio, "Eine Erneuerung gesellschaftsverändernder Kommunalpolitik? Zum Impuls der Jungsozialisten," in *Kommunalpolitik und Sozialdemokratie*, ed. Karl-Heinz Nassmacher (Bonn-Bad Godesberg: Verlag Neue Gesellschaft, 1977), 79-89.

41. See the report of the Sachverständigenrates, Adenauer-Stiftung, *Politik*, 1-32.

42. Gabriele Wurzel, *Gemeinderat als Parlament?* (Würzburg: Verlag Schmitt und Meyer, 1975), 108-9, 170-72.

43. Reuter, "Kommunalpolitik," 15.

44. Lehmbruch, "Der Januskopf," 8.

45. Albert Jakob, "Das Ende der Dorfpolitik," *Der Bürger im Staat*, 25 (March 1975):26; Gunlicks, "Gemeindevertreter," 299.

46. Kaack, *Geschichte*, 475; Lehmbruch, "Der Januskopf," 4-5.

47. Lehmbruch, "Der Januskopf," 5.

48. Ibid., 6-7.

49. Trachternach, *Parteien*, 47.

50. Josef Ziegler, *Bürgerbeteiligung in der kommunalen Selbstverwaltung* (Würzburg: Verlag Schmitt und Meyer, 1974), 77-80.

51. Kaack, *Geschichte*, 475.

52. Ziegler, *Bürgerbeteiligung*, 79.

53. Lehmbruch, "Der Januskopf," 5 and 7.

54. Cf. Ziegler, *Bürgerbeteiligung*, 79.

55. Lehmbruch, "Der Januskopf," 7.

56. Hans Herbert von Arnim, "Auswirkungen der Politisierung des öffentlichen Dienstes," in *Verwaltung und Verwaltungspolitik*, ed. Carl Böhret and Heinrich Siedentopf (Berlin: Duncker & Humblot, 1983), 223.

57. Ibid., 222.

58. Trachternach, *Parteien*, 236-37.

59. Ibid.

60. Zielinski, "Politik und Verwaltung," 160.

61. Cf. Kreiter, "Kommunale Entwicklungsplanung," 91–92.
62. Borchmann, "Kommunale Selbstverwaltung," 867.
63. Schönfelder, *Rat und Verwaltung*, 85.
64. Hans Herbert v. Arnim, "Ansätze, Chancen und Hemmnisse einer Drosselung öffentlicher Personalausgaben," in *Finanzpolitik im Umbruch: Konsolidierung öffentlicher Haushalte*, ed. Hans Herbert v. Arnim and Konrad Littmann (Berlin: Duncker and Humblot, 1984), 206.
65. Udo Bernbach, "Bürgerinitiativen gegen den Parteienstaat?" in *Bürgerinitiativen und Repräsentatives System*, ed. Bernd Guggenberger und Udo Kempf (Opladen: Westdeutscher Verlag, 1978), 92 and 95, claims that the citizen initiatives have more members than the parties; Uwe Thaysen, "Bürgerinitiativen, Parlamente und Parteien in der Bundesrepublik: Eine Zwischenbilanz (1977)," in ibid., 136, notes that all of these figures are rough estimates and calculates that the number of members in the citizen initiatives is considerably less than the membership of all parties.
66. Oscar W. Gabriel, "Bürgerinitiativen im lokalpolitischen Entscheidungsprozess: Entstehungsbedingungen und Aktionsmuster," in ibid., 261.
67. Ibid., and Reinhard Hendler, "Die Planungszelle als Instrument der Bürgerbeteiligung," *Aus Politik und Zeitgeschichte* B25/79 (23 June 1979):16–18.
68. Kreiter, "Kommunale Entwicklungsplanung," 109.
69. Ibid.
70. Bernbach, "Bürgerinitiativen," 97.
71. Adenauer-Stiftung, *Politik*, 28.
72. Gabriel, "Bürgerinitiativen," 265.
73. Thaysen, "Bürgerinitiativen," 137.
74. For detailed analyses of the origins, phases, reasons for coming into existence, and assessments of various "social movements" in the cities, see Dieter Rucht, "Die Bürgerinitiativbewegung—Entwicklungsdynamik, Politisch-Ideologisches Spektrum und Bedeutung für die Politische Kultur," in *Grossstadt und neue soziale Bewegungen*, ed. Peter Grottian and Wilfried Nelles (Boston and Stuttgart: Birkhäuser Verlag, 1983), 57–82.
75. Klaus G. Troitzsch, "Die Herausforderung der 'etablierten' Parteien durch die 'Grünen,'" in Kaack and Roth, *Handbuch*, 1:261–62 and 264.
76. Hans Meyer, "Kommunalwahlrecht," in *Handbuch der kommunalen Wissenschaft und Praxis*, vol. 2: *Kommunalverfassung*, 2d ed., ed. Günter Püttner (Berlin and Heidelberg: Springer-Verlag, 1982), 67–68.
77. For a brief discussion of this issue, with numerous citations, see ibid., 64, and Helmut Quaritsch, "Staatsangehörigkeit und Wahlrecht," *Die Öffentliche Verwaltung* 36 (January 1983):1–15.
78. Werner Sixt, *Kommunalwahlrecht in Baden-Württemberg* (Stuttgart: Richard Boorberg Verlag, 1980), 99–102.
79. Uwe Thaysen, *Bürger-, Staats- und Verwaltungsinitiativen* (Heidelberg and Hamburg: R. v. Decker's Verlag, 1982), 253–67.
80. Meyer, "Kommunalwahlrecht," in *Handbuch* (1982), 2:55.
81. Ibid., 58–59.

82. Dieter Nohlen, "Wahlsystem und Wahlen in den Gemeinden," in *Aspekte und Probleme*, 159–60.
83. For details of the electoral system in Baden-Württemberg, see Sixt, *Kommunalwahlrecht*.
84. Meyer, "Kommunalwahlrecht," in *Handbuch* (1982), 2:61.
85. Dieter Nohlen, "Das baden-württembergische Kommunalwahlsystem," *Der Bürger im Staat* 25 (March 1975):13–14.
86. Hans-Joachim Mann, "Wie wird gewählt? Das Kommunalwahlsystem in Baden-Württemberg," in *Kommunalpolitik in Baden-Württemberg*, ed. Hans-Georg Wehling (Stuttgart: Verlag W. Kohlhammer, 1979), 79.
87. Meyer, "Kommunalwahlrecht," in *Handbuch* (1982), 2:62–63.
88. Sixt, *Kommunalwahlrecht*, 33.
89. Meyer, "Kommunalwahlrecht," in *Handbuch* (1982). 2:56–57.
90. *Frankfurter Allgemeine Zeitung*, 13 June 1984, 5.
91. Ibid.

10. Local Government and Intergovernmental Relations

1. P. B. Spahn, "The German Model of Horizontal Federal Decentralization," in *Principles of Federal Policy Co-ordination in the Federal Republic of Germany*, ed. P. B. Spahn (Canberra: Centre for Research on Federal Financial Relations, Australian National University, 1978), 6–7.
2. Hartmut Klatt, "Parlamentarisches System und bundesstaatliche Ordnung," *Aus Politik und Zeitgeschichte* B31/82 (7 August 1982):3.
3. For a review of postwar developments in intergovernmental relations in the Federal Republic, see Bernd Reissert, "Responsibility Sharing and Joint Tasks in West German Federalism," in *Principles*, 25–26.
4. Wolfgang Zeh, "Spätföderalismus," *Zeitschrift für Parlamentsfragen* 8 (December 1977):475.
5. Ibid., 475–76.
6. Ibid., 489.
7. Fritz W. Scharpf, "Die Theorie der Politikverflechtung: Ein kurzgefasster Leitfaden," in *Politikverflechtung im föderativen Staat* ed. Joachim Jens Hesse (Baden-Baden: Nomos Verlagsgesellschaft, 1978), 26.
8. Konrad-Adenauer-Stiftung, *Staat und Gemeinden* (Cologne: Deutscher Gemeindeverlag, 1980), 15.
9. Ibid., 15–16.
10. Klaus Stern, "Die föderative Ordnung im Spannungsfeld der Gegenwart," in *Politikverflechtung zwischen Bund, Ländern und Gemeinden*, Schriftenreihe der Hochschule Speyer, vol. 55 (Berlin: Duncker & Humblot, 1975), 21 and 27.
11. Rudolf Hrbek, "Politikverflechtung macht an den Grenzen nicht halt," *Der Bürger im Staat* 29 (March 1979):39–40.
12. Schlussbericht der Enquete-Kommission, *Beratungen und Empfehlungen zur Verfassungsreform. Teil II: Bund und Länder* (Bonn: Presse- und Informationszentrum des

Deutschen Bundestages, 1977), 100.

13. Waldemar Schreckenberger, "Regierungsbeziehungen im Bundesstaat," in *Öffentliche Verwaltung in der Bundesrepublik Deutschland*, ed. Klaus König, H. J. von Oertzen, and Frido Wagener (Baden-Baden: Nomos Verlagsgesellschaft, 1981), 104.

14. Reissert, "Responsibility Sharing," 32-35.

15. Gerhard Lehmbruch, "Ein später Sieg Bismarcks?" *Der Bürger im Staat* 29 (March 1979):34-36.

16. Peter Becker, "Politikverflechtung in der Gemeinschaftsaufgabe 'Verbesserung der regionalen Wirtschaftsstruktur,' " in *Politikverflechtung II*, ed. Fritz W. Scharpf, Bernd Reissert, and Fritz Schnabel (Kronberg: Athenaeum Verlag, 1977), 37-38.

17. Hartmut Klatt, "Die Länderparlamente müssen sich wehren," *Der Bürger im Staat* 29 (March 1979):22.

18. Konrad-Adenauer-Stiftung, *Staat und Gemeinden*, 39.

19. Hans Boldt, "Politikverflechtung als Resourcenverwaltung," *Der Bürger im Staat* 29 (March 1979):14.

20. Konrad-Adenauer-Stiftung, *Staat und Gemeinden*, 22.

21. Frido Wagener, "System einer integrierten Entwicklungsplanung im Bund, in den Ländern und in den Gemeinden," in *Politikverflechtung*, Schriftenreihe Speyer, 55:133-35.

22. Hans-Erhard Havercamp, "Die kommunale Perspektive: Staatliche Regulation der kommunalen Entscheidungspolitik und-planung," in *Politikverflechtung im föderativen Staat*, 39.

23. Wagener, "System," 145.

24. Klatt, "Die Länderparlamente," 21.

25. Klatt, "Parlamentarisches System," 5.

26. Konrad-Adenauer-Stiftung, *Staat und Gemeinden*, 35-36.

27. Philip M. Blair, *Federalism and Judicial Review in West Germany* (Oxford: Clarendon Press, 1981), p. 2 and chap. 8.

28. Eberhard Laux, "Kommunale Selbstverwaltung als politisches Prinzip: Wege der Diskussion," in *Selbstverwaltung im Staat der Industriegesellschaft*, ed. Albert von Mutius (Heidelberg: R. v. Decker's Verlag, 1983), 74.

29. Hermann Scheffler, "Forderungen der Gemeinden zur Neuordnung ihrer Stellung gegenüber Bund und Länder," in *Politikverflechtung*, Schriftenreihe Speyer, 55:42.

30. Fritz W. Scharpf, Bernd Reissert und Fritz Schnabel, *Politikverflechtung: Theorie und Empirie des kooperativen Föderalismus in der Bundesrepublik* (Kronberg: Scriptor Verlag, 1976), 29.

31. Ibid., 209-10.

32. Enquete-Kommission, *Verfassungsreform*, 219.

33. For a criticism of the Commission's report, see Gerhard Lehmbruch, "Verfassungspolitische Alternativen der Politikverflechtung. Bemerkungen zur Strategie der Verfassungsreform," *Zeitschrift für Parlamentsfragen* 8 (December 1977):461-74.

34. Klatt, "Parlamentarisches System," 8-10.

35. Reissert, "Responsibility Sharing," 37.

36. Scharpf et al., *Politikverflechtung I*, 239-41.

37. Spahn, "The German Model," 12-13.

38. Ibid., 14.

39. For a review of different eras of federalism in the United States, see David B. Walker, *Toward a Functioning Federalism* (Cambridge: Winthrop Publishers, 1981), chap. 3.

40. Ibid., 81.

41. Ibid., 84.

42. Ibid., 90.

43. Ibid., 104.

44. Ibid., 109–10, 174.

45. Ibid., 111.

46. Ibid., 175–76.

47. Ibid., 176.

48. Ibid., 177–89.

49. ACIR, *Regulatory Federalism: Policy, Process, Impact and Reform* (Washington, D.C.: Advisory Commission on Intergovernmental Relations, 1984), 157.

50. Walker, *Toward a Functioning Federalism*, 193–99.

51. Ibid., 207–17.

52. Ibid., 220–21.

53. For an excellent review of federalism under the Reagan administration, see George E. Peterson, "Federalism and the States: An Experiment in Decentralization," in *The Reagan Record*, ed. John L. Palmer and Isabel V. Sawhill (The Urban Institute, Cambridge: Ballinger Publishing Company, 1984), 217–59.

54. For a listing of programs that were consolidated, see ACIR, *A Catalog of Federal Grant-in-Aid Programs to State and Local Governments: Grants Funded FY 1981* (Washington, D.C.: Advisory Commission on Intergovernmental Relations, 1982), 67–69.

55. Timothy J. Conlan, "Federalism and Competitive Values in the Reagan Administration" (Paper delivered at the 1984 Meeting of the American Political Science Association, Washington, D.C.), 2–3.

56. ACIR, *Regulatory Federalism*, 189, 198.

57. ACIR, *Regulatory Federalism*, 228–34.

58. Conlan, "Federalism," 8.

59. Ibid., 8–13.

60. Ibid., 14.

61. David B. Walker and Cynthia Cates Colella, "Federalism in 1983: Mixed Results from Washington," *Intergovernmental Perspective* 10 (Winter 1984):24–27.

62. Kenneth Howard, "De Facto New Federalism," *Intergovernmental Perspective* 10 (Winter 1984):4, 39.

63. Walker, *Toward a Functioning Federalism*, 220.

64. For a discussion of the role of Congress in contributing to the growth in federal programs, see Deil S. Wright, *Understanding Intergovernmental Relations*, 2d ed. (Monterey: Brooks/Cole Publishing Company, 1982), 162–64.

65. Ibid., 165–71.

66. Today thirty states and more than one hundred cities have permanent offices in Washington, where they lobby for funds and programs. See Charles Press and Kenneth Ver

Burg, *State and Community Governments in the Federal System*, 2d ed. (New York: John Wiley & Sons, 1983), 95.

67. Rainer-Olaf Schultze, "Entwicklungen des Föderalismus in Deutschland, Kanada und Australien: Wider den Fatalismus unbefragter Unitarisierungsannahmen," *Zeitschrift für Parlamentsfragen* 15 (June 1984):292–94.

11. Intergovernmental Relations and the Undermining of Traditional Administrative Systems

1. See, for example, Frido Wagener, "Äusserer Aufbau von Staat und Verwaltung," in *Öffentliche Verwaltung in der Bundesrepublik Deutschland*, ed. Klaus Koenig, H. J. von Oertzen, and Frido Wagener (Baden-Baden: Nomos Verlagsgesellschaft, 1981), 77.

2. Arnold Brecht, *Föderalismus, Regionalismus und die Teilung Preussens* (Bonn: Ferd. Dümmlers Verlag, 1949), 85. For the original English edition of this book, see his *Federalism and Regionalism in Germany: The Division of Prussia* (New York: Oxford University Press, 1945).

3. For example, Nevil Johnson, *Government in the Federal Republic of Germany: The Executive at Work* (Oxford and New York: Pergamon Press, 1973), 100–101.

4. K. C. Wheare, *Federal Government*, 4th ed. (London and New York: Oxford University Press, 1963), 33.

5. See, for example, David Caputo, *Urban America: The Policy Alternatives* (San Francisco: W. H. Freeman and Company, 1976), chap. 8. For a German example of the use of "vertical" in this atheoretical sense, see Werner Thieme, "Die Gliederung der deutschen Verwaltung," in *Handbuch der kommunalen Wissenschaft und Praxis*, vol. 1: *Grundlagen*, 2d ed., ed. Günter Püttner (Heidelberg, Berlin, and New York: Springer-Verlag, 1981), 149.

6. Gordon Smith, *Politics in Western Europe*, 4th ed. (New York: Holmes and Meier Publishers, Inc., 1984), 222, 225.

7. Ibid., 219, 222–25.

8. Joseph F. Zimmerman, *State-Local Relations: A Partnership Approach* (New York: Praeger Publishers, 1983), 31. Zimmerman notes that "the grass roots tradition is revered in the United States, yet local governments historically occupied a highly subordinate role in the governance system," which is to say that "states traditionally have inhibited the solution of substate problems by failing to delegate to political subdivisions sufficient authority to cope with the problems." Pp. 14, 87, and 160.

9. Peter H. Merkl has described German spatial federalism as "executive-legislative federalism" in his article, "Executive-Legislative Federalism in West Germany," *American Political Science Review* 53 (September 1959):732–41. Gordon Smith, on the other hand, uses the perhaps more descriptive term "administrative federalism." *Politics in Western Europe*, 231, 234.

10. See the citations in notes 1–3 and P. Bernd Spahn, "The German Model of Horizontal Federal Decentralization," in *Principles of Federal Policy Co-ordination in the Federal Republic of Germany*, ed. P. B. Spahn (Canberra: Centre for Research on Federal Financial Relations, Australian National University, 1978), 6–7.

11. For example, Caputo, *Urban America*, chap. 8.

12. See for example R. A. W. Rhodes, "The Changing Pattern of Local Government in England," in *Local Government Reform and Reorganization: An International Perspective*, ed. Arthur B. Gunlicks (Port Washington: Kennikat Press, 1981), 109–10, and, by the same author, "Centre-Periphery Relations in the United Kingdom," in *Centre-Periphery Relations in Western Europe*, ed. Vincent Wright and Yves Meny (London and Boston: Allen and Unwin, 1985).

13. Deil Wright, *Understanding Intergovernmental Relations*, 2d ed. (Monterey: Brooks/Cole Publishing Co., 1982), 6–8.

Index

Abitur, 147
Administration: of delegated functions, 48, 100, 110–11; of German federal government, 34, 37, 85–88; of *Land* governments, 101, 105; of local governments, 11, 98, 118; organizational structure of, 151–53
Administrative districts, 131; reduction in number of, 50. *See also Regierungsbezirk*
Administrative law and principles, 5
Administrative reform, 54, 56, 106–7, 109
Advisory Commission of Intergovernmental Relations (ACIR), 193
Affirmative action, 211
Agricultural administration, 89
Aid to Families with Dependent Children (AFDC), 196
Allgemeine Finanzzuweisung, 129. *See also* Grants-in-aid
Allied occupation, 1, 26, 30; democratic principles of, 27; German parties allowed under, 28; local government under, 28–31; military government, 27
Allzuständigkeit, 33, 40, 50, 84, 109, 118, 122, 207; of counties, 68, 71, 183; of municipalities, 68, 70, 183; in Prussia, 33. *See also Universalität des Wirkungskreises*
American local governments: direct grants by federal government to, 125; layoffs by, 139; metropolitan contrast to Germany, 63; nonpartisan elections in, 210; "nonsystem," 181; reforms, 61; revenues of, 135
Amt: as "association of municipalities," 10, 12, 41; as "office," 151; in Schleswig-Holstein, 53, 78
Angelegenheiten des eigenen Wirkungskreises, 96

Angestellten, 145; categories and rights of, 146; federal regulations concerning, 147; in higher ranks of city service, 147; training of, 148
Anglo-Saxon countries and *ultra vires*, 84, 85
Annexation and local reforms in Germany, 54
Anticyclical policies, 184
Arbeiter, 145–46, 149
Arbeitsgemeinschaft, 44
Areal organization, principles of, 200
Arrondissements, 33
Articles of Basic Law. *See* Basic Law
Association of villages, 103, 104
At-large election system, 210
Aufgaben, 94, 101, 103; distribution of, 123
Aufgabengliederungsplan, 151
Aufgabenverteilung, 118
Auftragsangelegenheiten, 40, 95–96, 110
Auftragsverwaltung, 90, 183, 198
Aufwandsentschädigung, 160
Augsburg, 6
Australia, federalism in, 190
Austria, 6, 11, 14, 17
Autobahnen, 86

Baden, 11, 15, 17, 18, 28, 42; French influence on local government, 78; liberalism in, 21; 1921 city charter law, 25
Baden-Württemberg, 36, 38, 41–43, 57, 69, 82, 94, 96–99, 150, 158, 161, 172–75, 178; contribution to equalization fund, 127; fiscal ranking, 129; *Landrat*, 81; form of local government in, 78–79
Basic Law: article 20, 50, 188–89; article 28, 48, 51, 68, 70–71, 119, 121, 128, 188, 189; article 72, 51, 121, 125, 127, 189;

article 91a, 123–25, 184, 189; article 91b, 123–24, 184; article 104, 51, 104, 124–25; article 106, 51, 69, 121–23, 125, 127, 128, 131; article 107, 69, 126; article 115, 69; general, 72, 84, 86, 102, 109, 114–15, 140–42, 164, 174, 183; section VIIIa, 123, 184
Basic Law, section X: articles 104a–115 on financing of local governments, 119; outline of tax system, 121
Bauleitplanung, 115–17
Bavaria, 11, 18, 25, 30, 36, 41, 53, 55, 57, 67, 69, 94, 95, 98, 101, 103, 128, 150, 156, 161–62, 175, 177–78; *Bezirke* and *Bezirkspräsident* in, 42–43; fiscal ranking of, 129; form of local government in, 25, 28, 78–79; formula grants, 129–30; *Landrat*, 81–82; *Regierungspräsident* and *Bezirksregierung* in, 92; size criteria of cities, 129–30
Beamte, 99, 146, 149; categories, pay scales, and educational requirements of, 139, 145; federal and *Land* regulations concerning, 149, 152; *höherer Dienst*, 147–48
Bebauungspläne (*Bebauungsplanung*), 115–17
Beigeordnete: in Hesse, 73; powers of, 76; of North German council form, 81
Belgium, 15
Berlin, 24, 34, 175, 202; lord mayor of, 24
Betriebsrat, 178
Bezirk (*Bezirke*), 41–43, 70, 165
Bezirkspräsident, 38, 43, 92
Bezirksregierungen, 131
Bezirksverband Pfalz, 42, 94
Bismarck, Otto von, 1–2, 16–17, 20, 67; and creation of *Bundesrat*, 185; and creation of federal state, 18
Bismarck Reich, 17–18, 34, 36; federalism in, 202; Kaiser and parliament in, 35; spatial administration in, 204
Bloc grants, U.S., 130
Blockwahlsystem, 175
Bonn, 35, 37; compensation for being capital, 123
Boundary reform, 52, 54
Bourgeoisie, 159, 168; and bourgeois parties, 165
Braunschweig (Brunswik), 43
Brecht, Arnold, 201, 203
Bremen, 6, 17, 28, 36, 156, 173; economic problems of, 127
Britain. *See* Great Britain
Brokdorf, 173
Bündelung, 107

Bundesrat: of Bismarck Reich, 35, 185; of Federal Republic, 36, 122, 124, 149, 183, 185–87, 198–99, 212
Bundesraumordnungsgesetz (BROG), 114–15
Bundestag, 35–36, 198
Bureaucracy: classical model of, 203; functional model of, 200; local, 151
Bürger, 7
Bürgerantrag, 174
Bürgerinitiativen, 172
Bürgermeister, 27, 83; Hesse, 73, 76; Rhineland-Palatinate, 78; system of government, 17, 25, 28, 30. *See also* Strong mayor form
Bürgermeisterverfassung, 10
Bürgernähe, 52, 60, 63
Business payroll tax, 123
Business tax, 126, 134, 137, 140, 210. *See also Gewerbesteuer*

California, mandates for local governments, 194
Candidate recruitment, 159–60, 162, 172
Carter presidency, 192
Categorical grants, United States, 192
Central places, 128, 130, 135
Centralization, 2
Centralized administration, 200; for taxes, 120
Chancellor's office, planning staff of, 186
Chefebene, 151
Christian Democratic Union (CDU), 35, 159, 162, 165, 166, 168, 178; CDU-FDP coalition and county reforms in Lower Saxony, 57, 64; in Hesse, 61; and local reforms, 56. *See also* Christian Social Union (CSU)
Christian Social Union (CSU), 56
Citizen initiatives, 171–72, 180
Citizen participation, 54
City administration, 109, 112–13
City charter law: of 1808, 2, 7, 9, 11–12, 14–18, 33, 67, 73, 84, 95; of 1831, 9, 16, 27, 29–30, 73; of 1850, 15–16; of 1853, 16–18; of 1856, 16–17, 76; of 1876, 20; of Hanover, 15. *See also Land*, general local government charter laws; *Land*, local government law
Civil servants, German, 98, 139, 211
Classical model of administration, 3, 33
Collectivism, 165
Cologne (Köln), 149, 151
Communists (communism), 26, 29, 161
Congress, U.S., 206; federal grant programs, 192, 193; under Reagan, 196; role in intergovernmental relations, 198
Congress of Vienna, 9

Constitution, German, 211. *See also* Basic Law
Constitution, U.S.: necessary and proper clause, 186; powers of, 204
Constitutional law: concerning local governments, 72, 103–4, 115–16
Constitutional reforms of 1969, 184
Cooperative federalism, 3, 60, 118, 123, 132, 142, 181, 184–85, 197, 199, 207–8; in United States, 3, 181, 191–92, 197, 199, 204–5
Corporation tax, 122, 126, 210
Councils, county, 19, 162
Councillors, 157–60, 167, 168, 171, 176, 179; distribution of seats, 156–57
Counter-cyclical investment, 132, 136
County (*Landkreis*), 88, 98–110, 117–18, 131–32, 151
County charter law, 69, 81; of 1812, 12–13; of 1872, 18–21, 81; *See also Kreisordnungen*
County finance, 131–32
County-free cities (*kreisfreie Städte* or *Stadtkreise*), 36
Creative Federalism, 192
Czechoslovakia, 29

Decentralization, 3, 33, 52, 68, 188–89, 200, 202
Democracy, 22–23, 30, 48
Die Demokratische Gemeinde (SPD publication), 166
Deutsche Angestellten Gewerkschaft (DAG), 146
Deutsche Gemeinde Ordnung (DGO), 26. *See also* German Municipal Charter Law of 1935
Deutscher Beamten Bund (DBB), 145
Devolution, 202
Dezernenten, 156; *Dezernatsleiter*, 151
D'Hondt method of calculation, 176, 178–79
Direktorialverfassung (city manager form), 80
Doppelbehörde, 99
Dual federalism, 2, 181, 190–91, 196–97, 201–2, 204–6
Dualism: between state authorities and local government, 2, 29, 95, 97, 188, 208; between local administrators and council, 168
Dysfunctional federalism: in United States, 194, 198

East Germany, 1–2
Economies of scale, 51–52
Educational reforms, 65
Eigene Angelegenheiten, 37
Eigener Wirkungskreis, 8, 40, 94–95, 186

Einheit der Verwaltung, 32, 202. *See also* Unity of administration
Einheitsgemeinden (unitary municipalities), 41, 53, 103
Einraümigkeit, 55, 59
Elazar, Daniel, 2–3
Elbe river, 6, 9, 11, 13; French influence west of, 10
Election laws/systems, local, 155, 174–79; in *Länder*, 161, 174
England, 5, 13, 39, 84–85, 188, 209. *See also* Great Britain
Environmentalists, 139
European Common Market, 89, 121, 183, 188
European Parliament, 173
Executive federalism, 185
Executive-legislative federalism, 203

Fachaufsicht, 39–40, 95–96
Fachhochschulen, 147
Federal bank, 86
Federal Constitutional Court, 69, 90
Federal Construction Law (*Bundesbaugesetz*), 114, 117
Federal Employment/Unemployment Office, 37, 87, 144
Federal Health Office, 87
Federal Register, U.S., 194
Federal Science Council, 87
Federal Social Insurance Office, 144
Federalism, 3; American, 142, 195, 200, 212; German, 18, 34, 47, 67, 114, 142–43, 199, 202–4, 212
Federalism, functional, 142, 199
Feudalism, 5
Finance reform law: of 1919, 24; of 1969, 123, 125, 132, 134, 140, 142, 181, 185
Finanzausgleich. See Fiscal equalization
First mayor, 78, 79. *See also* Lord mayor
Fiscal equalization, 119, 125, 127, 188, 210; of counties, 130–31; of *Länder*, 126, 128–29, 132, 140
Five-percent clause, 173, 178
Flächennutzungsplan (municipal land-use plan), 115, 117
Flächenstaaten, 36–37, 98, 100, 105, 118, 152
Ford, President Gerald, 192, 196
Foreign workers, 174
Forms of local government: in municipalities, 73–81; in counties, 81–82
Formula grants: for counties, 131
Fraktion; 156–58, 160, 162–64, 168, 170,

180, 210
Fraktionszwang, 164
France, 5-7, 10-11, 13, 18, 22, 27-28, 30-34, 38-40, 42, 47, 73, 78, 83, 95, 99, 188, 206; administrative system of, 1-3, 15, 208; and *Bürgermeister* form of local government, 12, 18, 25, 28; Communist party in, 164; Fifth Republic, 33; spatial administration in, 39, 66, 86, 204, 206; as unitary state, 213
Frankfurt, 6, 22, 43, 168
Frankfurt Constitution of 1849, 14-15, 67
Frankfurt National Assembly, 14
Free Democratic Party (FDP), 35, 56, 159, 162, 165, 179
Freie Liste, 175. *See also Lose gebundene Liste*
Führerprinzip, 26, 67
Functional administration, 49, 200, 203, 205, 212
Functional brotherhood, 186
Functional (dual) federalism, U.S., 142, 199
Functions, local government, 104, 106-8, 118
Fused administration, 202

Gaullists, 33
Gebietskörperschaft, 19, 70
Gehobener Dienst, 147
Gemeinde (Gemeinden), 27, 40. *See also* Municipality
Gemeindedirektor, 79-81, 83
Gemeindeordnungen, 69, 73. *See also* City charter law
Gemeindeprüfung, 102
Gemeinderatsverfassung, 25
Gemeindeverband, 53, 71, 94
Gemeindevorstand, 73, 77-78
Gemeinschaftsaufgaben, 86, 87, 90-91, 116, 123, 184
Gemeinschaftssteuer, 122-23
German Association of Cities, 147
German Democratic Republic (DDR), 1-2
German Empire, 6, 14, 18, 21-23, 34
German Federal Bank, 37
German Municipal Charter Law of 1935, 26. *See also Deutsche Gemeinde Ordnung* (DGO)
German Weather Service, 37
Germany, Federal Republic of, 1, 29; comparison with Weimar Republic, 35; government and administration of, 31, 34, 36-37, 46, 85-89, 91, 94, 96-97, 104, 112, 144, 149
Gesamtsteuer, calculation of, 130
Gesetzesflut, complaints of, 183

Gewerbesteuer, 121, 123
Giessen, 61-62
Gleichartigkeitsverbot, 122
Gleichschaltung, 26, 161
Grants-in-aid: and delegated functions, 124; description of, 129; by federal government, 141, 182, 184; in Germany, 132, 135, 182, 198; for infrastructure investment, 125, 129-31, 137; by *Länder* to local governments, 120, 123-24, 135, 138, 189; and mixed financing, 141; special purpose, 129-30, 140, 142; in United States, 198
Grass-roots democracy: in United States, 208
Great Britain, 8, 18, 22-23, 29, 31, 92, 155, 160; administrative system, 208; influence on German local government, 28, 73, 83; local elections, 179; local government reforms, 30; local property taxes, 210; occupation of northern Germany, 79; unitary state, 204, 213
Great Society, 192
Green party (Green movement, the Greens), 35, 171, 173-74, 179-80, 209
Grohnde, 173
Grundbetrag, calculation of, 130
Grundsteuer A and B, 121
Grüne Liste Umweltschutz, 173. *See also* Green party
Guilds, 7-8
Gymnasium, 112

Hamburg, 6, 17, 21, 36, 173; contribution to equalization fund, 127
Hameln-Pyrmont, 173
Hanover, 9, 15, 17, 22, 43
Hanseatic cities, 17, 21
Hardenberg, Prince von (chief minister), 9, 11-12, 32
Hare-Niemeyer method of vote calculation, 176-77, 179
Hauptsatz, calculation of formula grants, 130
Hauptschule, 148
Hebesatz, 123
Hesse, 36, 42, 61, 93, 96-97, 99-101, 109, 150, 156-57, 161, 168, 175, 178; contribution to equalization fund, 127; county charter laws of, 81; fiscal ranking, 129; introduction of *Bürgermeister* system in, 28; municipalities, 56, 73
Hessen-Nassau, 17
Hildesheim, 173
Hindenburg, President Paul von, 35
Hitler, Adolf, 27, 35

Höherer Dienst, 146
Honoratioren, 29, 159, 169. *See also* Notables
Horizontal administration, 203
Horizontal fiscal equalization, 69, 126-27
House committees, U.S., 212

Imperative mandate, 163-64, 170
Implementation deficit, 115
Implied powers, 201
Income tax, 122, 130, 210; distribution of, 126, 134
Industrialization (industrial revolution), 9, 14, 20-21, 23, 208
Innere Verfassung, 69, 150
Intergovernmental relations: comparison of German and American, 197-99, 213; German, 3, 166, 169, 189; U.S., 3, 181-83, 186-87, 190, 192-96, 205-8, 212
Intermediate levels of government, 13. *See also Mittelinstanz*
Intermunicipal cooperation, 50
Investments, municipal, 125, 138, 141, 185-86
Iron triangle relationships, 186, 201, 212

Jacksonian democratic tradition, 209
Jeffersonian democratic tradition, 209
Johnson, President Lyndon, 192, 199
Johnson, Nevil, 203
Joint action, kinds of, 183
Joint authorities, 52
Joint tasks, 123-25, 132, 184, 186; concerning higher education, 141; investment grants for, 137; planning for, 185; problem of financing, 140, 142. *See also Gemeinschaftsaufgaben*
Junker, 12-15
Jurists, 147

Kaiser (*Kaiserreich*), 23
Kommunale Gemeinschaftsstelle für Verwaltungsvereinfachung (KGSt), 151
Kommunalverwaltung, 94. *See also* Administration, of local governments
Kommunale Wahlbeamte, 150
Kommunaler Finanzausgleich, 128
Kommunalpolitische Blätter (CDU publication), 166
Kommunalpolitische Vereinigung, 166
Kommunalverband Ruhrgebiet, 43
Kommunen, 118
Köstering, Heinz, 108
Kreis, 11, 18, 27

Kreisausschuss (county executive committee), 19, 81
Kreisfreie Städte, 39, 49
Kreisordnungen, 69, 81. *See also* County charter law
Kreistag (county council), 81
Kreisumlage, 131
Kreisverband, 165
Krupp, Friedrich, 22
Kumulieren, 175, 177-78

Labour government, British, 28
Lahn (Lahnstadt), 61-62
Land (*Länder*), 24-31, 36, 49, 84, 85-87, 90, 95-101, 106, 109, 111-12, 117-18, 144-45, 148-49, 155, 164, 187-88, 207; autonomy of, 2, 48; Basic Law provisions relating to, 68; conferences of, 183; courts of, 34, 68; employees, 98, 139; elections in, 161, 171; field agencies in, 85, 88; general local government charter laws, 67, 76, 81, 158; general government and administration of, 31, 36-39, 55, 80, 85, 88-90, 92, 94, 97-99, 105, 149, 184, 199; local government administration of *Land* law, 71, 88; and local government law, 70, 72, 96, 156, 164; origin of, 7; parliaments of, 35, 55, 102-3, 130, 168, 173, 185-87, 212; population of, 53, 54; taxes in, 126, 130; unincorporated areas of, 70
Land agencies, 38, 47; employment office, 90; finance office, 91; social insurance office, 144; statistical office, 38; survey office, 38
Land Central Bank, 90
Land law, general, 40, 46; implementation by local governments, 84, 104; in relation to local autonomy, 149
Landeswohlfahrtsverband, 42; Baden, 94; Hessen, 93; Württemberg-Hohenzollern, 94
Landgemeindeordnung, 21
Landkreis, 18-19, 39, 42, 46; supervision of, 97
Landrat, 12-13, 17, 19-20, 26-27, 30, 33, 39, 81-83, 99, 150, 151; in Prussia, 12-13, 17, 19-20, 33
Landschaftsverband Hessen, 42; *Landschaftsverband Rheinland*, 42, 93; *Landschaftsverband Westfalen-Lippe*, 42, 93
Landtag, 37
Land-use planning, 51, 116; city, 113; *Land*, 114-15; federal, 114, 186; regional, 60, 63
Laufbahnbeamte, 150

Laufender Sachaufwand, 139
Lehmbruch, Gerhard, 185
Leistungsfähigkeit, 51
Liberals (Liberalism), 14–17, 20–22, 23, 25, 161
London School of Economics, 28
Lord mayor, 77, 79. See also First mayor
Lose gebundene Liste, 175. See also *Freie Liste*
Lower Saxony, 28, 30, 36, 39, 41–42, 53, 57, 69, 93, 95–96, 98, 100, 102, 128, 150, 161, 173, 175–76, 178–79; county administration in, 105; fiscal ranking of, 129; historical tradition, 55; *Land* Administration Office, 38; local reforms in, 56, 64; North German council form of local government in, 79–80; regional planning in, 59, 63, 115
Lübeck, 6
Luneville, Peace of, 6

Magistrat, 7–10, 13–14, 16, 20, 25, 28–30, 73, 76, 78, 81; in Hesse, 73; *unechtes*, 29, 73
Magistratsverfassung, 73, 77
Maire system, 76
Mattenklodt, Herbert-Fritz, 57
Mature federalism, 182
Mecklenburg, 17
Mecklenburg-Schwerin, 25
Medicaid, 196
Mehrwertsteuer (value-added tax), 137
Meldewesen, 112
Military administration, 144
Military government after World War II, 27
Minister-President, 115
Minister of the Interior, 38–40, 46, 88, 97, 99, 114, 187; functional and legal supervision of local governments, 72, 109; of North-Rhine Westphalia, 82; of Saarland, 39; of Schleswig-Holstein, 81
Minister of Labor and Social Welfare, 86
Ministry for Planning, Construction, and City Development, 114
Mischfinanzierung. See also Mixed financing
Mittelinstanz, 13, 38
Mitterrand, President François, 33
Mittlerer Dienst, 148, 153
Mixed financing, 140, 141; in North-Rhine Westphalia, 142
Monocratic city council, 25
Montesquieu, 7
Multimember district election system, 210. See also At-large election system
Municipal charter law: of 1850, 16; of 1935, 26, 67
Municipal socialism, 25, 208
Municipality, 27, 36, 40, 44, 88, 92, 98, 100–101, 104, 150–51, 170; administration of, 41, 94, 102–3, 105–8, 110, 118; constitutional protection of, 84, 109; planning, 116; supervision of, 96–97, 100. See also *Gemeinde*

Nachbarschaftsverband, 43
Napoleon I, 1, 6–7, 9, 11, 28, 30, 32–33, 42, 76, 204
Nazi (Nazism), 1, 26–27, 29, 67, 161, 209
Nebensätze: and calculation of formula grants, 130
New Deal, 181, 191
New Federalism, 192, 196–97
Nobility, 5, 11–12, 14–16, 19–21
Noncentralized administration, 3
Normative administration: regarding personnel, 149
North Carolina, mandates for local governments, 194
North German Confederation, 34
North German council form of local government, 73, 79–80
North-Rhine Westphalia, 28, 30, 36, 39, 41–42, 53–54, 56, 57, 93, 96, 97, 99–103, 110, 128, 146–47, 150, 161–62, 174–75, 178–79, 183; administration of counties and municipalities in, 69, 105–7; business payroll tax in, 123; contribution to equalization fund, 127; fiscal ranking of, 129; North German council form of local government in, 79–80; special purpose grants, 142
Notables, 29, 209. See also *Honoratioren*
Nuremberg, 6

Oberbürgermeister, 39; of Hesse, 73. See also Lord mayor
Oberkreisdirektor, 39, 82–83; in Lower Saxony and North-Rhine Westphalia, 82
Oberpräsident of Prussian provinces, 13
Oberschule, 148. See also *Gymnasium*
Oberstadtdirektor, 39, 80
Obligatory self-government functions, 104, 111
Offenbach, 43
Öffentlicher Dienst, 145
Öffentlicher Dienst, Transport und Verkehr (OTV), 146
Öffentlich-rechtliche Vereinbarung, 43
Office of Management and Budget (OMB), 196

Index 245

Oldenburg, 42, 94
Oldenburgischer Bezirksverband, 42, 93
Omnibus Reconciliation Act of 1981, 196
Organisationshoheit, 151
Organleihe, 39, 99
Örtliche Angelegenheiten, 104
Ortsbürgermeister, 78
Ortschaften, 42, 54, 60, 63, 70
Ortsgemeinden, 78
Ortsverein, 165
Ostfriesische Landschaft, 42, 93

Panaschieren, 175, 177-78
Pappermann, Ernst, 147
Paris, 33
Parliamentarization of local government, 164, 167-171, 179
Parliament(s): European, 173; federal, 173; *Land*, 35, 55, 102-3, 130, 168, 173, 185-87, 212; in Prussia, 14-15, 17, 20-21
Parties at local level, 156-71. *See also Fraktionen*
Party state, 169
Patronage politics, 155, 167, 170, 179
Payroll tax, 121, 134
Personalhoheit, 149-51
Personnel: division of administration functions, 98; costs, 139, 171
Pflichtaufgaben, 94, 110, 183; *nach Weisung*, 96-97; *Pflicht-Selbstverwaltungsaufgaben*, 95
Picket fence federalism, 186, 201
Planning: categorization of, 186; federal, 50, 114-15, 186; *Land*, 50, 114, 116, 118; local, 63, 117; regional, 60, 63, 114-15, 118; relevance to local reforms, 60, 62, 116-17
Plebiscitarian democracy, 164, 172
Plutocratic electoral system, 16, 19-20. *See also* Three-class electoral system
Politicization of local government, 163, 168, 170, 172-73, 179
Politikverflechtung, 182-83, 189, 206
Post-Graduate School of Public Administration in Speyer, 148
Potsdam conference, 27
Prefectorialism, 2
President's Task Force on Regulatory Relief, 197
Preuss, Hugo, 23-24
Prillwitz, Günther, 62
Private sector (privatization), 135, 162
Project grant, 131

Proportional representation, 175, 179, 209
Provincial Charter Law of 1875, 20
Prussia, 1, 2, 6-24, 28-31, 33-35; administration in, 2, 13-14, 33; administrative reforms, 32, 84; decentralization in, 41, 204; defeat by Napoleon, 6-7; industrial revolution in, 14, 20-21; influence of, 211; king of, 9, 11, 17, 19; provinces, 2, 12-14, 17, 20, 33-34, 42, 81; reforms in, 6-7, 11, 15, 17, 34; as unitary state, 13, 18, 202; victory over France in 1871, 18
Public administration, 94, 117, 148, 155
Public choice, 128
Public sector, 162
Public servants, 143-44

Quangos, 204

Railroads, 144
Das Rathaus (FDP publication), 166
Ratsverfassung, 28, 30
Räumliche Planung, 114
Reagan, President Ronald, 196-97, 199, 206, 213
Realschule, 148
Realsteuer, 121; in counties, 131
Rechtsaufsicht, 40, 95-96
Recruitment by party, 162-63, 169
Referate, 151
Referendarzeit: for law students, 146
Reform: administrative, 60; assessment, 62, 64; impact, 59, 62; implementation, 55; *Land* parliament, 56, 57, 211; local government, 52, 106; partisan divisions over, 54; political party effects on, 61; postal and telecommunications, 60; protests against, 61; rationale for, 49; voluntary changes, 55. *See also* Administrative reform; Territorial reform
Reform fatigue, 65
Regierungsbezirke, 13, 27, 33-34, 36, 38-40, 46, 57, 91-93, 131. *See also* Administrative districts
Regierungspräsident, 13, 38, 40, 92, 97
Regierungspräsidium, 38
Regional planning, 114-15, 118
Reich cities, 5-6, 11
Reichsrat, 35
Reichstag, 22, 24, 31, 35
Representative democracy, 164, 174
Ressortkumpanei, 186
Reuter, Ernst, 31
Revenue sharing, U.S., 130

Revolution of 1848, 14
Rhine (Rhineland), 1, 6, 10, 12, 15–16, 25, 28, 30
Rhineland-Palatinate, 28, 36, 41–43, 69, 78, 81, 95–96, 98–99, 101, 150, 161–62, 175, 177; fiscal ranking of, 129; French influence, 76, 99; local government reform in, 50, 56, 57; strong mayor form of local government, 76, 77
Ridley, F. F., 2, 4
Ritter, Gerhard, 9
Robson, William, 28
Roosevelt, President Franklin D., 181, 191, 205
Rural government, 11, 15, 18–19, 21, 34
Russia, 11

Saarbrücken, 100
Saarland, 28, 36, 38–40, 46, 57, 78, 81, 95, 99–100, 127–29, 150, 161–62, 175, 178; fiscal ranking of, 129
Sales tax, 134
Samtgemeinden, 10, 12, 41, 53, 64, 103
Saxony, kingdom of, 18, 22, 25
Scales of economy, 64
Scharpf, Fritz W., 182
Schiller, Karl, 186
Schleswig-Holstein, 17, 22, 28, 30, 36, 38–41, 43, 69, 79, 81, 96–97, 99–102, 150, 156, 161–62, 173–74, 178; fiscal ranking of, 129; local reforms in, 56; *Magistrat* form of local government in, 76; strong mayor, 78
Schmidt, Chancellor Helmut, 61
School reforms, 166
Selbstverwaltungsangelegenheiten, 40, 95, 100
Senat, 37
Senate, U.S., 212
Single-member district/ward system, 210
Sitzungsgelder, 160
Smith, Gordon, 201, 202
Social Democratic Party (SPD), 22–23, 25–26, 35, 57, 159–60, 165–67, 170, 173–74, 178; candidate recruitment, 162; in Hesse, 61; local government reforms, 56, 64; socialist youth organization, 209
Social welfare, 85–86, 89
Southern, David, 145
South German form of local government, 73, 78, 80
South Germany, 15, 17, 25, 94, 98–102, 112, 158, 161, 167, 169
Sozialhilfe, 112, 139

Spahn, P. Bernd, 203
Spain, 5, 18
Sparkassen, 72
Spatial administration, 32, 34, 38–39, 42, 46–50, 66, 72, 84, 92, 100, 142, 200, 202–7, 212
Spatial-federal system, 51, 60, 71, 85–86, 117, 142, 181, 199, 206
Spatial-unitary system, 86, 206
Special grants, 123
Special-purpose authorities, 144, 200. *See also Zweckverband Staatskanzlei*, 115
Stadtdirektor, 80
Stadtkreis, 18–19, 39–42, 46, 97–98, 100, 102, 109, 117
Stadträte, 73
Stadtstaaten, 36–37, 94
Stadt-Umweltverband, 43
Stadtverband Saarbrücken, 43
Stadtvorstand, 77–78
Stare Liste, 175
Stein, Baron vom, 1, 2, 7–9, 11, 13–15, 18, 20, 23, 25, 29–30, 32–33, 55, 65, 67, 84, 95, 211
Strong mayor form of local government, 73. *See also Bürgermeister*
Süddeutsche Ratsverfassung, 73, 78, 80
Sun Belt, 212
Supervision (supervisory authorities), 5, 95–98, 100, 102, 117–18
Supreme Court, U.S., 191
Sweden, 85
Switzerland, 188

Taxes (tax system), 91, 120–22, 126, 130, 134, 137
Teilortswahlen, 178
Territorial corporation, 71
Territorial reform, 56, 83, 107–8, 117, 149, 156, 160, 162, 178. *See also* Reform
Thieme, Werner, 62
Third column thesis, 71–72
Third Reich, 1, 26, 31, 153
Three-class electoral system, 15–16, 19–20, 22
Thuringia, 25
Tutelage, 8

Überörtliche Aufgaben, 68, 105
Übertragender Wirkungskreis, 40, 95, 186
Ultra vires, 84
Umlandverband Frankfurt, 43
Unitary municipalities, 54

Unitary organization of the state, 68, 200, 202, 204, 213
Unity of administration, 48–49, 52, 60, 64, 70, 204. See also Einheit der Verwaltung
Unity of living conditions, 121, 123–24, 127
United States, 3, 8, 22, 27–28, 31, 39–40, 49, 53, 68, 70–71, 92, 96, 108, 119, 122, 125–26, 132, 135, 143–44, 148, 152, 155–56, 159–60, 163–64, 169, 174, 180, 211; dual federalism, 202; functional administration in, 203, 208–9; functional federalism in, 51, 191; grants-in-aid, 130, 198; home rule, 84; intergovernmental relations, 206; local politics, 161, 179; local self-government, 209; picket fence federalism, 201; planning in, 199; political parties in, 209; taxes, 210; *ultra vires* doctrine, 84
Universalität des Wirkungskreises, 68, 84. See also *Allzuständigkeit*
Universities, 145–48, 150

Value-added tax, 122–23, 126, 130, 210
Verband Grossraum Hannover, 43
Verbandsgemeinde, 41, 53, 78
Vertical administration, 201, 203
Vertical fiscal equalization, 120, 122, 126
Vertical joint planning, 186
Vertikaler Finanzausgleich, 120. See also Vertical fiscal equalization
Verwaltungsgemeinschaft, 41, 53

Verwaltungsgliederungsplan, 151
Verwaltungsverflectung, 206
Virginia, 39
Volunteerism, 56
Vorbereitungsdienst, 146

Wagener, Frido, 87, 186, 201, 203, 224 (n.17)
Wahlbeamte, 151–56, 167
Wählergruppen, 63, 157, 175
Walker, David, 193–95, 198
Washington, D.C., 193, 198
Weber, Max, 4, 160
Weimar Republic, 1, 23–24, 30, 34–35, 67, 161, 178, 209
Weisungs- und weisungsfreie Pflichtaufgaben, 96
Welfare state, 68, 83, 85, 172, 187–88
Wertschöpfungssteuer, 137
West Berlin, 31, 36–37
Westphalia, 10, 12, 16
Wetzlar, 61
Wheare, K. C., 201
Wissenschaftsrat, 187
World War I, 18, 21–23, 25, 29–31, 155, 159, 161, 179, 209
World War II, 31, 48, 78–79, 191, 209–10
Württemberg, 11, 18, 21–22, 25, 28, 30
Württemberg-Hohenzollern, 28, 42

Zweckverband, 44, 46, 49, 63, 113

Arthur B. Gunlicks is professor of political science at the University of Richmond. He is editor of *Local Government Reform and Reorganization: An International Perspective* (1981).